RAF BOMBER COMMAND

1939–45

COVER IMAGES: Main image – Bomber Command air operations over north-west Europe, 30 November/1 December 1944, primary target Duisburg. *(Ian Moores)*; below left: Flt Sgt Don Whitehead and his 75 (NZ) Squadron crew with Short Stirling AA-K at Newmarket, June 1943 *(the late Don Whitehead)*; centre: Avro Lancaster on final approach to land; below right: Handley Page Halifax pilot in the cockpit.

First published in August 2018

A catalogue record for this book is available from the British Library.

ISBN 978 1 78521 192 8

Library of Congress control no. 2018935487

Published by Haynes Publishing,
Sparkford, Yeovil, Somerset BA22 7JJ, UK.
Tel: 01963 440635
Int. tel: +44 1963 440635
Website: www.haynes.com

Haynes North America Inc.,
859 Lawrence Drive, Newbury Park,
California 91320, USA.

Printed in Malaysia.

Senior Commissioning Editor: Jonathan Falconer
Copy editor: Michelle Tilling
Proof reader: Penny Housden
Indexer: Peter Nicholson
Page design: James Robertson

Acknowledgements

UK National Archives, US Library of Congress, US National Archives, National Archives of Australia, Library and Archives of Canada, Bundesarchiv, Rolls-Royce Heritage Trust, Lee Barton/ Air Historical Branch (RAF), Getty Images (Popperfoto, Fox Photos, Hulton Archive, PhotoQuest, Hans Wild/LIFE, SSPL, Underwood Archives, Leonard McCombe/ Picture Post, Haywood Magee/Picture Post), Alamy, Interfoto/Alamy, Studiegroep Luchtoorlog 1939–1945, Peter Smith, Philip Jarrett, Steve Smith/218 Squadron Association, Michael Arrieta, the Purdy family, M.W.G. Thomas, Marcel Baillargeon, Andy Thomas, the late Ken Merrick, Phil Gallant, Alan Wilson/Wikimedia Commons, Alan Alexander/New Zealand Bomber Command Association, Jean-Paul Corbeil and Pierre Lagacé, Josh Hodgson, Iain Murray, Martin Smith, David Worrow, Piotr Forkasiewicz (www.peterfor.com), L. Budge, Kay Gould/ Aitken family, 505 Games, Vincent Holyoak, Len Manning, Dave Welch, www.627.co.uk, www.secondworldwar.nl.

RAF BOMBER COMMAND

1939–45

Operations Manual

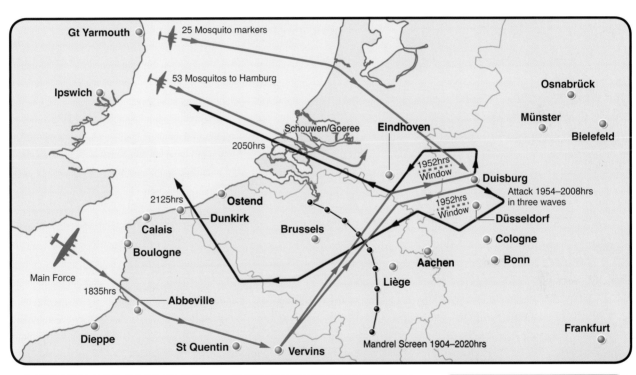

Gt Yarmouth

25 Mosquito markers

53 Mosquitos to Hamburg

Ipswich

Osnabrück

Münster

Bielefeld

Schouwen/Goeree Eindhoven

2050hrs

1952hrs
Window

Duisburg

Attack 1954–2008hrs
in three waves

2125hrs

Ostend

Dunkirk

Calais

Boulogne

Brussels

1952hrs
Window

Düsseldorf

Cologne

Bonn

Aachen

Main Force

1835hrs

Abbeville

Liège

Dieppe

St Quentin Vervins

Mandrel Screen 1904–2020hrs

Frankfurt

Insights into the organisation, equipment, men, machines, technology
and tactics of the RAF's bomber offensive 1939–45

Jonathan Falconer

Silent sentinels: the Bomber Command Memorial in London, unveiled 67 years after the end of the Second World War. *(Author)*

Contents

Introduction

Bomber Command was conceived in 1936 as a daylight bombing force along the lines of contemporary strategic thought, which confidently asserted that 'the bomber will always get through'. But when the Second World War broke out the reality was rather different. Unsustainable losses during the early months proved that heavy bombers operating by day were expensive cannon fodder, forcing most of the Command's efforts into a night offensive for which its crews were ill-prepared and inadequately trained. Meanwhile, its small force of light bombers continued to fly daylight operations against heavily defended targets in occupied Europe, suffering dreadful losses at the hands of a determined enemy. By 1945, however, Bomber Command had adapted to the exigencies of the fast changing air war over Germany and was equipped with some of the best combat aircraft in the world, which were flown by well-trained and highly motivated crews.

Strategic bombing was the major innovation of the Second World War, wielded by the Allies to break the will of the German people and hasten the collapse of their war economy. The bomber offensives of the RAF and the USAAF placed huge demands on the young aircrew that flew the aircraft, many of whom were in their late teens. Just as the debate still rumbles on about whether strategic bombing actually shortened the war, the question remains as to whether the great sacrifices asked of them were justified.

Some 47,000 Bomber Command aircrew died on operations. A further 8,000 or so were killed in non-operational and training accidents. To give this figure a perspective, more RAF bomber crewmen were killed on operations between 1939 and 1945 than British Army officers who died in the hell of the trenches in the First World War (over 41,000). That 19 Victoria Crosses were awarded to British and Commonwealth bomber aircrew speaks volumes about the gallantry shown by men of the wartime command. One of the RAF's oldest squadrons, No 7, saw unbroken service throughout the war and its crews became not only the most decorated in Bomber Command, but also in the RAF as a whole, receiving 438 Distinguished Flying Crosses (DFC), 161 Distinguished Flying Medals (DFM), 3 Conspicuous Gallantry Medals (CGM) and 40 Distinguished Service Orders (DSO).

BELOW In the beginning: Wellington crews of 149 Squadron pose for the camera at Mildenhall after returning from the first raid by British bombers on Berlin, 25/26 August 1940.

This book has its roots in the author's *Bomber Command Handbook 1939–1945*, which was first published in 1998. Twenty years have passed since its publication but popular interest in the wartime command continues with a steady output of new books and magazine features. In the main these are biographical accounts that explore personal stories of individuals and crews, or examine particular events and operations, as well as the aircraft at the tip of the spear that was Bomber Command.

Taking the *Handbook* as its basis, the Haynes *Bomber Command Operations Manual* is a fully revised and redesigned new book. The author has retained roughly half of the original content to which he has added five new chapters that give readers a broader appreciation of Bomber Command's war. They cover the massive works programme to build new bomber airfields in England; the complex German air defence network protecting the Reich from the 'RAF terrofliegers' (as they were known by the Germans); what happened to the bomber crews that failed to return from operations and the steps taken to discover their fate; the 'make-do and mend' Home Front ethic that was applied to repairing damaged bombers to keep frontline squadrons operational; and how the back-room data analysts and number crunchers in Bomber Command's Operational Research Section played a crucial role in informing the commander-in-chief's decision-making. The book also benefits from a comprehensive re-illustration with new photographs and other imagery.

Bomber Command was in existence from 1936 until 1968 when it became part of the new Strike Command, which combined the RAF's other famous wartime commands of Fighter and Coastal under a single authority, followed in 1972 by Air Support Command. Strike Command, too, was not going to live forever and it eventually joined forces with Personnel and Training Command to create the single RAF Air Command in 2007. Somehow, this new name does not have the same ring of authority, power or prestige of any of its illustrious forebears.

It took 67 years for the sacrifice of Bomber Harris's 'old lags' (as he called his crews) to be recognised with a national memorial to Bomber Command in London's Green Park. It was unveiled by Her Majesty the Queen in a memorable ceremony on a blisteringly hot June day in 2012. Why it took almost a lifetime for the memorial to become a reality is a national disgrace.

Thanks to the vision in 2007 of Bomber Command Association secretary Douglas Ratcliffe and chairman Tony Iveson, the Heritage Foundation charity's chairman David Graham and its president for 2008 Robin Gibb, what had started out as an impossible dream became a reality within five years. The resulting memorial is a moving tribute to all who served with Bomber Command in the Second World War and in particular the 55,000 aircrew who perished.

In *The Lost Command* (1971), which tells the story of Bomber Command in the Second World War, Alastair Revie makes the poignant observation that '… bombers came and went in 50 years. There was only one such force as Bomber Command and there can never be another in history.' Visit the memorial in London, stand in the cloister and remember this lost generation.

ABOVE In memoriam: the BBMF Lancaster releases a cloud of poppies over the Bomber Command Memorial in London during the unveiling ceremony on 28 June 2012. *(Author)*

'We are going to scourge the Third Reich from end to end. We are bombing Germany city by city and ever more terribly in order to make it impossible for her to go on with the war. That is our object; we shall pursue it relentlessly.'

Sir Arthur Harris, radio address, 28 July 1942.

Chapter One

Reaping the whirlwind

RAF Bomber Command was born in the turbulent years of the 1930s as Britain frantically rearmed to meet the threat of another European war. From hesitant beginnings after war broke out in 1939, by 1945 the Command had grown into a powerful leviathan capable of inflicting massive material damage on Germany and its allies.

OPPOSITE 'Strike hard, strike sure', the motto of RAF Bomber Command, is epitomised in this atmospheric photograph taken at RAF Scampton as dusk falls on a February evening in 1943. Lancasters of 57 Squadron await the arrival of their crews before taking off for a night raid on Germany.

The rise of the bomber

The cult of the bomber was very much a phenomenon of the interwar period. Its new mass destructive role witnessed during the closing stages of the First World War strongly affected military thinking in the years that immediately followed.

From as early as 1913 in Great Britain the possibilities of air power had preoccupied William Joynson-Hicks, the Conservative MP for Brentford. From the back benches in the House of Commons his well-informed and outspoken commentary to parliament on military matters culminated in 1916 with a 'shilling volume' pamphlet of his speeches to the House criticising the British government for its lacklustre aerial policy. It was called *The Command of the Air, or prophecies fulfilled, being speeches delivered in the House of Commons*, with a foreword by Brigadier General Sir David Henderson, Director General of Military Aeronautics, later to become instrumental in establishing the RAF in 1918 as an independent service. The gradual evolution of British air power during the First World War owed much to Joynson-Hicks's lobbying and criticism of the Lloyd George coalition government. (Joynson-Hicks went on to greater things as Home Secretary in the second Baldwin government between 1924 and 1929.)

Joynson-Hicks and his air-minded oratory has been largely forgotten in popular memory, but three of his contemporaries continue to be recognised as originators of the theories of air warfare: General Giulio Douhet of Italy, Air Marshal Sir Hugh Trenchard of Great Britain, and Brigadier General William ('Billy') Mitchell of the USA. The early air theorists argued that the object of war was to destroy the will of the enemy nation as well as his ability to resist, and then to impose one's own will upon him. In the conflict of the future these three men believed naval and ground forces would no longer

have the decisive role. With the advent of the aeroplane, the obstacle of the enemy's surface forces could be jumped and attacks could be staged by air to hit at the enemy's population, or at the industry and economy that supported it. Gone were the days of air forces being merely auxiliary to the Army or Navy.

In Douhet's view, expounded in his book *The Command of the Air* published in 1921, the best way to attain victory was to destroy air bases, supply points and centres of production on which the enemy depended. His strategic bomber force would have two separable functions: it must be able to win command of the skies and be able to exploit that command. The immediate aim of air warfare, as Douhet clearly saw, was the need to defeat totally the opposing air force.

Air Marshal Sir Hugh Trenchard, the 'Father of the RAF', argued that the heart of air power lay in strategic bombing of an independent character. He asserted that operations in direct support of the Army and Navy were subsidiary and diversionary. However, Brigadier General William 'Billy' Mitchell made a big mistake: his almost religious advocacy of autonomy for the air arm made him powerful enemies on Washington's Capitol Hill (which destroyed his military career) and aroused American democracy's strong distaste for the military establishment and its theories of total war. This effectively put paid to any ideas of an independent air force in America until after the Second World War.

Throughout the interwar period various international conventions were held with the intention of banning the bomber. In 1922 the Washington Conference on the Limitation of Armaments strongly condemned aerial bombardment. The Hague Rules of Aerial Warfare of 1923, although never ratified, attempted to provide definition of what constituted a military target, what could be suitably subjected to air bombardment, and what could not. Military targets included:

> … *military forces, works, establishments or depots, factories constituting important and well-known centres engaged in the manufacture of guns, munitions or distinctively military supplies, lines of communication or transportation for military purposes.*

One of the important reasons for the failure to reach an agreement can be attributed to the fact that the Hague Rules saw aerial bombardment as legitimate, but only when directed against military objectives. The difficulty lay in defining and reaching agreement on what constituted a military objective. The rules therefore left it to the attacker to decide whether a military target was important enough to warrant a bombardment. In 1928 Trenchard produced a paper in which he acknowledged that, although bombing of civilians could be contrary to the rules of warfare, 'it is an entirely different matter to terrorise munitions workers

BELOW Architects of strategic air power: (left) Italy's General Giulio Douhet, (centre) Air Marshal Sir Hugh Trenchard of Great Britain, and (right) the USA's Brigadier General William 'Billy' Mitchell.

(men and women) into absenting themselves from work or stevedores into abandoning the loading of a ship with munitions through fear of air attack upon the factory or dock concerned'.

From the early 1930s much of Britain lived in fear of a catastrophic blow from the air by bombers. The statesman Harold Macmillan wrote in his memoirs: 'We thought of air warfare in 1938 rather as people think of nuclear warfare today.' Further attempts to restrict air warfare failed in 1932 when a disarmament conference organised by the League of Nations assembled in Geneva. By the time Germany withdrew from the conference in 1933 there had been no significant progress. It became increasingly obvious to Baldwin and his Cabinet that Germany, under Hitler, was rearming at a rapid rate and preparing for war.

In 1934 the British Army's funding allocation was halved in the new rearmament programme, since it had been decided to rely primarily on the deterrent effect of a larger air force. By 1938 the RAF's share of the combined services budget had risen from 17% to a massive 40%, with the bomber-building programme taking the lion's share. The plans were for the UK-based air force to be increased to 84 squadrons by March 1939, as detailed in Expansion Scheme 'A' for the RAF, which was approved by the Cabinet in July 1934. To concur with the policy of the Air Staff, 41 bomber squadrons – but only 28 fighter squadrons – were to be included. However, these figures were revised upwards and downwards at least eight times between 1933 and 1939 and were based on somewhat ambiguous information supplied to parliament by the Air Ministry.

In July 1936 Bomber Command came into existence when the Air Defence of Great Britain was replaced by four new Commands: Fighter, Bomber, Coastal and Training. In the same year the trio of twin-engine monoplane medium and heavy bombers that would eventually bear the brunt of the RAF's early bomber offensive made their maiden flights. The Whitley, Wellington and Hampden were ground-breaking designs of their

time and were conceived as the aircraft with which Bomber Command would undergo its expansion. While the factories were tooling up to mass-produce these aircraft, important decisions were being taken by the Air Staff leading to the design and production of the next generation of heavy bombers that would see Bomber Command through the Second World War – the four-engine Stirling, Halifax and Lancaster.

In the meantime, before the first trio of medium and heavy bombers entered squadron service, an odd assortment of monoplane bombers entered limited production and equally limited service with Bomber Command. These were the Vickers Wellesley, Fairey Hendon and Handley Page Harrow, all of which were obsolete even before they had been taken on strength by the RAF. Although the Vickers Wellesley medium bomber offered a vast improvement in performance over the Fairey Gordon and Hawker Audax biplanes which it replaced, it quickly became apparent to its crews that it was neither fast enough nor sufficiently well armed to survive in combat against new German fighter aircraft. The first Wellesleys entered squadron service in April 1937 but most had been transferred to squadrons in the Middle East before war broke out. Only one bomber squadron was equipped with the five-man Fairey Hendon, the RAF's first low-wing monoplane heavy bomber. Fourteen production Hendon IIs entered RAF service in November 1936 with 38 Squadron at Mildenhall (and later at Marham) and remained operational until January 1939 when they were superseded by Wellingtons.

The Harrow was the last of the stop-gap bombers intended to equip RAF heavy bomber squadrons during the expansion period. It served with five bomber squadrons and the first aircraft was delivered to 214 Squadron at Feltwell in

RIGHT The twin-engine Vickers Wellington was classed as a medium bomber when it entered service in October 1938 at the time of the Munich Crisis. These early Mk Is are from 9 Squadron and were photographed in 1938. Note the presence of the Vickers power-operated nose turret, which was superseded from the Mk Ia onwards by the Frazer-Nash FN5 two-gun turret.

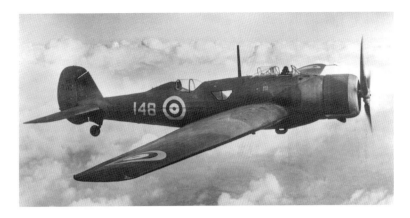

ABOVE Stop-gap bomber: scientist, engineer and inventor Barnes Wallis was more usually associated with the bouncing bomb, but his innovative geodetic lattice structure was used in the fuselage and wings of the single-engine Vickers Wellesley. The aircraft's modest 2,000lb bomb load was carried in external panniers underneath the wings. K7717 is shown while serving with 148 Squadron at Stradishall in 1937.

BELOW In 1937 the Armstrong Whitworth Whitley became the first monoplane medium bomber to be introduced into RAF service. The initial prototype Whitley Mk I, K4586, which is shown here, conducted its maiden flight from Baginton aerodrome near Coventry on 17 March 1936.

April 1937. Harrows were replaced in late 1939 by Wellingtons and then reassigned to RAF transport squadrons. It was not entirely surprising, therefore, that in 1935 no British bomber then in service could reach the nearest target in Germany, drop a bomb larger than 500lb and return to its base in England. These lamentable shortfalls in quality, quantity and strike capability existed up until 1938 when the Wellington and Hampden began to arrive on the squadrons.

With the bomber cast to play the leading role in the Air Staff's plans for any future war, such a large increase in the RAF's bomber force would inevitably cause problems with airfield accommodation. At the end of the First

World War there had been some 300 military aerodromes in the UK, yet by 1924 this number had dwindled to 27. The need clearly existed for a programme of rapid airfield construction to accommodate the growing air force. In 1935 the RAF's Expansion Scheme really took off with an ambitious airfield-building programme that continued unabated up to the outbreak of war four years later (of which more in Chapter 3, Airfield building).

The six-year offensive

When war was declared on Germany in September 1939, the RAF was faced with the problem of how to wage a viable strategic air offensive with so few and inadequate aircraft, of which about 280 were serviceable and with crews on a given day. Air Chief Marshal Sir Edgar Ludlow-Hewitt, who was then Commander-in-Chief of Bomber Command, tried in vain to open the eyes of the Air Staff to the serious shortcomings in aircraft, armament and equipment, and not least aircrew training to even the most basic level. After the

BELOW On daylight operations with Bristol Blenheim Mk IVs in May and June 1940, 40 Squadron suffered heavy casualties and at one stage two of its COs were lost within eight days. The experience was much the same on other Blenheim bomber squadrons – some 956 sorties were flown during this period by the 9 Blenheim squadrons in 2 Group for the loss of 57 aircraft, an attrition rate of 6.3%, or the equivalent to four entire squadrons from the Group – proving that day bombing was a prohibitively costly business. This Mk IV is about to leave RAF Wyton for a raid on France in June.

first costly daylight bombing raids on enemy targets in September and December 1939, the pre-war theory that the bomber would always get through was quickly proved wrong and Bomber Command realised that if it wanted to avoid heavy casualties, the only way to pursue an effective bombing campaign was under the cover of darkness.

Over the winter of 1940-41 it was believed that raids on the small but vital enemy oil refineries would reduce Germany to impotence, but the attacks proved a dismal failure. The first signs of the 'area' offensive yet to come became visible on 16 December 1940 when the centre and suburbs of Mannheim were bombed. By March 1941, however, the U-boat menace in the Atlantic had reached crisis point and Bomber Command was diverted for three months from direct attacks on Germany to bomb naval targets elsewhere, in the hope of relieving the enemy's stranglehold on Atlantic supply routes to Britain.

With its aircrew untrained and untried in night bombing, it was not until mid-1941 that Bomber Command was forced to face up to its grave shortcomings. The Butt Report of August 1941, commissioned by Churchill's scientific adviser, Lord Cherwell (Frederick Lindemann), revealed that few if any of its bombers had reached what they thought was the target, and fewer still had actually dropped their bombs anywhere near it. Hundreds of brave aircrew had died in the process, and to little effect, but with the formation in 1942 of a specialist target finding and marking force, 8 (Pathfinder) Group, the first of several measures were taken to remedy this situation. The Pathfinders' task was to guide squadrons of the main force to the target, which they had marked in advance with coloured flares and target indicators, thereby enabling accurate bombing to take place.

However, the problems encountered by the Command's heavy bomber squadrons of finding and hitting a target by night did not stop the medium bomber squadrons of 2 Group from continuing to mount daring but often costly daylight raids against enemy targets in occupied Europe and in Germany itself. Locating a target in daylight and hitting it from low level did not pose the same problems for navigation and bombing accuracy as a bombing operation by night over

ABOVE Wellingtons of 3 Group took part in one of the first RAF night bombing raids on Italy on 15 June 1940. From a forward operating base at Salon in Provence, aircraft from 75 (NZ), 99 and 149 Squadrons flew to Genoa where violent thunderstorms prevented all but one of the crews from finding their target. The others returned to base with their bomb loads intact. On the following night, 16/17 June, 99 and 149 Squadrons attacked the Caproni factory in Milan. These Wellington Mk Is are from 75 (NZ) Squadron in 1940.

BELOW While Bomber Command's heavy bomber squadrons operated by night, the Blenheim light bombers of 2 Group continued to fly daring low-level operations in daylight against heavily defended targets in Germany and occupied Europe. Here, on 16 July 1941, 36 Blenheims attack the docks at Rotterdam, where 4 aircraft fell to the intense flak.

a longer distance and at higher altitude. From May 1943, control of 2 Group passed from Bomber Command to the 2nd Tactical Air Force in preparation for the Allied invasion of north-west Europe and from thereon in the Command became an exclusively 'heavy' force.

In the latter half of 1941, Bomber Command suffered increasingly heavy losses. The exceptionally harsh winter that followed was doubtless to blame for some of these casualties, but when on 7 November 1941 37 aircraft failed to return from a force of 400 dispatched, Churchill ordered that bombing operations be suspended until the following spring. In some respects this gave the Command a welcome respite, with time to regroup and reassess the direction of the

bomber offensive, but it also served to show it up to its critics in the Admiralty and the War Office as being a bottomless pit into which considerable resources had been thrown, and for little return.

However, it was not all gloom for Bomber Command in 1941, for the first of the new generation of four-engine bomber aircraft that would transform its striking power began to come on stream with front-line squadrons, beginning in February with the Short Stirling, followed swiftly in March by the Handley Page Halifax and by the Avro Lancaster in March 1942. They gradually replaced the obsolescent twin-engine Wellington, Whitley and Hampden that had so valiantly borne the brunt of the early offensive.

On 22 February 1942 Bomber Command and

OPPOSITE The salvation of Bomber Command and the RAF's strategic bomber offensive, the Avro Lancaster flew its first operation in April 1942 and at the war's end it equipped 52 heavy bomber squadrons. No 103 Squadron's Lancaster B Mk I, PM-D2/W4364, 'Billie', became the first Lanc to complete 50 sorties, which is when this photograph was taken at RAF Elsham Wolds on 23 August 1943. Four days later 'Billie' and her crew failed to return from ops to Nuremberg, victims of a night-fighter.

ABOVE RIGHT Another new bomber also entered service with the RAF in 1942. It was a private-venture design manufactured by the de Havilland company at Hatfield and was built mainly out of wood, a material that went against the grain with the Air Ministry's preference for aircraft made from metal. Even so, the Mosquito became one of the most successful Allied aircraft of the war. An unarmed two-man Mossie could carry a 4,000lb bomb to Berlin and return within four hours – in half the time taken by a Lancaster.

RIGHT Throughout the Second World War Britain's factories turned out thousands of aircraft for Bomber Command. In this photograph taken at the Cricklewood factory of Handley Page in north London during March 1942, tail surfaces are fitted to a Halifax B Mk II Series 1 (W7656). Similar scenes were repeated on many production lines at aircraft factories across the country.

the bomber offensive gathered fresh momentum with the appointment of a new and dynamic commander-in-chief, Air Marshal Sir Arthur 'Bomber' Harris. He immediately set about stifling criticism from his detractors by launching the first 1,000-bomber raid in May the same year, which simultaneously proved to the Germans and enemies nearer home that Bomber Command meant business and was far from being a spent force. During 1942, three scientific research projects began to reach fruition, enabling Bomber Command to improve radically its navigation and

RIGHT A cartoon from the *Daily Express* newspaper graphically illustrates the sheer weight of the 1,000-bomber raid on Cologne.

THE FIRST THOUSAND

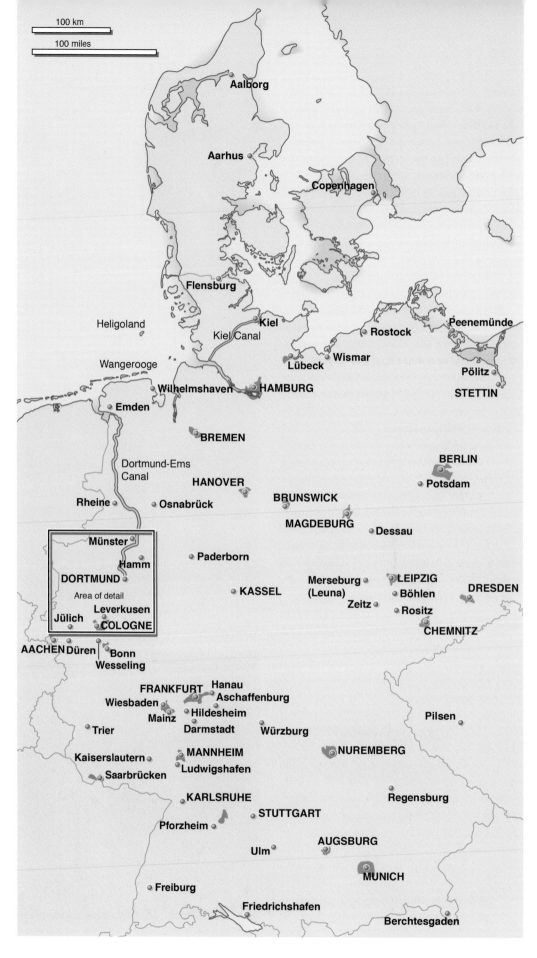

RIGHT Bomber Command targets in Germany. *(Ian Moores)*

100 km

100 miles

Aalborg

Aarhus

Copenhagen

Flensburg

Heligoland

Kiel

Kiel Canal

Rostock

Peenemünde

Wangerooge

Wismar

Lübeck

Pölitz

Wilhelmshaven

HAMBURG

STETTIN

Emden

BREMEN

BERLIN

Dortmund-Ems
Canal

HANOVER

Potsdam

Rheine

Osnabrück

BRUNSWICK

MAGDEBURG

Dessau

Münster

Paderborn

Hamm

Merseburg
(Leuna)

LEIPZIG

DRESDEN

DORTMUND

KASSEL

Böhlen

Area of detail

Zeitz

Rositz

Leverkusen

CHEMNITZ

Jülich

COLOGNE

AACHEN Düren

Bonn
Wesseling

FRANKFURT

Hanau

Aschaffenburg

Wiesbaden

Hildesheim

Pilsen

Mainz

Trier

Darmstadt

Würzburg

Kaiserslautern

MANNHEIM

NUREMBERG

Saarbrücken

Ludwigshafen

KARLSRUHE

Regensburg

STUTTGART

Pforzheim

AUGSBURG

Ulm

Freiburg

MUNICH

Friedrichshafen

Berchtesgaden

bombing accuracy. These were 'Gee' which first saw use in February 1942, followed later that year in December by 'Oboe', and in January 1943 by 'H2S'.

The year 1943 marked the watershed for the fortunes of Bomber Command. At this midpoint in the war it possessed a heavy bomber force made up almost exclusively of four-engine aircraft, flown by better-trained crews using the latest in radar technology for navigation and target finding, and guided over land and sea by the Pathfinders, enabling them to drop their bombs squarely on target, thanks to accurate target marking, improved bombsights and better bombs.

During the war not all Bomber Command's efforts were channelled into mass attacks on urban targets. A number of high-profile precision raids on key targets were flown both in daylight and at night by small forces of heavy bomber aircraft. Perhaps the best known was the attack on the Ruhr dams in May 1943 by Lancasters of 617 Squadron led by Wg Cdr Guy Gibson. The dam busters, as they became known, continued to bomb high-prestige targets from mid-1943 until the end of the war in Europe, accompanied later by the Lancasters of 9 Squadron.

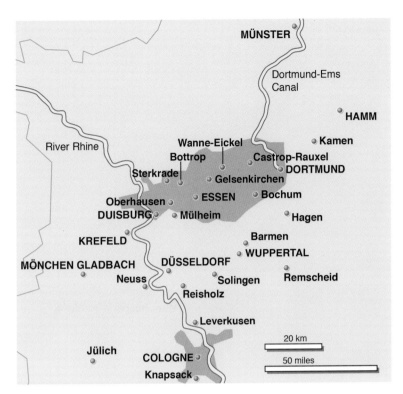

Bomber Harris believed that bombing held the key to the defeat of Germany. Strategic bombing on a large enough scale, relentlessly pressed home, would lead to the collapse of German industry and the morale of its population. The Casablanca Directive, drawn

ABOVE Detail of targets in the Ruhr conurbation. *(Ian Moores)*

LEFT Although largely committed to the area bombing of Germany, several Bomber Command squadrons were tasked with mounting precision raids on key targets. Probably the best known is 617 Squadron, which acquired the nickname of 'the dam busters' after its daring and much publicised attacks on the Ruhr dams on 16/17 May 1943. This is the gaping breach in the wall of the Möhne dam pictured soon after their attack using the famous bouncing bomb. *(BA 1011/637/4192/23)*

ABOVE Bomber Command has sometimes been called a blunt instrument, owing to Bomber Harris's commitment to area bombing, but when the main force was called upon to deliver a precision attack led by the Pathfinders and with a Master Bomber to control the raid, the bombing was invariably accurate and the results were often spectacular. This is the top secret rocket research establishment at Peenemünde on the Baltic coast before and after the raid on 17/18 August 1943.

up by the Combined Chiefs of Staff in January 1943, gave him the authority he required to prove his contention with a sustained assault on German cities. In the first of a series of carefully planned area attacks, the industrial cities of the Ruhr were pounded in 31 major raids between March and July, causing huge material damage and heavy loss of civilian life, but at the cost to Bomber Command of 1,045 aircraft and more than 5,500 aircrew killed or missing.

The climax of the area bombing campaign came in July and August the same year when the RAF launched four major night attacks on Hamburg, raising a terrific firestorm that devastated the city and killed more than 41,000 people. Speaking after the war, Hitler's Armaments Minister, Albert Speer, remarked that further attacks of this nature straight away on six more cities might have forced Germany into defeat, but Harris failed to grasp the significance of the repetitive attacks which had made the immense destruction possible.

In the meantime, the state of the U-boat war had improved greatly and a change in bombing priorities was authorised by the Combined Chiefs of Staff. The Pointblank Directive issued on 10 June 1943 amended the earlier Casablanca Directive, making the German aircraft industry first priority during the autumn of 1943, but Harris ignored the implication to attack specific key, or 'panacea' targets as he called them. Instead, in August he launched the Battle of Berlin (although sustained bombing of the capital did not actually get under way until mid-November). What he had done to Hamburg could be repeated on the capital of the Reich, and he believed it would cost Germany the war.

The greater part of the battle was fought in atrocious winter weather against a target at the extreme range of the bombers' endurance. Berlin's sheer size meant that it was hard for H2S-equipped aircraft to home directly on to a precise aiming point within the city limits. The absence of sufficiently distinctive landmarks in the general area of the target meant that dead reckoning runs were pretty much out of the question, and its great distance from England meant that accurate timing over the target was difficult. If these trials were not enough on their own, the strength of Berlin's formidable flak, searchlight and night-fighter defences also created serious problems for the aircrews.

Despite concentrating the offensive on a decisive target, the predicted collapse in German morale did not materialise. Although huge areas of the capital had been devastated, Bomber Command's loss rate was disastrous: in 19 major raids between August 1943 and March 1944, more than 600 aircraft were lost and 2,690 aircrew killed. But worse was still to

ABOVE With its tail up and four Merlin XXs bellowing at full take-off power, a 102 Squadron Halifax B Mk II laden with fuel, bombs and its seven-man crew strains to leave Pocklington's runway behind – destination Germany.

BELOW LEFT A bombers'-eye view of Hamburg at 01.00hrs on 28 July 1943, during the second of three devastating raids on the city by the RAF. Freak local weather conditions and the first use of 'Window' to jam German early warning radar, were combined with high explosives and incendiaries dropped by some 787 aircraft to whip up a terrific firestorm that killed tens of thousands and destroyed much of the ancient Hanseatic port.

BELOW Back from a gruelling 6½-hour trip to bomb Frankfurt on 4/5 October 1943, Flt Lt Arthur Carey RNZAF and his 102 Squadron Halifax crew look forward to bacon and eggs after their intelligence debriefing, and then to bed and the solace of sleep – such was the disjointed existence of an RAF bomber crew. The Carey crew survived the war.

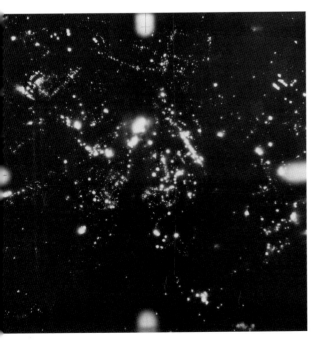

ABOVE The sky is a big place: after D-Day in the summer of 1944 Bomber Command flew thousands of tactical bombing sorties in daylight against European targets in support of the Allied advance. This photograph, which was taken by 75 (NZ) Squadron pilot John Aitken from the cockpit of his Lancaster, shows more than 40 Lancs in a loose gaggle. *(Courtesy of the Aitken family)*

BELOW Allied air superiority in European skies grew as its ground forces advanced towards Germany. When enemy early warning radar sites were overrun, the Germans increasingly lost the command and control of their air defences, leaving them at the mercy of round-the-clock bombing by the RAF and USAAF. In this photograph Münster is seen under attack in broad daylight by 112 Halifaxes on 12 September 1944. Only a few months earlier such an operation by day would have been suicidal.

come. When 795 aircraft of Bomber Command raided Nuremberg on 30/31 March 1944, 95 of their number failed to return, making it the Command's heaviest loss of the war on one operation. Mistakes in route planning at Bomber Command headquarters and freak meteorological conditions encountered on the outward journey to Nuremberg combined to serve up the bomber force on a plate to waiting German night-fighters.

The strategic offensive was curtailed from March to September 1944 while the squadrons of Bomber Command were switched to bombing communications targets in France and Belgium in the run-up to Operation Overlord, the Allied invasion of north-west Europe. In the weeks and months following the Normandy landings on 6 June, they were used in the tactical bombing role to support Allied troops in their breakout from the beachhead, and against the V-1 flying bomb sites in the Pas de Calais area. The diversion from bombing Germany was almost total, with only 8% of the tonnage dropped in June being upon Germany itself.

With the Allied advances on the Western Front the Germans lost much of their early warning system as they retreated back towards Germany. This fact became more significant by the time the strategic offensive resumed in strength in the late summer because it also worked for the bombers on another level: the Allies were now able to provide ground stations in Europe for their air navigation systems like Gee and Oboe, which meant the transmitters were that much nearer to the targets in Germany, with the obvious benefit of greater accuracy coming from closer range.

The RAF and US Army Air Force (USAAF) succeeded in gaining a measure of air superiority over mainland Europe, with long-range fighters like the American P-51 Mustang able to provide powerful escort defence for daylight raids as far afield as Berlin. This development enabled Bomber Command's heavies to attack German targets by day with a greatly diminished risk of assault by enemy fighters, although the Command continued to operate extensively by night.

By far the greatest damage inflicted upon Germany was achieved in the last six months of war, at which point Bomber Command was able to strike massive and highly destructive blows against both area and precision targets. On 14 and 15 October 1944, it flew more than 2,000 sorties to Duisburg in less than 24 hours. Towards the end of November 1944 precision attacks on communications and oil targets were beginning to paralyse German industry, while area attacks continued to lay waste the industrial cities of the Ruhr. By the end of January 1945, Germany's national grids of gas, electricity and water were wrecked, the rail network was in chaos, and every type of fuel was in very short supply. High-octane aviation fuel became increasingly scarce and it was not long before most of the Luftwaffe fighter force had been grounded due to lack of fuel.

In the spring of 1945, Bomber Command reached its peak wartime strength with an average daily availability of 1,609 aircraft with crews, but this period was also the most controversial of the war in terms of the morality of the RAF's bomber offensive. For many, the destruction of the medieval city of Dresden on 13/14 February 1945 represented the moral balance rejected. A city of minor industrial significance crammed with refugees, it was razed by a terrific aerial bombardment and the ensuing firestorm incinerated between 35,000 and 135,000 people, the exact number remains undetermined. Dresden was one of the few remaining large, built-up but un-bombed German cities and was thus singled out for destruction because there were few selective targets left.

Although Bomber Command could smash Germany's cities to rubble and dust, it failed to break the will of its people, just as the Luftwaffe had failed to break the inhabitants of London in the Blitz of 1940–41. On 16 April 1945 Chiefs of Staff announced the cessation of area bombing. Ironically, Bomber Command's final sorties of the war were humanitarian in nature, dropping much-needed food supplies to the starving population of Holland and the repatriation of Allied former prisoners of war from camps in Europe.

The hard-fought six-year bomber offensive against Germany had cost the lives of 55,000 Bomber Command aircrew and more than 8,000 aircraft had been destroyed. It had brutally remodelled the face of urban Germany and caused much material damage to the towns and cities of France and the Low Countries. Whether

ABOVE Dutch civilians in western Holland wave jubilantly to an overflying Lancaster of 635 Squadron during Operation Manna, some time between 29 April and 7 May 1945. A truce was arranged with the local German commander to allow Lancasters of 1, 3 and 8 Groups to drop food supplies to the starving civilian population. *(www.secondworldwar.nl)*

it hastened the end of the war in Europe remains a hotly debated issue, but the bravery of the men who flew by day and night with Bomber Command is an undisputed fact.

BELOW The heavy raids on Dresden and Pforzheim in February 1945 raised some searching questions about the morality of strategic bombing. This apocalyptic vision on a devastated street in Dresden was photographed after the RAF raid of 14/15 February by 796 Lancasters and 9 Mosquitoes that left more than 40,000 dead in a devastating firestorm, similar to the one that razed Hamburg in July 1943. Six Lancasters were lost. *(BA 183 R72625)*

'At 1130 the target broadcast came through on the blower from Group, giving the phasing and timing of the attack and the method of marking the target by the pathfinder force.'
William Jones, Intelligence Officer, RAF Kirmington, 1943.

Chapter Two

Organisation

From the boardroom of the
Air Council in London to the
windswept dispersals of a
Lincolnshire bomber airfield, the
chain of command was highly
effective at interpreting the policy
of the War Cabinet in Whitehall
and putting it into practice at
squadron level. At the sharp end,
at various times during the Second
World War some 130 squadrons
flew operationally with Bomber
Command in north-west Europe.

OPPOSITE Air Chief Marshal Sir Arthur 'Bomber' Harris is seen here in conference at Bomber Command's Headquarters (HQ) at High Wycombe in late February 1944. On the wall is a photographic mosaic of Stuttgart and its environs, the city having been raided by the RAF on the night of 20/21 February. The flight lieutenant on the right (with his back to the camera) is probably Harris's personal staff officer, Flt Lt Jean-Paul Etienne Maze DFC. In the foreground are WAAF photographic interpreters. *(Popperfoto/Getty Images)*

BELOW Towards the end of 1941, the Chief of the Air Staff, Sir Charles Portal, became increasingly dissatisfied with the performance of Sir Richard Peirse as Bomber Command's C-in-C (from October 1940), eventually posting him away in January 1942 to command the Allied Air Forces in South-East Asia. Peirse (on the left) is pictured with Bomber Command's Senior Air Staff Officer Robert Saundby.

BELOW RIGHT Air Chief Marshal Sir Arthur Harris was C-in-C of Bomber Command from February 1942 until the end of the war. Widely known by his nickname 'Bomber', his crews (whom he referred to affectionately as his 'Old Lags') tended to refer to him as 'Butch'. He is arguably the most controversial of Britain's wartime leaders due to his single-minded determination to pursue the systematic destruction of Germany through bombing.

The chain of command

From the outbreak of the Second World War, bombing policy directives were handed down from the Chief of the Air Staff at the Air Ministry to the Commander-in-Chief Bomber Command. These directives invariably stemmed from the higher authority of the War Cabinet (later, the Defence Committee), which received advice from the Chiefs of Staff of the three services. In January 1943 policy directives for Bomber Command became subject to the authority of the Combined Chiefs of Staff in the wake of the Casablanca Directive, which set in motion plans for a combined RAF and USAAF bomber offensive. These plans received final endorsement by the Combined Chiefs of Staff at the Trident Conference in Washington in May 1943.

In the first instance the general policy directives handed down from the Air Ministry were received by the commander-in-chief at Bomber Command's subterranean headquarters at High Wycombe in Buckinghamshire. From them the C-in-C interpreted his response and chose the ways, means and timing of operations. His staff then communicated the general plan to individual group headquarters, each of which was commanded by an air vice-marshal. The group commanders were responsible for drawing up comprehensive orders to be passed to their squadrons. These orders contained details of

the target for attack, the number of aircraft to be dispatched, the weight and composition of the bomb load, the route into and out of the target area, and so on. Group commanders were given a considerable degree of autonomy within the limits set in planning an attack. The next tier of command was at station level, each of which was commanded by a group captain or, when the 'base' system came into existence, an air commodore.

Late in 1942, with the rapid growth in the number of bomber airfields, it became apparent that it would be impracticable to control efficiently up to 15 airfields from a single group headquarters, and that some form of intermediate link was required. Thus, in the spring of 1943, the base system came about to ease this strain and to offer greater local control to stations and their satellite airfields.

Centred around a parent or base station, usually one of the pre-war permanent types hosting the base administrative apparatus for the control of six heavy bomber squadrons (or three heavy conversion units – HCUs), two substations of temporary wartime construction were located close by, each commanded by a group captain. The base system enabled the centralisation of many specialist and administrative functions previously undertaken on an individual station basis, although 8 (Pathfinder – PFF) and 100 (Bomber Support – BS) Groups were the exceptions to this rule. These stations were organised on an independent basis due to the widely varying tasks of their resident squadrons, although a form of centralised major servicing was introduced for their aircraft. From 1943 the PFF operated a scheme of planned maintenance for its Lancasters and Mosquitoes, which kept the number of aircraft available for operations at a higher level than any other group in the Command.

Each base headquarters was identified by a two-digit code, the first digit identifying the parent group and the second the base itself. For example, Pocklington in Yorkshire was designated as 42 Base Headquarters and its four satellite stations – Elvington, Full Sutton, Snaith and Burn – each became known as a 42 Base Substation. From 16 September 1943 until the end of the war, all bases were known by number and not their geographical location.

At any one time RAF bomber stations could house either one or two squadrons, an operational training or heavy conversion unit and/or a number of smaller miscellaneous units. However, front-line and training units would never have occupied the same station simultaneously, except for a short spell in 1941–42 when squadron conversion flights existed alongside their operational parent to convert new crews on to four-engine bombers. Each individual station provided its resident squadrons or units with technical and domestic housing, mess facilities, flying control, emergency and medical services and airfield security.

A squadron, usually commanded by a wing commander and with a total complement (on average) of some 24 aircraft with 3 in reserve, was responsible for its own aircraft maintenance and administration. But from July 1944, administrative functions were centralised at station level whereby the station was organised into three wings: flying, administrative and servicing. All personnel not directly involved with flying were taken off the squadron and reallocated to either the administrative or servicing wings and therefore came under the control of the station for all purposes. The squadron was now composed of operational commanders, aircrew and a handful of specialist and administrative personnel, thus reducing it in effect to a flying echelon incapable of undertaking operations independently of the station organisation.

At the sharp end of the squadron, individual aircraft, aircrews and groundcrews were allocated to a particular flight – A, B or C – each made up of some eight aircraft and occupying its own assigned corner of the airfield. Individual aircraft had their own dispersal pan situated on the airfield perimeter, with an aircrew of seven (generally) and a dedicated groundcrew staff with a flight sergeant ('chiefy') in charge.

All routine servicing, fuelling, arming and bombing-up was carried out in the open air on the dispersal pan, whatever the weather and time of day, night or year. Maintenance personnel on each station were organised into a Repair and Inspections Squadron (R&I Squadron) and a Daily Servicing Section (DSS). The DSS carried out daily inspections and

RIGHT The Air Council in session at the Air Ministry building, Adastral House, in Kingsway, London, during the Second World War, chaired by Sir Archibald Sinclair, the Secretary of State for Air.

THE CHAIN OF COMMAND 1939–45

(Dates of appointment in brackets)

War Cabinet
Prime Minister
Secretary of State for Air

Air Council
Secretary of State for Air
   Sir Kingsley Wood (May 1938)
   Sir Samuel Hoare (Apr 1940)
   Sir Archibald Sinclair (May 1940)
Parliamentary Under-Secretary of State for Air
   Capt Harold Balfour (May 1938)

   Lord Sherwood (Jul 1941)
   Cdr R.A. Brabner (Nov 1944)
   Maj Quintin Hogg (Apr 1945)

Air Staff
Chief of the Air Staff
   ACM Sir Cyril Newall (Sep 1937)
   ACM Sir Charles Portal (Oct 1940)
Vice-Chief of the Air Staff
   AM Sir Richard Peirse (Apr 1940)
   ACM Sir Wilfred Freeman (Nov 1940)
   AVM C. Medhurst (Acting) (Oct 1942)
   AM Sir Douglas Evill (Mar 1943)

RIGHT Sir Archibald Sinclair was Secretary of State for Air from May 1940 until the end of the war. As leader of the Liberal Party from 1935 to 1945, Sinclair was a prominent figure in British politics and in the 1930s he was an outspoken critic of appeasement.

FAR RIGHT Just six months into the job as Ludlow-Hewitt's successor at Bomber Command in 1940, 'Peter' Portal was singled out for high office and appointed Chief of the Air Staff.

Air Ministry

Air Member for Personnel
 AM Charles Portal (Feb 1939)
 AM Sir Ernest Gossage (Apr 1940)
 AM Philip Babington (Dec 1940)
 AM Sir Bertine Sutton (Aug 1942)
 AM Sir John Slessor (Apr 1945)
Air Member for Supply and Organisation
 AM W. Welsh (Sep 1937)
 AM Sir Christopher Courtney (Jan 1940)
Air Member of Training
 AM Alfred Garrod (Jul 1940)
 AM Sir Peter Drummond (Apr 1943)
Permanent Under-Secretary of State for Air
 Sir Arthur Street (June 1939)

Bomber Command
Commander-in-Chief – Air Marshal

Group
Air Officer Commanding – Air Vice-Marshal

Base
Commanding Officer – Air Commodore

Station
Commanding Officer – Group Captain

Squadron
Commanding Officer – Wing Commander

remedied petty unserviceability, while the R&I Squadron carried out minor inspections and performed major repairs. An aircraft would only return to the hangars on the airfield's technical site for major maintenance by the Base Major Servicing Section (BMSS), which also carried out initial checks on aircraft when they were delivered. However, Bomber Command ground servicing staff were hampered by inadequate technical accommodation and equipment up until the end of the war, but to a large extent this situation was alleviated from 1943.

Once the squadron had been briefed for operations and the aircraft readied for the task ahead, the crews would embark and the aircraft would be marshalled from the dispersal pans by their groundcrews on to the perimeter track, around which they would taxi to the threshold of the runway in use. Once there they would await their turn for the green light from the airfield controller's caravan, clearing them for take-off and sending them hurtling down the runway and off into the night.

For a two-squadron Lancaster station like Mildenhall in Suffolk operating 15 and 622 Squadrons in September 1944, it would have taken a little over half an hour on a maximum effort raid to get all aircraft of both squadrons airborne.

The groups

In September 1939 Bomber Command's front-line force was made up of 29 home-based squadrons divided between 4 groups and spread across 17 airfields from Yorkshire to Oxfordshire. Each group was equipped with a particular type of twin-engine bomber aircraft dedicated specifically to the light, medium or heavy bombing roles.

No 2 Group was based in the Norfolk area and equipped with the shapely Bristol Blenheim light bomber; 3 Group's squadrons were centred on the Cambridge and Huntingdon areas and were equipped with Dr Barnes Wallis's 'geodetic' medium bomber, the Vickers Wellington; the North and West Riding of Yorkshire-based 4 Group's mainstay was the slab-sided Armstrong Whitworth Whitley heavy bomber; 5 Group was based in south Lincolnshire and Nottinghamshire and was equipped with

RIGHT Geographic
distribution of bomber
groups in England and
Scotland 1939–45.
(Ian Moores)

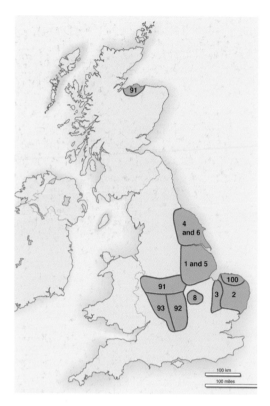

the 'flying panhandle' – the Handley Page
Hampden medium bomber. No 1 Group, with
ten squadrons of single-engine Fairey Battle light
bombers, had moved to France on 1 September
to form part of the Advanced Air Striking Force
(AASF) and did not come under Bomber
Command's operational control again until June
1940, whereafter its squadrons were based in
the south of Yorkshire and north Lincolnshire.

From comparatively small beginnings at
the onset of war, by 1945 Bomber Command
had grown into an awesome leviathan capable
of laying waste to Nazi Germany's cities
and industrial might. In September 1939,
the Command could muster a daily average
of 280 aircraft crews flying from 27 grass

airfields; in the closing months of the war it
could field a daily average of 1,069 aircraft
with crews, drawn from 97 squadrons flying
from more than 60 airfields (all but two of
which had paved runways) and under the
control of seven operational groups. By this
late stage of the war it was a predominantly
heavy bomber force.

Looking at the disposition of its groups in
1945, the geographical locations of the groups
was little different from 1939; but what had
changed was the Command's sheer size and
destructive power. No 1 Group operated an all-
Avro Lancaster force; 2 Group's light bombers
had been hived off in May 1943 to join the
2nd Tactical Air Force, in preparation for the
D-Day landings in June 1944; 3 Group, like
1 Group, was an all-Lancaster affair; 4 Group's
squadrons flew Handley Page Halifaxes while
5 Group was predominantly an all-Lancaster
force (although it did operate a number of de
Havilland Mosquitoes in the target-marking role,
for which it was unique in the Command). This
target-marking force was made up of three
squadrons 'on loan' from 8 (PFF) Group.

The decision to amputate a vital part of
the PFF's body and transplant it elsewhere
in the Command was the source of some
considerable displeasure at 8 (PFF) Group's
headquarters. But this was just a continuation
of the infighting between the main force
groups and the PFF, which had begun in
1942 when four of the best squadrons, one
drawn from each of the four front-line groups,
had been allocated to the newly formed 8
(PFF) Group.

Moving upcountry to the North Riding of
Yorkshire and County Durham, the Canadian
squadrons of 6 (RCAF) Group flew a mixed

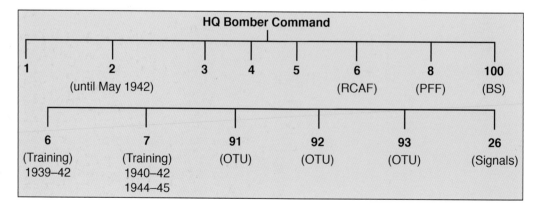

RIGHT Front- and
second-line groups
under the operational
control of Bomber
Command, 1939–45.

HQ Bomber Command							
1	2	3	4	5	6	8	100
	(until May 1942)				(RCAF)	(PFF)	(BS)
6	7	91	92	93			26
(Training)	(Training)	(OTU)	(OTU)	(OTU)			(Signals)
1939–42	1940–42						
	1944–45						

force of Halifaxes and Lancasters. Bomber Command's specialist target-marking force was 8 (PFF) Group – the Pathfinders – which flew a mixed force of Lancasters and Mosquitoes from airfields around Ely in Cambridgeshire's fenlands. Finally, another specialised force existed for bomber support duties in the shape of 100 (BS) Group, which flew electronic and radio countermeasures and intruder sorties with a mixed force of Mosquitoes, Halifaxes, Lancasters, Stirlings, Liberators and Flying Fortresses from airfields in north Norfolk.

Front-line groups

No 1 Group

Formed at Abingdon (then in Berkshire), on 1 May 1936, 1 Group began life with three stations and ten squadrons; by the war's end this had risen to 14 of each. At the outbreak of war the group moved to France with its Fairey Battle squadrons where it became HQ Advanced Air Striking Force. After suffering severe losses in the Battle of France, the AASF returned to England in June 1940 and 1 Group was then re-formed at Hucknall, Nottinghamshire, as a main force bomber group with bases in the East Midlands and Lincolnshire. By the end of the year its squadrons were in the middle of casting off their obsolete Fairey Battles in favour of Vickers Wellingtons. In January 1942 the group comprised ten Wellington squadrons, of which four were Polish and two Australian. Group headquarters was moved again in July 1941, this time to Bawtry Hall in Yorkshire, and the group eventually established its wartime bases in Lincolnshire and Yorkshire. By the end of November 1942 its squadrons had begun to convert to Lancasters, which they retained for the duration of the war. No 1 Group flew a total of some 57,900 sorties during the war and dropped 238,356 tons of bombs, for the loss of 8,577 aircrew.

Air Officers Commanding (with dates of appointment)
AVM A.C. Wright – Sep 1939
Air Cdre J.J. Breen – Jun 1940
AVM R.D. Oxland – Nov 1940
AVM E.A.B. Rice – Feb 1943
AVM R.S. Blucke – Feb 1945

LEFT In 1942 Edward Rice took over command of 1 Group from Robert Oxland. A chance meeting between Rice and the head of the Lincolnshire engineering firm Rose Brothers led to the design of the successful Rose-Rice twin .50in Browning tail turret for the Lancasters of 1 Group.

No 2 Group

Formed on 20 March 1936, also at Abingdon, 2 Group then comprised just two squadrons, one each of Hawker Harts and Hinds. On 3 September 1939 it made history by dispatching the first operational sortie of the war, and the next day mounted the first bombing raid on Germany. In October the group consisted of ten squadrons of Bristol Blenheims and finally settled its headquarters at Castlewood House, Huntingdon, where it was to remain for the next four years. No 2 Group was established as a medium bomber group and equipped variously with the Bristol Blenheim, de Havilland Mosquito, Lockheed Ventura, Douglas Boston and North American Mitchell. (The exception to this was 90 Squadron, which was equipped with the Boeing Fortress I heavy bomber between May 1941 and October 1942.) The achievements and exploits of the group are many and varied, but the more daring include the first daylight raid on Berlin, several precision attacks on Gestapo and SS buildings in occupied Europe and Scandinavia, and the low-level daylight raid on Bremen in which Wg Cdr Hughie Edwards won the VC. At the end of May 1943, 2 Group was transferred from Bomber Command to the newly formed 2nd Tactical Air Force in preparation for the invasion of Europe.

RIGHT The establishment of the Commonwealth Air Training Plan in Canada before the Second World War owes much to the foresight of James Robb, the Air Officer Commanding (AOC) of 2 Group from 1940 to 1941. He became C-in-C Fighter Command in 1945.

BELOW During the Second World War Richard Harrison was three times mentioned in dispatches and was appointed AOC of 3 Group on 27 February 1943, taking over from Sir Ralph Cochrane who assumed command of 5 Group.

The group flew over 57,000 sorties during the war for the loss of 2,671 aircrew.

Air Officers Commanding (with dates of appointment)
AVM C.T. Maclean – May 1938
AVM J.M. Robb – Apr 1940
AVM D.F. Stevenson – Feb 1941
AVM A. Lees – Dec 1941
AVM J.H. D'Albiac – Dec 1942
AVM B.E. Embry – Jun 1943

No 3 Group

Formed at Andover, Hampshire, on 1 May 1936, 3 Group headquarters moved to Mildenhall before finally settling in Exning, Suffolk, in March 1940. The group achieved a number of firsts early in the war: it was the first group to be completely equipped with the Wellington; 115 Squadron made the RAF's first attack on a mainland target, Stavanger/Sola airfield, on 11/12 April 1940; and 7 Squadron became the first in Bomber Command to equip with one of the new generation of four-engine heavy bombers, the Short Stirling, in August 1940. No 3 Group was equipped variously with the Vickers Wellington, Short Stirling and Avro Lancaster and its squadrons flew as part of the main force for the whole of the war, taking part in all of Bomber Command's campaigns. During 1943–44 its Stirling aircraft played an important role in resistance operations, dropping agents and equipment into occupied Europe and Scandinavia. The group also had a leading part in the introduction of the radar bombing aid G-H in November 1943 and was later earmarked to become Bomber Command's sole G-H-equipped heavy bomber group. No 3 Group flew some 66,613 sorties during the war for the loss of 1,668 aircraft.

Air Officers Commanding (with dates of appointment)
AVM J.E.A. Baldwin – Aug 1939
AVM The Hon R.A. Cochrane – Sep 1942
AVM R. Harrison – Feb 1943

No 4 Group

Formed on 1 April 1937 at Mildenhall, Suffolk, the group headquarters moved twice more before settling at Heslington Hall near York in April 1940. At the outbreak of war the group's eight heavy bomber squadrons were equipped with the Armstrong-Whitworth Whitley and based in Yorkshire. They flew the first night sorties of the war when they dropped leaflets on German cities on 3/4 September 1939. Further leaflet-dropping and anti-shipping sorties followed before 4 Group made its first attack on a land target, Hornum on the island of Sylt, in March 1940. In June, five squadrons of Whitleys made the first long-range bombing raid of the war on an Italian target, Turin. As part of the main force, the group's squadrons flew on all of Bomber Command's campaigns of the war including tactical bombing in support of the invasion of Europe. Equipped initially with the Whitley, 4 Group began to re-equip with the four-engine Halifax in early 1941, the aircraft type with which it remained for the duration of the war. Two Wellington squadrons also formed part of the group in 1941–42. In summer 1944, two all-French squadrons, 346 and 347, joined the group and flew Halifaxes from Elvington until the end of the war. In May 1945 the group transferred from Bomber to Transport Command with which it remained until disbanded in 1948. In total, 4 Group's squadrons flew 57,407 sorties during the war and dropped more than 200,000 tons of bombs for the loss of 1,509 aircraft.

Air Officers Commanding (with dates of appointment)
AVM A. Coningham – Jul 1939
AVM C.R. Carr – Jul 1941
AVM J.R. Whitley – Feb 1945

No 5 Group

Formed on 1 September 1937 at Mildenhall, Suffolk, as an offshoot of 3 Group, 5 Group's wartime activities became more widely publicised than any of its rivals. The group contributed not only to the main heavy bomber offensive but was also responsible for many of the more specialised and most dramatic attacks of the war. These included the Ruhr dams raid by 617 Squadron, successive breachings of the Dortmund–Ems Canal, the daylight raid on Augsburg and the sinking of the battleship *Tirpitz*. At the outbreak of war, with its headquarters at St Vincents in Grantham, 5 Group controlled five stations and ten squadrons equipped with the Handley Page Hampdens. By the war's end it had 17 squadrons of Lancasters and one of Mosquitoes under its command. The group pioneered target marking (it had its own independent target-marking force) and minelaying techniques and was the only group in Bomber Command to use the 12,000lb Tallboy and 22,000lb Grand Slam earthquake bombs operationally, and in daylight. After VE-Day, 5 Group prepared for service in the Far East with the 'Tiger Force', but the dropping of the atom bomb put paid to this and the group was finally

disbanded in December 1945. During the war it had been equipped variously with the Hampden, Manchester, Lancaster and Mosquito, and flew 70,357 sorties for the loss of 1,888 aircraft.

Air Officers Commanding (with dates of appointment)
Air Cdre W.B. Calloway – Aug 1937
AVM A.T. Harris – Sep 1939
AVM N.R. Bottomley – Nov 1940
AVM J.C. Slessor – May 1941
AVM W.A. Coryton – Apr 1942
AVM The Hon Sir R.A. Cochrane – Feb 1943
AVM H.A. Constantine – Feb 1945

No 8 (Pathfinder Force) Group

Formed on 15 August 1942 with headquarters at Wyton (then in Huntingdonshire) and known as the Pathfinder Force, the group was officially redesignated 8 (PFF) Group on 13 January 1943. Its headquarters later moved in June 1943 to Castle Hill House, also in Huntingdonshire. Created at the instigation of the Air Ministry with the intention of leading the main force and marking the target, although initially opposed by Bomber Harris who feared the creation of a *corps d'élite* would lead to the fostering of jealousy within the other groups of his command, it was made up of five squadrons, one from each of the operational bomber groups. By April 1945 the force comprised 19 operational squadrons. At

first the constituent squadrons of the group flew their original aircraft (Wellington, Stirling, Halifax, Lancaster and Mosquito) but eventually it standardised on the Lancaster and Mosquito only. Pathfinder crews were all volunteers who were experts in their respective aircrew trades and who had agreed to fly another tour of operations – volunteers within a volunteer force. The navigational skills of the Pathfinder Force were legendary and, combined with navigation and blind-bombing aids such as Oboe and H2S, they perfected target-marking techniques. With the use of coloured pyrotechnics they made possible the visual pinpointing and accurate bombing of targets by the main force crews who followed. Pathfinder Mosquitoes were also part of the Light Night Striking Force (LNSF), which flew high-speed nuisance raids against German industrial centres armed with 4,000lb HC 'Cookies'. By the war's end the Pathfinders had flown 51,053 sorties against 3,440 targets, for the loss of more than 3,700 aircrew and 675 aircraft. It was disbanded in December 1945.

Air Officers Commanding (with dates of appointment)
AVM D.C.T. Bennett – Jan 1943 (Bennett, as an air commodore, had been appointed to command the PFF in Aug 1942)
AVM J.R. Whitley – May 1945

No 6 (RCAF) Group

Formed on 25 October 1942 at Allerton Park (popularly known as 'Castle Dismal'), near Knaresborough in Yorkshire, 6 (RCAF) Group was unique in Bomber Command, being manned almost entirely by Canadians and paid for by the Canadian government. In January 1943 the group became operational with nine heavy bomber squadrons equipped with the Wellington, some of which were detached to the Middle East from June to November. Flying from airfields in North Yorkshire and County Durham, 6 (RCAF) Group's squadrons played a full part in the bomber offensive up until the very end of the war in Europe; the group was disbanded in August 1945. Equipped variously with the Wellington, Halifax and Lancaster, the group flew 39,584 sorties and dropped 126,122 tons of bombs and mines for the loss of 784 aircraft and almost 10,000 aircrew.

Air Officers Commanding (with dates of appointment)
AVM G.E. Brookes – Oct 1942
AVM C.M. McEwen – Feb 1944
Air Cdre J.L. Hurley – Jun 1945

No 100 (Bomber Support) Group

Formed on 28 November 1943 at Radlett, Hertfordshire, the headquarters of 100 (BS)

Group finally settled at Bylaugh Hall near Swanton Morley in Norfolk. This specialist – and very secret – group was an eclectic mix of heavy bomber and night-fighter aircraft and crews whose task was to wield a host of newly invented electronic and radio countermeasures equipment to confound the German night-fighter and air defence systems, thereby reducing the losses being inflicted upon Bomber Command's main force and Pathfinder squadrons. Using air and ground radars, homing and jamming equipment and special radio and navigational aids, the group's bomber aircraft jammed and deceived the German defences, while its night-fighter intruder aircraft roamed the night skies over Europe to seek out and destroy Luftwaffe night-fighters. By the war's end 100 (BS) Group had largely succeeded in paralysing the German night-fighter network. With 13 squadrons equipped with Halifax, Fortress, Stirling, Liberator, Wellington, Mosquito, Beaufighter and Lightning aircraft, the group operated from a clutch of airfields in north Norfolk. By the end of the war it had flown 7,932 radio countermeasures sorties for the loss of 47 aircraft and 8,814 'Serrate' and intruder sorties for the loss of 75 aircraft; it suffered more than 500 aircrew casualties. The group was disbanded in December 1945 but its contribution to the 'new' war of electronic

countermeasures had far-reaching implications for conflicts yet to come.

Air Officer Commanding (with date of appointment)
AVM E.B. Addison – Nov 1943

Training groups

No 6 (Training) Group

Formed on 2 September 1939 at Abingdon (then part of Berkshire), 6 (Training) Group controlled 14 so-called 'group pool' squadrons responsible for the operational instruction of newly trained aircrew. Aircraft of the same type as those in current use with front-line squadrons were allocated to the group. From early in 1940 these group pool squadrons became known as operational training units. On 11 May 1942, 6 (Training) Group became 91 (Operational Training Unit – OTU) Group.

Air Officers Commanding (with dates of appointment)
Air Cdre W.F. McN. Foster – Sep 1939
Grp Capt H.S.P. Walmsley – Mar 1942

No 7 (Training) Group

On 15 July 1940 a second operational training group, No 7, was formed with headquarters

at Bicester, Oxfordshire, to cope with the increase in demand for operational training. Its headquarters moved to Winslow Hall, Buckinghamshire, on 1 September 1941 where it was renumbered 92 (OTU) Group on 11 May 1942. No 7 (Training) Group was re-formed on 20 September 1944 with headquarters at St Vincents, Grantham, Lincolnshire, to control the growing number of Bomber Command heavy conversion units that were previously under the control of individual bomber groups. The group was finally disbanded on 21 December 1945 and control of its units passed to 91 (OTU) Group.

Air Officers Commanding (with dates of appointment)
Acting Air Cdre L.H. Cockey – Jul 1940
AVM E.A.B. Rice – Feb 1945

No 91 (OTU) Group

Formed on 11 May 1942 at Abingdon by renumbering 6 (Training) Group, 91 Group continued to administer bomber operational training units until disbandment in March 1947.

Air Officers Commanding (with dates of appointment)
Grp Capt H.S.P. Walmsley – May 1942
AVM J.A. Gray – Feb 1944

No 92 (OTU) Group

Formed on 14 May 1942 at Winslow Hall, by renumbering 7 (Training) Group, 92 Group continued to administer bomber operational

training units until its disbandment on 15 July 1945.

Air Officers Commanding (with dates of appointment)
Grp Capt H.A. Haines – May 1942
AVM H.K. Thorold – Mar 1943
AVM G.S. Hodson – Feb 1945

No 93 (OTU) Group

Formed on 15 June 1942 at Egginton Hall, Derby, 93 Group became the third operational training group to be established in order to cope with the huge demands for bomber aircrew operational training. With the eventual downturn in requirements as the war drew to a close, the group was absorbed into the remaining two OTU groups in January 1945.

Air Officers Commanding (with dates of appointment)
Grp Capt C.E. Maitland – Jun 1942
Air Cdre A.P. Ritchie – Feb 1943
AVM O.T. Boyd – Feb 1944
AVM G.S. Hodson – Aug 1944

The squadrons

At various times 130 bomber squadrons flew with Bomber Command in north-west Europe during the Second World War. Some could trace their lineage with pride back to the early years of the First World War, before the formation of the RAF in 1918.

The RAF's squadron numbering system

began with the formation of the service on 1 April 1918 and the initial sequence for RAF squadrons ran from 1 to 299; however, with the rapid expansion of the RAF during the Second World War and the incorporation of individual Commonwealth and Allied personnel and units, new block sequences of squadron numbers were made available, as follows: 300–352 Allied (*eg*, Polish, Dutch, French); 353–399 RAF; 400–449 Canadian; 450–484 Australian; 485–499 New Zealand; 500–509 Special Reserve; 510–599 RAF; 600–616 Auxiliary Air Force; 617–650 RAF; 651–673 Army; 674–699 RAF.

Under Article XV of the British Commonwealth Air Training Plan (BCATP) it was agreed that trained Canadian, Australian and New Zealand air- and groundcrews would be provided to serve with the RAF, but in return the RAF had to pay and equip them. These squadrons were actually RCAF, RAAF and RNZAF, but served under British operational control for the duration of the war and were therefore regarded as being part of the RAF's organisation. They were often referred to as 'Article XV squadrons'. Twenty-five such squadrons served at various times with Bomber Command and constituted a quarter of the Command's effective strength. Australian squadrons were the most numerous, with eight, and then there were two New Zealand squadrons, but the contribution from the antipodes was topped by the RCAF which supplied a whole bomber group (No 6) of – ultimately – 15 squadrons, from January 1943.

Although fewer in number, the nine squadrons from Allied countries overrun in the opening stages of the war contributed in no small way to Bomber Command's campaign. To some extent, their men had a stronger and more personal reason to hit back at Nazi Germany. Of these squadrons, four were Polish, four French (although two went to 2nd Tactical Air Force in May 1943, soon after their formation in the UK) and one Czech.

For a number of reasons – political, national security and just simple prejudice – the use by the RAF of personnel from Allied countries, particularly Czechoslovakia, was the source of much high-level discontent within the British government and at the Air Ministry.

Some squadrons had a name included in their titles. Allied squadrons like 311 (Czech) Squadron incorporated their nationality, while others adopted a regional title from their mother country; for example, the Free French 342 (Lorraine) Squadron. RAF squadrons manned largely by personnel from a Commonwealth country contained this recognition in their title, such as 44 (Rhodesia) Squadron or 139 (Jamaica) Squadron. Canadian squadrons incorporated the names of wild animals, birds – usually ones indigenous to Canada – or native Canadian tribes, like 431 (Iroquois) Squadron, or the name of an adoptive city, 405 (Vancouver) Squadron and so on. The practice established during the First World War of naming RAF squadrons after countries who had presented aircraft or made gifts of money to fund a particular squadron, continued during the Second World War; for instance, 97 (Straits Settlement) Squadron and 214 (Federated Malay States) Squadron.

ABOVE No 635 (Pathfinder) Squadron was formed on 20 March 1944 from C Flight 97 Squadron and B Flight 35 Squadron.

'Where cattle had grazed for centuries the scene changed to a landscape of hangars, bomb dumps and petrol storage tanks, squadron offices and other administrative buildings, messes and living quarters, control tower, radio and radar establishments – and a cinema.'

Alex Thorne, Lancaster pilot, 635 (Pathfinder) Squadron, describing RAF Downham Market.

Chapter Three

Airfield building

Eastern England became a giant springboard from which Bomber Command could launch its raids on Germany and occupied Europe. A huge network of frontline and training airfields were built, beginning in 1935 and gathering pace after war broke out. Operating from 33 permanent RAF stations in 1939, by the end of the war in 1945 Bomber Command's squadrons had flown from more than 170 airfields across England and Scotland.

OPPOSITE RAF Skellingthorpe was one of dozens of new airfields that sprung up across eastern England in the first years of the war. 'Skelly' was built on virgin countryside 3 miles west of Lincoln and opened for operations as a satellite to Swinderby in 1941, playing host to 50 and 61 Squadrons until the end of the war. Since the base closed in 1955 most traces of its wartime identity have almost completely vanished, obliterated by a 1970s housing estate. Pictured in the summer of 1942, 50 Squadron's Avro Lancaster B Mk I, R5689/VN-N, waits on the perimeter track, while seven other Lancasters can be seen at their dispersals. *(Fox Photos/Getty Images)*

By the end of the war in Europe in May 1945, over 170 airfields in England and Scotland had seen use by Bomber Command at various times in the six-year-long offensive against Germany, but the RAF's massive airfield-building programme had really taken off in 1935 with Expansion Scheme 'C'. A carefully planned construction schedule provided for some 100 new military airfields, which continued without interruption up until the outbreak of war four years later.

Scheme 'C' was approved in March 1935 and emphasised the need for the RAF's bomber force to be able to reach Berlin in a latitudinally straight line. The eastern counties of England, particularly in Lincolnshire and Yorkshire, became the obvious choices for the construction of these new airfields, sowing the seeds for the rapid growth of what in future years would become known as the 'Bomber Counties' of the Second World War.

Even before the League of Nations' Geneva Disarmament Conference in 1932, plans were afoot at home to construct new airfields for the RAF. In the early 1930s the Air Ministry Works Directorate (AMWD) was formed as the body responsible for the planning and organisation

BELOW Elevation drawings of a typical Expansion Scheme officers' mess and quarters building. A standardised design of well-proportioned Georgian-style architecture was applied across all expansion period RAF stations, with careful attention given to the locality in the choice of colour, texture and pointing of stone and brickwork, and the choice and colour of roof tiles.

of these new airfields. A subsidiary of the AMWD was created in 1934, known as the Air Ministry Aerodromes Board (AMAB). Its task was to work in close liaison with the Air Ministry Lands Branch (AMLB) in the selection of suitable sites for new airfields. An important part of the AMAB's brief was to create a standard architectural style for both airfield and domestic facilities, and to prepare plans for the modification of existing airfields.

The environmental impact of all this new land development, much of it in the heart of the English countryside, attracted the attention of a number of monitoring groups. All plans for permanent buildings on new airfields had to be approved by the Royal Fine Arts Commission, while the siting of airfields in the countryside involved consultations with the Society for the Preservation of Rural England.

Expansion Scheme bomber stations

Work on the first of the RAF's Expansion Scheme bomber stations – Cranfield (Bedfordshire), Feltwell, (Norfolk), Harwell (Oxfordshire), Marham (Norfolk), Stradishall

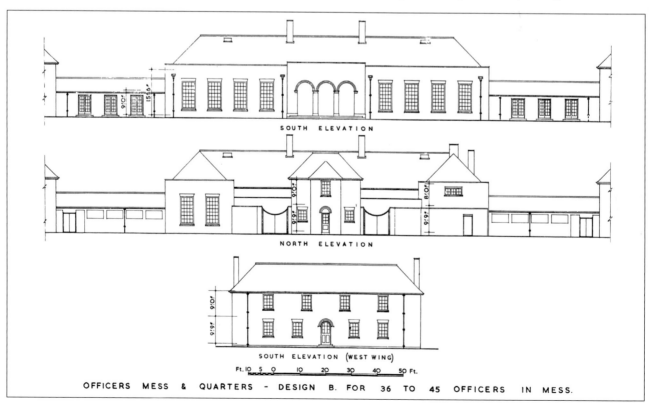

SOUTH ELEVATION

NORTH ELEVATION

SOUTH ELEVATION (WEST WING)

Ft. 10 5 0   10   20   30   40   50 Ft.

OFFICERS MESS & QUARTERS - DESIGN B. FOR 36 TO 45 OFFICERS IN MESS.

(Suffolk) and Waddington (Lincolnshire) – began in 1935. At the same time a number of existing bomber stations, like Upper Heyford in Oxfordshire, underwent a modernisation programme. Work on further new permanent stations was begun in 1936: Dishforth, Driffield, Finningley and Leconfield (Yorkshire); Hemswell and Scampton (Lincolnshire); Upwood and Wyton (Huntingdonshire) – names that would soon assume well-earned places in the annals of the RAF.

Expansion Scheme stations were characterised by their high standard of construction, distinctive and comfortable neo-Georgian headquarters buildings, messes and quarters and solid C-Type aircraft hangars. Technical buildings were generally located alongside and to the rear of the hangars. Accommodation was centralised and laid out to a roughly circular arrangement and not dispersed over a large area like the dozens of hostilities-only 'prefab' bomber stations that were built during the course of the Second World War. The last permanent bomber stations to be built before the outbreak of war included: Middleton St George (County Durham – the most northerly of the front-line bomber airfields); Leeming and Topcliffe (Yorkshire); Binbrook, Coningsby and Swinderby (Lincolnshire); Newton and Syerston (Nottinghamshire); Bramcote (Warwickshire); Oakington and Waterbeach (Cambridgeshire); North Luffenham (Rutland); and Oulton and Swanton Morley (Norfolk).

Hangars

The Air Ministry decided that a new standard hangar was needed for its bomber stations with a clear span of 150ft, clear length of 300ft and a clear height of 35ft. These generous dimensions would allow new specifications to be issued to aircraft manufacturers to design heavy bomber aircraft with wingspans greater than 100ft (in 1939 the Short Stirling at 99ft 1.12in and the Handley Page Halifax at 98ft 8in, followed in 1941 by the Avro Lancaster at 102ft span).

ABOVE The Airmen's Mess at RAF Scampton (which opened in 1936) has secured a place in aviation history as the building inside which the aircrew briefings for the dams raid were held on 16 May 1943. In the background can be seen the station's water tower and the hipped roof of one of its four C2-Type hangars.

RIGHT In this aerial view of the Pathfinder base at RAF Wyton in Huntingdonshire, the general layout of an Expansion Scheme airfield and its three-runway layout can be appreciated.

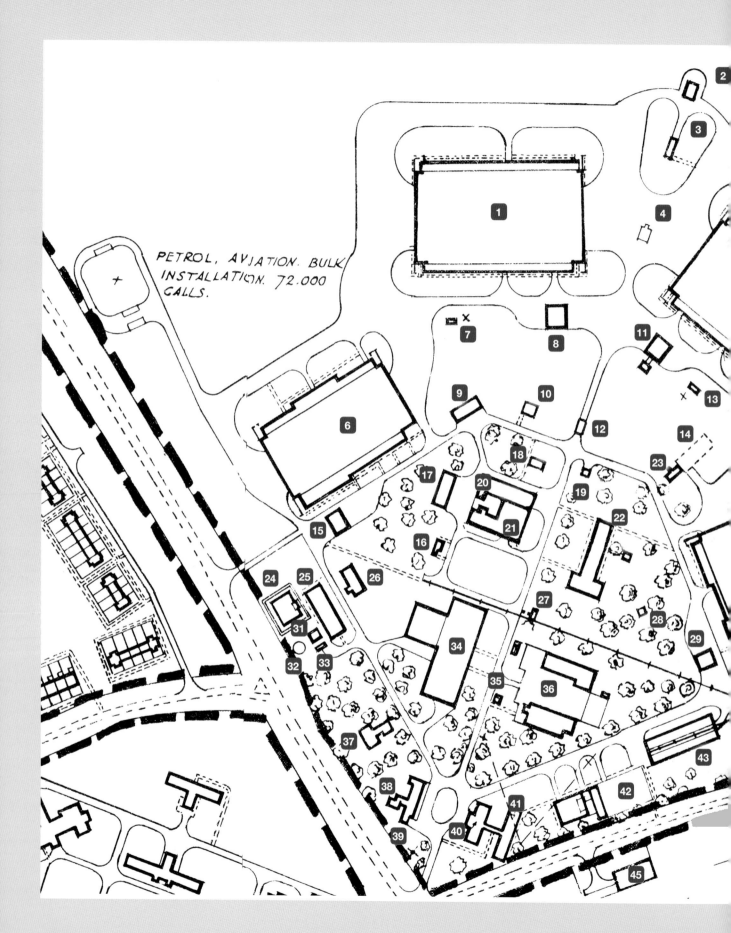

PETROL, AVIATION. BULK
INSTALLATION. 72.000
GALLS.

RAF BICESTER, CENTRAL AREA SITE PLAN

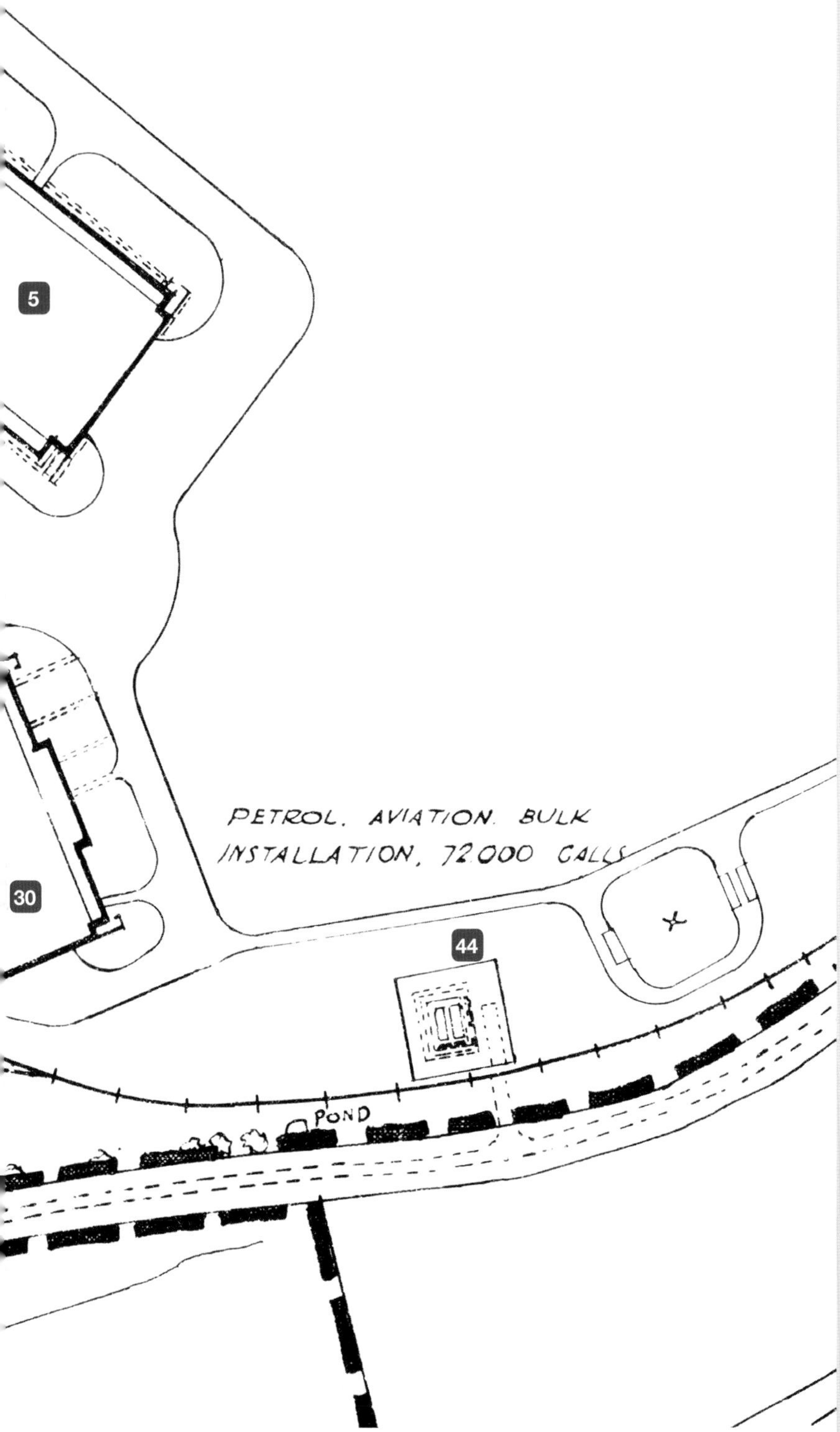

RAF Bicester in Oxfordshire can trace its origins back to 1916 as a Royal Flying Corps training airfield. As a result of the Expansion Scheme the airfield underwent a significant modernisation programme in 1937, which saw the construction of two new hangars, a bomb dump, additional quarters for officers and airmen and a new control tower, among other buildings. Its layout is a fairly typical example of a permanent airfield from this period.

Key

1 C-Type hangar
2 Watch office with tower
3 Fire tender shelter
4 Watch office
5 C-Type hangar
6 C-Type hangar
7 Pyrotechnics store
8 Petrol tanker shed
9 Engine test house
10 Link trainer hut
11 Petrol tanker shed
12 Workshops
13 Pyrotechnics store
14 Machine-gun test butt
15 Petrol tanker shed
16 Inflammables stores
17 Lubricants and liquid container stores
18 Latrines, technical
19 Fire tender and Hucks starter shelter
20 Gymnasium
21 Main workshops
22 Armoury, lecture rooms and AML Teacher
23 Shelter, practice bombs
24 Reservoir (100,000gal)
25 Power house
26 Parachute store
27 Oil, lubricant, bulk installations, 2,000gal
28 Group XII ammunition store
29 Petrol tanker shed
30 C-Type hangar
31 Cooling pond
32 Elevated water tank, 30,000gal
33 Crude oil store
34 Main and church stores
35 Bulk MT fuel underground installation, 12,000gal
36 MT sheds
37 Fire party house
38 Guard and fire party house
39 Flagstaff
40 Offices, station headquarters and camera obscura
41 Operations block
42 Works services buildings
43 Fuel stores
44 Bulk aviation fuel installation, 24,000gal
45 Pyrotechnics bulk store.

PETROL. AVIATION. BULK INSTALLATION, 72000 GALLS

POND

ABOVE RAF Dishforth in Yorkshire was among the new permanent bomber stations that were begun in 1936. It had five C-Type hangars, each of which was able to accommodate several heavy bombers like a Lancaster or a Halifax. These Halifax Mk IIIs of 426 (Thunderbird) Squadron are parked inside and beyond the station's No 2 hangar in March 1945.

The design chosen to meet these criteria became known as the C-Type and following a succession of modifications it became the standard permanent RAF hangar, being erected at virtually all of the early Expansion Scheme stations from Lossiemouth in Scotland to Upwood in Huntingdonshire. A typical RAF heavy bomber station had two C-Type hangars per squadron (a station typically housing two squadrons).

Initially C-Type hangars were built with a steel framework clad in brick, but from 1936 when fears of war began to circulate this was changed to reinforced concrete. The wall stanchions supported lattice roof girders separated by hipped roof trusses consisting of timber purlins and boarding with asbestos slates. Large glazed panels were fitted to each bay to allow natural light into the hangar, and there were rows of windows down each side. Sets of heavy lifting gear were also provided, which were capable of lifting stores and equipment weighing between 1½ and 6 tons. Enclosing the ends of the hangar were two sets of six-leaf doors constructed with steel plates on both sides and the cavity filled with gravel to a height of 20ft as a protection against shrapnel. Single- or two-storey side annexes were added as squadron office accommodation.

In 1938 the C-Type was redesigned to make it more economical to build, with a reduction of 5ft in the roof height and steel cantilevered roof frames with asbestos sheet cladding; it became known unofficially as the C1-Type.

A new airfield-building programme

As Europe began its rapid descent into war during the summer of 1939, the British government and parliament reacted to the signing of the Nazi–Soviet Pact of 23 August by passing the Emergency Powers (Defence) Act within 24 hours. Among the many far-reaching provisions of this Act, the Air Ministry was given authority to requisition suitable land across the country for use by the RAF. Civilian building contractors were invited to tender for contracts and an ambitious new programme of airfield building quickly got under way.

Big construction companies like Laing, Costain, Taylor-Woodrow and Wimpey (now Taylor Wimpey plc), which are well known today as house and infrastructure builders, were involved in the airfield-building programme. A greater number of smaller contractors were also involved and where individual firms possessed insufficient plant of their own, machinery was loaned to them by the AMWD so that all companies, big and small, could play their part in the massive undertaking. Once tenders had been accepted and issued, work began on clearing and levelling sites. Armies of workmen with heavy plant moved in to remodel the English rural landscape into launch pads for hundreds of Allied bomber aircraft and accommodation for the thousands of RAF personnel who would make this possible.

At the outbreak of war Bomber Command was operating from 27 permanent airfields in England and Scotland, all of which were grass surfaced. A significant number of large, permanent airfields were also nearing completion at this time, legacies of the Expansion Scheme. As a result of the sudden

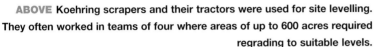

ABOVE Koehring scrapers and their tractors were used for site levelling. They often worked in teams of four where areas of up to 600 acres required regrading to suitable levels.

BELOW Mechanical compacting and spreading machines like this American supplied Blaw-Knox equipment were used for runway paving. They were self-propelled and spread, levelled and tamped the surfacing material in one operation. These laying machines produced a high-quality finish that eliminated surface 'waves' on runways and could work to a tolerance of ¼in in every 10ft of length.

ABOVE Proper consolidation of subgrades and foundations was particularly important where the construction of runways and taxiways was concerned. Several different kinds of machine were used for this task, of which the sheepsfoot roller (pictured) was probably the best as its high pressure of up to 300lb/sq in enabled a greater degree of soil compaction than would have been possible with smooth-wheeled rollers.

BELOW Construction workers and plant are pictured laying runways at an airfield 'somewhere in England' during the war. Many of the runways from which RAF bomber squadrons operated between 1943 and 1945 were founded on blitz brick and masonry hardcore from bomb-damaged British towns and cities.

changes in Air Ministry requirements brought on by the outbreak of war, major specification changes were considered necessary at these half-finished airfields to provide additional barrack blocks, bomb stores and ancillary buildings. Comprehensive camouflage schemes were put into operation using paint, netting and other materials in order to make runways, hangars and other buildings as inconspicuous as possible from the air.

Runways and dispersals

Bomber airfields built before the war, when grass landing strips were the norm, had no paved runways. With the introduction to service of heavier bomber aircraft the need for metalled runways to allow an unhindered all-weather operational capability became clear. Grass airfields were generally quite adequate in the summer, but with the onset of winter poor drainage of surface water led to waterlogging

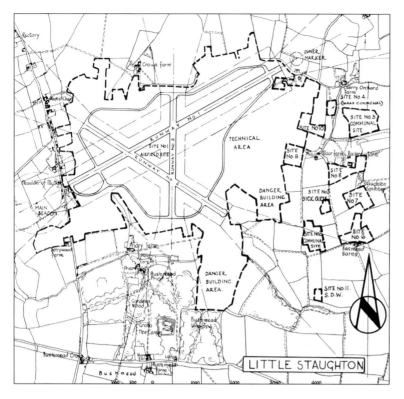

LITTLE STAUGHTON

and serious problems for an airfield's operational effectiveness. The advantages of tarmac and concrete runways became apparent and in 1939 work began to gradually re-equip most of the Command's airfields with a new three-runway layout, perimeter tracks and concrete dispersal pans.

The new dispersal pan system allowed squadron aircraft to be scattered around an airfield perimeter to save them from damage or destruction in the event of enemy air attack. Aircraft were usually only returned to the hangars for major engineering or repair work, although a shortage of hangars was the principal reason behind this practice.

From December 1940 all new bomber airfields were constructed with one paved main runway of 1,400yd and two subsidiaries each of 1,100yd in length. By February 1941 this scale was amended with an increase in length of the main runway to 1,600yd. In October the same year, requirements had changed still further, extending the main runway length to 2,000yd with subsidiaries each of 1,400yd, thereby setting the standard for runway dimensions until the end of the war. In practice the subsidiary runways were rarely used and towards the end of the war doubts were expressed about whether a three-runway layout was needed at all on heavy bomber stations.

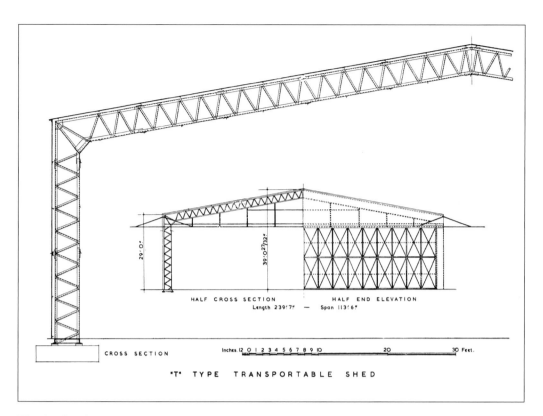

29'.0"

39'.0²⁷/₃₂"

HALF CROSS SECTION
Length 239'.7" — Span 113'.6"

HALF END ELEVATION

CROSS SECTION

Inches. 12 0 1 2 3 4 5 6 7 8 9 10   20   30 Feet.

"T" TYPE TRANSPORTABLE SHED

Technical accommodation

Because of the large aircraft they operated, bomber stations needed more large hangars and technical accommodation than fighter stations, although what they did have remained inadequate for much of the war. In fact, the rapid growth in the bomber force and the increasing complexity of its new and heavier aircraft outstripped a hoped-for parallel growth in ground support services and equipment. As a result, powerplant, workshop and other technical accommodation fell far short of the Command's minimum requirements, at least until the end of 1943.

Prefabricated buildings

To keep pace with the rapid rate of airfield construction a range of prefabricated structures was developed that combined ease and speed of erection with cost-effectiveness and durability. Prefab Nissen and Romney huts sprung up around the new airfields with a new type of steel-fabricated hangar of welded and bolted construction covered with galvanised corrugated iron sheeting. Called the T-Type hangar, the design was refined over several years and in its T2 version it became the standard temporary

hangar for the RAF during the Second World War with some 906 built for RAF stations at home and overseas.

BELOW An idea of the T-Type's metal framework can be gained from this unusual photograph that shows how a third-hand example was rebuilt in 2015 at Schiphol in the Netherlands for use as a bus station. The hangar had been among many that were surplus to RAF and USAAF requirements when the war ended and it was bought second-hand in the 1950s for £350 (including dismantling and transport to the Netherlands) to use at Zestienhoven Airport in Rotterdam. *(Studiegroep Luchtoorlog 1939–1945)*

LEFT Completed in 1943, the 100 (BS) Group airfield at North Creake in north Norfolk is situated 2½ miles east of the village from which it takes its name. In this view, looking north-north-east, the airfield's technical site and control tower are evident, along with a stretch of perimeter track, a variety of prefab buildings and a pair of T2 hangars.

CENTRE Nissen huts were a common sight on many 'hostilities only' wartime bomber airfields. They were one of the principal forms of temporary buildings and were used for all kinds of accommodation. Semi-circular in section, they came in three spans – 16ft, 24ft and 30ft, all of which were covered with 26-gauge corrugated iron sheeting. They could be built to any length in multiples of 6ft-bays. This is one of the dispersed sites at RAF Ludford Magna near Louth in Lincolnshire that opened in June 1943.

Lighting systems

The need became clear for a standard night-landing lighting system on all airfields in the Command. The result was the Mk II System, which was controlled from the watch office and was highly effective in reducing the time taken to land heavy bombers at night. It also increased the number of aircraft it was possible to operate from one airfield.

LEFT Creature comforts could be few and far between in the Spartan accommodation on a wartime bomber airfield. Here, Plt Off Trevor Charlesworth (left) and his 44 Squadron Lancaster crew ham it up for the camera as they pretend to warm themselves on the coke stove in their Nissen hut at Dunholme Lodge after returning from a raid on Stuttgart, 2 March 1944. It is shocking to note that by the end of the month all but one of these men had been killed on operations. Only bomb-aimer Sgt Mike Fedoruk (foreground, wearing the Canada flash) survived being shot down over the Netherlands with another crew on 24/25 March on ops to Berlin, successfully evading capture.

A programme fraught with problems

Such a large upsurge in airfield construction needed huge numbers of workers, but supply and demand were not always a good fit and there were inevitable labour shortages. On top of this came two knotty problems that continued to thwart the AMWD for much of the war in its desire to maintain a smooth-running construction programme.

In the first problem, the Air Ministry's regular changes concerning the dimensions and levels of accommodation on bomber airfields meant that alterations in airfield layout and dispersal schemes had to be made in mid-contract, with all the disruption to work and the re-tendering of contracts this entailed.

With the second, the Ministry of Works' tight control on payments and an emphasis on quick completion meant there was a tendency for contractors to rush through the work without adequate supervision, which often resulted in the mix of concrete for runways and perimeter tracks falling below the required standard. With this unrelenting pressure on contractors to speed up, their work was often carried out when the weather was unsuitable for laying concrete – for example in a frost or in heavy rain. The consequence was that owing to the constant pounding by heavy bomber aircraft taking off and landing day and night, many runways and perimeter tracks showed signs of disintegration after only brief use, requiring their closure for repairs – with all the knock-on effects this had for flying operations.

By 1942 the pace of runway construction had gathered such momentum that an average completion time from foundations down to receiving the first bomber aircraft was from five to seven months. To complete an entire 'A'-class (Heavy Bomber) airfield with all facilities it would take a 1,000-strong labour force about 18 months. Such was the rapid rate of construction that in the peak year for airfield building in 1942 an average of one new airfield was coming into use with the RAF every three days at an average cost of about £1 million each.

During the war the Air Ministry was by far and away the biggest user nationally of cement, ballast and stone for airfield and runway construction. At a conservative estimate the airfield-building programme in the UK consumed more than 60 million tons of these materials.

Very Heavy Bomber upgrades

During 1943 the RAF identified a number of its airfields as suitable for improvement to Very Heavy Bomber (VHB) standard in order to take the expected Boeing B-29 Washington (or Superfortress in USAAF parlance) and the projected Vickers Windsor (never to enter service). Lakenheath, Marham and Sculthorpe in East Anglia were earmarked to become the first VHB airfields and were closed for major reconstruction work during 1944–45.

The end of the war

Within months of peace being declared in the summer of 1945, the RAF began to wind down its huge force of men and machines, airfields and weapons. Squadrons were disbanded, air- and groundcrews demobbed, hundreds of aircraft were scrapped and thousands of redundant bombs dumped into the seas around Britain; and dozens of airfields which had once been home to the most powerful conventional bomber force the world had yet seen were returned to the ploughshare and Mother Nature, from whence they had come.

BELOW Still recognisable as an airfield more than 70 years after its closure, North Killingholme was one of a clutch of 1 Group bomber bases built on the flatlands south of the Humber Estuary. It has largely avoided the fate of many other bomber bases, most of which have either been returned to agriculture or ripped up for redevelopment. This evocative photograph was taken in August 2014 from the Canadian Warplane Heritage's Lancaster during its UK tour. *(Peter Smith)*

'Life on the squadron was seldom far from fantasy. We might, at eight, be in a chair beside a fire, but at ten, in an empty world above a floor of cloud. Or at eight, walking in Barnetby with a girl whose nearness denied all possibility of sudden death at twelve.'

Don Charlwood, Lancaster navigator, 103 Squadron, 1942–43.

Chapter Four

Bomber boys

Bomber Command was truly international in its make-up, with crews drawn not only from the mother country but also from the nations of the Empire and Dominions overseas. Canada was unique in supplying an entire bomber group, while exiles from the Nazi-occupied countries of Europe also played their part, with one Czech and four Polish-manned squadrons formed in Bomber Command.

OPPOSITE RAF bomber boys: the seven-man crew of an Avro Lancaster wait near the locker room at Waddington for transport out to their aircraft at dispersal in October 1942. At this time the Lincolnshire airfield was home to a pair of Lancaster squadrons – Nos 9 and 44.

ABOVE 1940 – Handley Page Hampden medium bomber crew. Sqn Ldr David Drakes and his 49 Squadron crew of four – Plt Off William Cheetham, air gunner; Plt Off Victor Beaney, navigator/bomb-aimer; Sqn Ldr David Drakes, pilot; and Flt Sgt William Watson, air gunner. They failed to return from a shipping strike off the Frisian Islands on 1 November 1941.

the far corners of the Empire and from the Nazi-occupied countries of Europe and Scandinavia. A typical RAF bomber crew was a microcosm of Bomber Command itself, reflecting this broad international and social mix of humanity. In fact by January 1945 nearly half of Bomber Command's pilots were from Canada, Australia or New Zealand.

All RAF bomber aircrew were volunteers, and in the case of the Pathfinder Force many were volunteers within a volunteer force. Canada contributed a complete bomber group, No 6, while other countries supplied entire squadrons. By the war's end most of Bomber Command's aircrew was made up of men who were volunteers (that is, not regulars) and who at the beginning of the war had still been at school. Those who had been regulars in the pre-war RAF and who had survived the culling of six years of war, were by now in a distinct minority.

Bomber aircrew trades

The bomber crew

RIGHT 1944 – Avro Lancaster heavy bomber crew. This is the eight-man crew of WO John Laurens DFM (far left) pictured at Ludford Magna with Lancaster DV267/SR-K, before leaving on one of the Berlin raids in early 1944. The eighth crewmember, special operator Sgt Jim Davies, stands next to him. The crew failed to return from an operation to Leipzig on 19/20 February, their aircraft crashing near Groningen in the Netherlands. Laurens and two of his crew died, but five (including Jim Davies) survived.

(Getty Images)

Bomber Command and the aircrews who served in it were probably unique in the history of warfare. The Command itself was a truly cosmopolitan affair, attracting men from

At the outbreak of war the aircrew of a typical twin-engine light bomber such as the Blenheim Mk IV was made up of a pilot, an observer/bomb-aimer and a wireless operator/air gunner. By the war's end the crew of a four-engine heavy bomber like the Lancaster could number up to eight men: pilot, navigator, flight

engineer, bomb-aimer, wireless operator, mid-upper gunner, tail gunner and perhaps an extra gunner, navigator or 'special operator'.

As the war gathered momentum, the growing size and complexity of bomber aircraft made it necessary to restructure the bomber crew, bringing in new and specialised crew trades while revising the duties of existing ones. In 1939 a medium or heavy bomber like the Wellington or Whitley had two pilots, one the captain and the other a novice gaining experience under his instruction. This practice was later considered wasteful and discontinued in 1942 because the Air Ministry insisted that it was impossible to train sufficient pilots to carry two per aircraft in Bomber Command. A single-pilot policy was therefore adopted throughout the Command, but Don Bennett, AOC of the Pathfinder Force, took a very different view of this change in policy, which was beginning to have its greatest effect just when the PFF was created: 'Had junior pilots been brought in to act as flight engineers for, say, fifteen trips before they went for their final conversion training to fly in command of heavies, a tremendous improvement in efficiency and a reduction in losses would have resulted.' Nevertheless, this was but one of the ways in which the role of the bomber pilot gradually evolved from the pre-war duties of flying and navigating the aircraft to one of purely piloting, the other jobs being taken over by specialist aircrew trades.

The pilot was identified by the flying brevet with two wings either side of a laurel wreath surrounding the letters 'RAF', surmounted by a king's crown. The same design applied to pilots from Canada, Australia and New Zealand, with the letters replaced by RCAF, RAAF or RNZAF respectively.

Defence of the bomber against enemy fighters lay in the hands of the air gunner. Before the war he was an armament tradesman who could be called upon to fly as an air gunner, for which he was paid only for the time he spent in the air. He wore a brass winged bullet on each sleeve, but for him flying was a secondary duty. Not until May 1940 did the Air Ministry officially decree that all aircrew tradesmen (that is, air gunners and wireless operator/air gunners) should be promoted from

the ranks to at least sergeant. This promotion applied to all other ranks who had completed training in their aircrew trade category and who were flying operationally. There were two aircrew trades that came under the air gunner category: wireless operator/air gunner and straight air gunner. Both were identified by the twelve-feather half-wing brevet with a laurel wreath surrounding the letters 'AG'. Wireless operators were identified by the addition of 'sparks' badges on each sleeve above their stripes, although a few 'WAG' brevets were issued.

With the move to night operations in 1940, bomber aircraft began flying ever-increasing distances and it became clear that a navigation specialist was required. Although the aircrew category of observer (designated by the flying 'O' half-wing brevet, but without the laurel wreath) had been around since the First World War and performed the duty of second aircrew member responsible for navigation, bomb-aiming and any other task called upon to do by the pilot, it was clearly insufficient because the pilot was still the primary navigator. Not until the introduction of the specialist navigator category in 1942, identified by the 'N' half-wing brevet, did the situation change. Now that the roles of pilot and navigator had been more clearly defined, a requirement for further specialist categories became apparent – that of the air bomber ('B') and flight engineer ('E').

A greater range of bombs were now in use by the RAF and with them came more complex bombsights and bomb-release mechanisms. Analysis of early raids had identified the need for two specialists in bomber crew: the navigator to take the bomber to the target area and an air bomber to take over and make the final run-in to the target where he would release the bombs. Along with the flight engineer category, that of the air bomber was introduced at about the same time as the navigator.

The advent of the four-engine bomber, the first of which was the Short Stirling, led to the creation of the flight engineer trade to handle the mechanical, hydraulic, electrical and fuel systems during flight. He also acted as a link between the aircrew and the groundcrew. The first officially trained flight engineers began arriving on the squadrons in April 1941, although it was not until September 1942 that official recognition was forthcoming with the introduction of the specialist 'E' flying brevet.

Up until the autumn of 1944, flight engineers for Canadian heavy bomber squadrons in England were in short supply because the RCAF did not train aircrew in this trade. As a palliative for this situation the RAF supplied trained flight engineers on attachment to 6 Group's bomber squadrons. Towards the end

of 1943 the Canadians began training their own flight engineers in response to an Air Ministry request for this aircrew category to serve with RCAF heavy crews, but it was late in 1944 before the first appeared on the squadrons.

From mid-1943 the importance of radio countermeasures to the bomber offensive became increasingly plain. To the newly designated special duty squadrons of 100 (BS) Group a new aircrew category was added. Known as a 'special operator', or 'spec op' for short, his duty was to operate the onboard electronic jamming equipment with which to block German communications. Spec ops were selected from all aircrew categories and every man was a German-language speaker; some were German-born, while others were German Jews, who took an extra personal risk whenever they flew over enemy territory.

On the main force squadrons it was also not uncommon for an extra (eighth) crew-member to be carried to operate the H2S set. He was usually a navigator and was known as the 'Y' operator, 'Y' equipment being another codename for the H2S radar.

Bomber aircrew commissioning policy

Since the earliest days of the RAF when it became clear that more than one person was needed to crew a large aircraft, the most important figure in any aircrew has always been the pilot. In most cases he was a commissioned officer and was designated the captain of the aircraft. Along with two other key crew-members – the navigator and the bomb-aimer – the leadership qualities of these three men were vital to the cohesion of a Second World War RAF bomber crew.

The Air Ministry's aircrew commissioning policy, which held good for much of the Second World War, reflected this need for leadership, and was based largely on its pre-war perception of the RAF as a small elite band of regular officers, the question of who was in charge of a bomber aircraft, and its views on social class which reflected those of British society in the 1940s. The benchmark for an aircrew commission in the RAF during the pre-war years had been leadership – or displaying

RIGHT Standing at his engineer's panel in a Stirling of 75 (NZ) Squadron, Sgt A.R. Gunn grins for the camera. Initially, the lack of a proper job description for the flight engineer meant that some crews considered him superfluous, but when the Air Ministry got wind of this they moved quickly to formalise the important role.

'officer-like qualities' – which reflected strongly the public school ethos of the period. But during the Second World War when NCOs made up the greater part of the RAF's bomber crews, change was forced on to a reluctant Air Ministry.

More pilots, navigators and bomb-aimers were commissioned on completion of their flying training than were the other aircrew categories – the so-called 'tradesmen' like air gunners, wireless operators and flight engineers. Of those who were commissioned out of the former group, many were likely to have been educated at public school. More than a few who served in RAF bomber aircrew during the war suspected that the 'old school tie' network lay behind commissioning policy, but it is equally true to say that many officers in the RAF and Bomber Command in particular were not public school educated. In an aircraft piloted by an NCO where there were commissioned officers in the crew, in some instances the navigator or bomb-aimer (who was commissioned) would be designated as the captain of the aircraft. However, it was not uncommon to find all-NCO aircrews. In any case, if a man survived a tour of 30 bomber operations he would almost certainly be put forward for a commission, the reasoning probably being that he must have had officer-like qualities to get him through a tour unscathed – a back-handed compliment if ever there was one.

The RCAF, which from 1942 was a large supplier of trained bomber aircrew to the RAF, suggested there should be more fairness in granting commissions to all who shared the same dangers as aircrew, arguing that NCO rank was not compatible with the heavy responsibilities of a pilot. Needless to say, the Air Ministry was unconvinced by the argument. But the need for aircrew continued to grow as the bomber offensive gained momentum and the original supply of public school candidates soon diminished, forcing the RAF to open its aircrew ranks to a wider social catchment. Soon, it was the turn of men who were products of the grammar and secondary modern schools to swell the ranks of the RAF's bomber crews. Young men like Michael Beetham and Ivor Broom joined up almost straight from school and served the RAF well. They each became distinguished bomber pilots

in their own right during the war and rose to high office in the postwar RAF – Sir Michael Beetham became Marshal of the RAF, Sir Ivor Broom an air marshal and group commander in Strike Command.

Training new crews

At the outbreak of war one of the main tasks of Bomber Command's small regular force of officers and men was to train the huge influx of aircrew volunteers. Some of the older volunteers for flying duties had experience of flying from before the war with University Air Squadrons or the Volunteer Reserve, but the vast majority had never flown before.

To train these volunteers, from August 1939, 13 squadrons were reserved for operational training duties and became known as Group Pool Squadrons under the control of 6 (Training) Group, although from April 1940 they were renamed Operational Training Units (OTU). They provided six-week courses in which individuals were welded into crews and converted on to type; 55 hours of flying for those earmarked for heavy bombers, 60 for light/medium bombers. In July 1940 a second OTU group, No 7, was formed to cope with the increase in demand for operational training. These two groups were later renumbered 91 and 92 Groups when a third OTU group, No 93, was formed in May 1942. (With the downturn in the operational training requirements of the Service Flying

ABOVE NCOs made up more than 70% of RAF bomber crews, but in a reflection of the social inequalities of the period, awards of the Distinguished Flying Medal (DFM) accounted for less than a quarter of the combined total of almost 27,000 Distinguished Flying Crosses (DFC) and DFMs awarded during the Second World War.

ABOVE Fresh-faced aircrew recruits march off smartly to collect their kit from the RAF's No 3 Aircrew Reception Centre (ACRC) at Lord's cricket ground in 1942. The men were billeted in requisitioned blocks of flats nearby in St John's Wood and Regent's Park, which were collectively known as RAF Regents Park. At its wartime peak, ACRC processed 1,700 recruits per week. One can wonder not only how many of these young men would pass the selection for aircrew, but also how many more would survive the war. From Lord's they were posted to an Initial Training Wing (ITW) for further specialist training.

BELOW Aircrew basic training included flight theory and navigation and was undertaken in England at more than 35 Initial Training Wings around the country, many of which were located in requisitioned hotels in resort towns. This is C Flight, 1 Squadron of 17 ITW, billeted at Belvedere House on the Esplanade at Scarborough in North Yorkshire, pictured in July 1943. How many of these smiling faces lived to see the peace in 1945?

ABOVE Aircrew under training could be identified by the white flash in the front of their forage caps. It was worn until training was complete, when they received their 'wings' at Elementary Flying Training School.

Training Schools (SFTS) as the war drew to a close, 93 (OTU) Group's flying units were eventually absorbed into the remaining two training groups in January 1945.) Bombers of the same types as those being used in the front-line squadrons were allocated to the OTUs and tour-expired aircrew were 'rested' at them as instructors to pass on their first-hand

knowledge of operational flying to the novice crews. Training crews for heavy bombers made the biggest demand on the OTU system, with only two supplying trained crews to the light bomber squadrons of 2 Group from an average total of 22 OTUs.

However, before volunteers could be posted to Bomber Command they needed to undergo basic theoretical and flying training in Training Command. Aircrew basic training was undertaken at one of the many Initial Training Wings (ITW) scattered across England, where drill and PT were combined with classroom work to prepare minds and bodies for the next stage in the training programme. After completion of the passing-out examinations, and various psychological and aptitude tests, successful graduates were shipped overseas for flying training. As a result of the Empire Air Training Agreement much of this was carried out at SFTS thousands of miles away from the shores of Great Britain in the safer and less congested skies of the Dominions and the USA. (The exception was for flight engineers who were trained at 4 School of Technical Training, St Athan, in South Wales.) Those bomber crews who trained overseas will never forget the colourful names of their training airfields in the Dominion countries like Canada, for example – airfields named Moose Jaw, Medicine Hat and Portage la Prairie, set in the expansive flatlands of Canada's prairies.

At the peak of the scheme in September 1943, there were 333 Flying Training Schools of which 153 were in the UK, 92 in Canada, 26 in Australia, 25 in South Africa, 10 in South Rhodesia, 9 in India, 6 each in New Zealand and the Middle East, 5 in the USA and 1 in the Bahamas. Of course, these schools trained aircrew for the RAF as a whole, but Bomber Command was a major beneficiary.

Flying Training Command produced pilots, navigators, bomb-aimers, wireless operators and air gunners, and handed them over to Bomber Command, whose job it then was at the OTUs to fuse them into fighting crews and then convert them on to the operational types they would soon be flying into battle.

The 'crewing-up' process at OTU was a haphazard affair but was in most cases highly successful. Hundreds of young men fresh out

of flying training were herded into hangars and told to sort themselves out into crews. What attracted individuals to one another ranged from physical appearance to smoking or drinking habits and the crews that resulted from this strange 'marriage' of individuals were often of mixed nationality and social background, comprising men from the four corners of the Empire and from all walks of life. Once on a squadron, the very nature of their shared experiences and mutual danger quickly bonded them into tightly knit crews who grew together. In many of those who survived the war, these bonds endured into old age. In early 1943, however, only about 17%

ABOVE More Bomber Command aircrew were trained in Canada under the British Commonwealth Air Training Plan (BCATP) than anywhere else. No 31 Elementary Flying Training School (EFTS) operated from Calgary on the prairies of Alberta in western Canada, one of 92 flying training schools in the country.

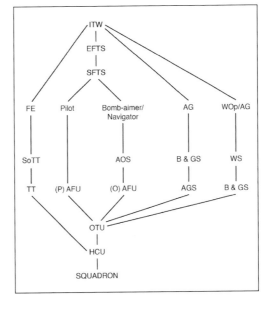

LEFT RAF bomber crew training in 1944.

of RAF bomber crews could expect to finish a 30-operation tour.

By early 1942, the length of the OTU training stood at 80 hours during a ten-week course, a figure which it remained at more or less for the rest of the war. Intakes were fortnightly with between 11 and 16 crews arriving at a time. The principal and most numerous aircraft type on which crews trained at OTU was the Wellington and a single OTU would have on strength some 50 aircraft. In the main these were hand-me-downs from the front-line squadrons, worn out and in need of considerable engineering support to keep them flying safely. Needless to say, the exigencies of war meant that many OTU aircraft were kept flying long after they should have been grounded and became virtual death traps. This, combined with the youthful inexperience of their crews, meant that fatal accidents during operational training were high: some classes lost as many as 25% of their strength in three or four months. The churchyards of many a small town in the Vales of Evesham and York pay mute testimony to the thousands of trainee aircrew who never made it on to an operational squadron, victims of clapped-out aircraft and their own inexperience.

With the downturn in operational training requirements as the war drew to a close, 93 (OTU) Group's flying units were eventually absorbed into the remaining two training groups in January 1945.

Two difficulties arose when the new four-engine bombers started arriving on the squadrons at an ever-quickening pace to replace the twin-engine Whitleys, Wellingtons and Hampdens. The first problem was to

convert the operational crews from the old type to the new by withdrawing the squadron from the line, but after that the new incoming crews also had to be converted. The second complication concerned the Wellingtons which now predominated at the OTUs, because they had neither mid-upper turrets nor flight engineers, both of which were features and requirements of the new four-engine bombers. Thus the conversion of new crews on to four-engine bombers was soon beyond the practical capability of front-line squadrons.

With ever more squadrons converting to four-engine bombers, an interim solution was arrived at where one heavy conversion unit (HCU) per bomber group was established, plus one conversion flight (CF) of four aircraft per squadron, generally equipped with Halifaxes or Stirlings. This second stage in the operational training chain converted crews on to the heavy bomber types they would soon fly operationally. In a course lasting five weeks – which covered a variety of skills and procedures combined with 20 hours of flying instruction – pilots achieved a minimum of 350 hours before joining a heavy bomber squadron. This was also the point at which the flight engineer joined a crew from his trade training at St Athan in South Wales. A review of Bomber Command's advanced training took place in 1942 which led to the disbandment of individual squadron conversion flights and the amalgamation of their resources to form HCUs. These had a mixture of aircraft types which comprised the Halifax, Manchester, Stirling and Lancaster, but within a few months they had been resolved into units containing, for the most part, one type only. Like those on the OTUs, most of

these aircraft were worn-out hand-me-downs with poor serviceability records and this, combined once again with the novice crews' inexperience, could have tragic results.

When the first Lancasters came into service in 1942 the problems of conversion training became even more complicated. There was a natural reluctance on the part of Bomber Command to relegate any of these fine – and at first fairly scarce – aircraft to conversion training, and so a number of HCUs were established with 50-50 Halifax and Lancaster strengths, but this was soon found to be unsatisfactory and the arrangement was abandoned in 1943. The Lancasters were withdrawn and crews being posted to Lancaster squadrons were sent for a short period to Lancaster Finishing Schools (LFS) for a further 12 hours of flying. This practice ceased at the end of 1944 when the supply of Lancasters became better and the appropriate HCUs were equipped with them.

The number of HCUs increased steadily during 1943 and many moved to satellite stations where they could continue the crew conversion process unimpeded by the demands of an operational station. Each bomber group allocated a base station and a number of satellites for use by the HCUs associated with it. For example, 4 Group in Yorkshire allocated Marston Moor as 42 Base Station (1652 HCU), with its satellites at Rufforth (1663 HCU) and Riccall (1658 HCU). With a daily serviceability rate of about 40 aircraft, the strength of a typical HCU was considerably higher than that on an operational bomber squadron, but HCUs also suffered much the same troubles as OTUs with the dangerous mix of clapped-out aircraft and inexperienced crews, as the following personal diary excerpt reveals. It was kept by 19-year-old flight engineer Sergeant Les Fry while he was undergoing conversion training on to Halifaxes at 1666 HCU, Wombleton, in the early summer of 1944:

Saturday 27 May: *We had only been here 5 minutes when I saw the first plane I have seen go up in flames. It was burning for almost an hour. There were three F/Es in it: one of them had his leg broken and the other his jaw. The rest of the crew got out OK. [Halifax II, HR834.]*

Monday 5 June: *Another kite crashed. Everyone was ok.*
Wednesday 7 June: *Another kite crashed. All were killed. [Halifax II, LW279.]*
Sunday 11 June: *The kite we were on last night was lousy. We had to change kites because we had an oil leak.*
Wednesday 14 June: *Tonight I did my first solo if one can call it that. It was about 5 hours, but we had to change kites. I have not been in a kite yet that is first class.*
Thursday 22 June: *We got about nine hours in today and are going hard at it. I had an engine cut out on landing yesterday, but it picked up a bit when we started to level off.*
Friday 23 June: *On fighter affil for four hours this afternoon. I had the hydraulic system go U/S.*
Monday 26 June: *They lost another kite on Saturday night. Only the first F/E and the tail gunner got out. The rest were killed. [Halifax II, JD106.]*

By mid-1944, the length of an HCU course had been increased to five weeks, with one week of ground instruction and four weeks of flying training. The flying element of the HCU course had risen to nearer 40 hours (nearly double when compared to the syllabus used in 1942), while the cumulative total across the whole flying training process had risen to an average of 440 hours for pilots, and some 200 hours of flying for navigators – over twice that provided in 1941. During the summer months, ten to eleven new crews were posted in every week, although this figure usually dropped to about seven during the winter.

The Mosquito squadrons in Bomber

ABOVE Plt Off Denis Brown and his crew are pictured beside their Stirling at 1657 Heavy Conversion Unit (HCU) at RAF Waterbeach, Cambridgeshire, during the final stage of their training. They subsequently joined 218 Squadron but were lost over Denmark on 29 April 1943 when their Stirling (BF447) was shot down by a Messerschmitt Bf 110 night-fighter of II./NJG3, one of 32 aircraft lost that night. Two of the seven-man crew managed to bale out, but the remaining five perished, including Brown. He was an only son, and as with so many other grieving families, his loss would have been felt very deeply.

Command presented a particular problem when it came to conversion training. Like the Lancaster, the 'Wooden Wonder' was an aircraft in short supply and therefore could not be spared from the front-line squadrons. Another difficulty arose due to its high performance because there was nothing comparable to a Mosquito for conversion training purposes – except of course another Mosquito. The interim solution was to form a small Mosquito Training Unit (No 1655, from the Mosquito Conversion Unit) in the Pathfinder Force in October 1942 where only pilots and navigators with previous operational experience, and who were likely to learn quickly, were sent in. Once the supply situation had improved sufficiently, an existing OTU (No 16) was re-equipped with Mosquitoes in late 1944.

Other special training units were formed from time to time to give particular instruction on new equipment and techniques, for example G-H and H2S training, and the Pathfinder Navigation Training Unit (formed in June 1943), which gave special instruction in target-marking techniques.

Tour length, survivability and morale

Based on the British Army's combat experience in the First World War, the RAF of the Second World War soon realised that to sustain a bomber offensive over a long period of time some form of front-line crew rotation would be necessary. At first 200 hours was established by the Air Ministry as the cut-off point, whereafter a bomber crew could be rested at an operational training unit, or other flying training establishment. In 1941 the notion of an absolute number of operations constituting a tour of duty came into being: 30 sorties, not exceeding 200 flying hours, was regarded as sufficient for completion of a tour, with a six-month break from operations at a flying training establishment followed by a second tour. Pathfinder Force crews committed themselves to a 45-sortie tour. On the medium bomber squadrons of 2 Group, however, a tour of daylight operations was set at 20 sorties during the autumn of 1942, with few crews actually getting beyond 15. Whether this 20-op limit had been set 'unofficially' at group or squadron level is not known, but it would certainly reflect the high level of casualties experienced at the time by crews flying daylight sorties.

The grim realities of operational flying put the survival prospects for bomber crews into sharp perspective. In 1942 less than half of all heavy bomber crews would get through their first tour, one in five would live to fly a second. By 1943 the odds against survival had lengthened further still with one in six expected to survive their first tour, while a slim one in 40 would come through two tours.

Aircrew survival depended upon many different factors, which included the operational experience of a crew, their degree of alertness and vigilance when flying, the type of aircraft, whether day or night operations were being flown, the point in the war at which they were operating – and luck. 'It can never happen to me' was the mantra that kept many thousands of aircrew flying – until, of course, it did.

Once a heavy bomber crew had completed 12 operations, their chances of going on to complete a full tour of 30 ops without becoming casualties was good.

To improve their chances of survival, they might have taken some of the following precautions: observing strict R/T (radio-telephony) procedure; flying a gentle, weaving course rather than remaining straight and level for long periods; gently banking the aircraft from side to side to enable the gunners to check the blind spots beneath the wings for an enemy

BELOW Flt Lt Arnold King DFC, RNZAF, and his crew began their first operational tour with 218 Squadron in October 1943. At that time the losses on 3 Group's Stirling squadrons were running dangerously high, forcing Bomber Harris to withdraw all Stirlings from Bomber Command operations over Germany the following month. The King crew flew most of their ops on Stirlings before converting to Lancasters in August 1944, flying three more missions to bring their tour to a successful conclusion. *(Steve Smith/218 Squadron Association)*

LEFT Although the de Havilland Mosquito had the lowest attrition rate of all Bomber Command aircraft, it was still no guarantee of survival against the odds. Flg Offs Ken King DFC and Cecil Arrieta DFM of 128 Squadron were an experienced bomber crew flying a Mosquito Mk XX (KB199) on a sortie to Berlin on 30 September/1 October 1944 when they took a catastrophic hit from flak. King force-landed the Mossie in Germany in the darkness but died in the crash, while Arrieta, who was badly injured, finished up as a POW after months of hospital treatment. *(Michael Arrieta)*

CENTRE New Zealander Sgt Ken Stentiford RAFVR (standing, second from right) was a flight engineer with Plt Off Arthur Grant's 408 (Canadian) Squadron crew, flying Halifaxes from Leeming. Of Maori descent, Ken had been flying operationally with the RAF since 1940, and as such he was an experienced airman. On ops to Düsseldorf on 11/12 June 1943 the crew's Halifax Mk II (JB972) was hit by flak. It was attacked by a Bf 110 night-fighter of Stab I./NJG 1 flown by ace Major Werner Streib while making its bombing run and crashed near Krefeld, killing Grant and the two air gunners. Stentiford and three others baled out and survived to become POWs. *(Courtesy the Purdy family)*

RIGHT After his parachute was set on fire and rendered useless during a night-fighter attack at 18,000ft over Germany on 24 March 1944, Flt Sgt Nicholas Alkemade chose to jump from his burning 115 Squadron Lancaster. Sudden death on the ground was preferable to being slow-roasted alive in his gun turret. He free-fell 3½ miles in the darkness and survived. By pure luck Alkemade landed in the branches of a fir tree that broke his fall, before tumbling into a snow drift underneath. He spent the rest of the war as a POW in Stalag Luft 3.

fighter moving into position for attack; gunners keeping a constant lookout for enemy night-fighters, continually scanning the night sky while traversing their turrets from side to side; and maintaining a high level of concentration on the way home, when the temptation was to relax.

A Blenheim crew operating in daylight during 1940–41 would have had a very slim chance of survival, whereas a Mosquito crew flying operationally in the spring of 1945 would have stood a very high chance of coming through unscathed.

Although the Lancaster was the best of the RAF's trio of heavy bombers, it was more difficult to bale out of quickly and successfully than either the Halifax or the Stirling. This was because the latter two aircraft were roomier inside the nose compartment and where the escape hatch in the floor was easier to access.

Why did a crew that followed all of the precautions listed above suddenly 'fail to return' one night? Why did highly experienced and successful bomber pilots like Alec Cranswick, Charles Pickard and Guy Gibson – who between them had well over 300 operations to their credit – eventually die on operations? Why did a Lancaster gunner survive a fall from 18,000ft without a parachute after his aircraft had been blown apart, his fall broken by the snow-laden branches of a fir tree? Was it all down to luck, fate, a combination of circumstances? There is no simple answer.

'Lack of Moral Fibre'

RIGHT Taking off on another op, who knows what was preying on the minds of the seven-man crew inside this Lancaster, alone with their thoughts as they headed out towards the North Sea and the night terrors over Germany? The RAF was a whole world war behind the British Army when it came to understanding the causes of 'operational twitch' in the Second World War, which the Junior Service branded 'Lack of Moral Fibre'. British soldiers who lost their nerve and had suffered 'shell-shock' in the First World War were harshly treated by the Army, but by the time the Second World War came around the powers that be recognised it as a genuine psychological condition that required medical treatment. There was no such luck for a hapless RAF bomber crewman if and when his nerve finally broke – and he was punished for it.

Although all RAF bomber aircrew were volunteers, the process did not work in reverse, which meant that one could not 'volunteer out' if flying was not to one's liking, if the pressures were too great, or if an individual later found himself psychologically unsuited to flying duties.

Operational flying imposed a tremendous strain on aircrew that affected all men to a greater or lesser degree, but some took it worse than others. Operational twitch, loss of nerve, emotional exhaustion, shell-shock, aeroneurosis – it took many forms and descriptions – was not entertained by those in authority within the RAF. The official term was 'Lack of Moral Fibre' (simply abbreviated to 'LMF'), which was first introduced by senior RAF commanders in 1940 and which quickly became a policy as well as a system for dealing with aircrew who refused to fly.

The main cause of LMF was an airman's exposure to, or the immediate prospect of, life-threatening experiences. Lack of Moral Fibre was adopted as a term to avoid the use of psychiatric labels such as 'aeroneurosis' and 'flying stress', which it was argued encouraged aircrew to expect nervous symptoms and gave them an honourable way out from operational flying without loss of face or privilege. In a war for survival, during which the RAF expended a great deal of time and money training aircrew, the LMF policy reflected the anxieties of senior officers who feared that any refusal to fly could rip through entire stations like wildfire.

In a statement from the Air Council in April 1940 infamously dubbed the 'waverer letter', which formally introduced the LMF policy to the heads of all home-based and overseas Commands, a distinction was drawn between two types of aircrew who refused to fly: the 'waverer' and those 'lacking moral fibre':

a: [the waverer] The case of a man who is doing his best to fight against his weakness and is maintaining a show of carrying out his duties, but has nevertheless lost the confidence of his commanding officer.
b: [LMF] The case of a man who has not only lost the confidence of his commanding officer in his courage and resolution but makes no secret of his condition and states openly that he does not intend to carry out dangerous duties.

For the former, it was believed that with the right encouragement there was a chance of rehabilitation at an Aircrew Refresher Centre. If the authorities deemed a man 'cured' he might be re-mustered to ground duties on his release, or in some instances returned to flying duties; for the latter, however, it was a sentence of humiliation and vilification by the RAF before being drummed out of the service.

By the standards of the 21st century, the punishment dispensed to those who could no longer take the strain of operations is harsh and inhumane, the intention being to prevent others of questionable morale from avoiding combat duties. Nevertheless, the RAF was very loath to court-martial a man (particularly if he was an officer) accused of LMF for fear of the adverse publicity such a trial might generate. In fact some high-ranking officers and politicians, including the Secretary of State for Air, Sir Archibald Sinclair, considered parts of the LMF policy indefensible from a popular point of view.

At operational level the treatment of LMF cases varied from station to station. Some commanding officers preferred to deal with the matter discreetly by posting away the offender on other grounds, while others took a more Draconian view and followed the Air Ministry's ruling on LMF cases to the letter. A network of 12 psychiatric units was opened across the country to assess and treat aircrew removed from flying duties. They were called NYDN centres – 'Not Yet Diagnosed Nervous' – which worked on the assumption that a man was a coward unless he could prove himself otherwise. Men who refused or were unable to return to operational flying after treatment at one of these centres were sent to an Aircrew Disposal Unit (initially at Uxbridge, later at Chessington and finally at Keresley Grange near Coventry) where they awaited a decision by the Air Ministry on their fate. Their verdict was based on information received from the squadron medical officer and the psychiatric assessor at an NYDN centre.

If found guilty of cowardice, aircrew officers were cashiered, NCO aircrew reduced to the ranks or discharged from the service, while some were transferred to either the Army, the Navy or sent to work in the coal mines. Flying badges were forfeited since they were regarded by the air force as signs of continuing qualification rather than symbols of training graduation. However, the humiliation of the letters 'LMF' did not stop there, because they were stamped on a man's personnel record and discharge documents, and could follow him wherever he went for employment thereafter.

The demeaning treatment meted out to an anonymous flier who had fallen foul of the LMF policy was witnessed on 8 June 1944 by Campbell Muirhead, a Lancaster bomb-aimer on 12 Squadron at RAF Wickenby:

By order – no exceptions. The entire Station strength on parade. To witness what to me anyway was a sad, sad sight. We were well away from the action so I couldn't hear exactly all of what was being said. But I certainly could see what was being done. This sergeant had refused to fly on an op. He had been accused, and found guilty, of LMF, which is Lack of Moral Fibre. There he was standing out there in front, all on his own, in full view of every person on the unit,

to be stripped of his wings (or his half-wing – I couldn't see) followed by his sergeant's stripes. Reduced from sergeant to AC2 in the space of a minute (they would all be unstitched beforehand, of course). All this followed by an immediate posting elsewhere.

The policy's harshness accounts for the comparatively small number of LMF cases in Bomber Command during the Second World War, which ran at approximately 200 per year, although

COPY OF ENCLOSURE 2E
FROM AIR MINISTRY FILE 663

ENCLOSURE 1E

From:- Officer Commanding, No. 101 Squadron.

To:- Officer Commanding, R.A.F. Station, Ludford Magna.

Date:- 7th April, 1944.

Ref:- 101S/04/P4   CONFIDENTIAL.

                    Sgt.   A/Gunner.

The above mentioned N.C.O. has been taken off all flying and his name is submitted under the terms of Air Ministry memorandum S.61141/S7d(1) dated 1st June, 1943, para. 5 (i) for the reasons stated below.

2.   Following his last Operational sortie on the 24th February, 1944, this N.C.O reported sick and stated that he considered he was unfit for duty in the air. The medical Officer could find no evidence of physical illness and arranged for an appointment with a specialist. The Medical authorities report is attached and Sgt.   is found fit for full flying duties.

3.   I interviewed Sgt.   and came to the conclusion that he lacked the moral fibre to face up to Operational flying. I informed him of this and the consequences of my submitting his name under the terms of the Air Ministry memorandum quoted above. Sgt.   then admitted that he did not wish to continue operational flying.

4.   He declined to make a statement but desires an interview with the Air Officer Commanding.

5.   He was given 24 hours to reconsider the matter, but remains firm in his decision.

6.   I therefore recommend that this N.C.O. should revert to his basic trade of A.C.H., and be posted away from the Squadron at the earliest opportunity.

7.   He has carried out 4 successful operational sorties making a total of 32.50 operational flying hours, all in Lancaster aircraft, and a total of 148.40 flying hours.

                              R.A.ATYCAND W/Cdr.
                    Commanding No 101 Squadron R.A.F.

surviving records are not sufficiently comprehensive to confirm this figure. However, the true figure is probably higher because many men who experienced psychological problems associated with combat flying, but who were fearful of being branded LMF, kept their fears bottled up and either completed their tours – or simply failed to return.

Many should not have continued to fly, their state of mind making them a danger for safety reasons to the rest of their crews. Compared with the USAAF's more enlightened attitude

that most LMF cases were psychological in origin and should therefore be treated medically, the RAF's policy, based as it was on its questionable views on character deficiency and cowardice, was harsher and designed to act as a deterrent. Yet at no time in the war was the problem of LMF significant enough to compromise Bomber Command's operational effectiveness, even during the darkest moments of the battles of the Ruhr and Berlin in 1943–44 when casualties among aircrew ran high.

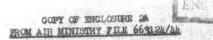

COPY OF ENCLOSURE 2A
FROM AIR MINISTRY FILE 663124/44

ENCLOSURE 1A

Headquarters No. 1 Group,
Royal Air Force,
Bawtry Hall,
Bawtry, Yorks.

Ref:- 1G/745/498/P4.

25th April 1944.

Sgt.   - Air Gunner, No. 101 Squadron.

Sir,

        I have the honour to forward herewith reports from the Officers Commanding R.A.F. Station Ludford Magna, No. 101 Squadron, certificate from the N.C.O. concerned, Medical Officer's reports, list of operational sorties together with a letter from the Base Commander Headquarters No. 14 Base, in respect of the above named N.C.O. who has been taken off flying duties at his own request.

2.   This Australian N.C.O. appeared before me today. He made no effort to conceal the fact that he is scared of his duties as an Air Gunner. He has an idea fixed in the back of his head that he would make a satisfactory offensive pilot in a single-seater aircraft. I cannot subscribe to any such suggestion for I feel that basically the man has not got the stamina required to back up the bluff that he is putting to himself.

3.   While it is obviously clear that he has made a big effort to conquer his inherent fears I am quite certain that no useful purpose could be served in persevering with his training in any category of aircrew and I am compelled therefore, to classify him under the terms of para 5 (i) of Air Ministry Memorandum S.61141/S.7.e (1) dated 1st June 1943.

4.   Sgt.   is being posted to the Aircrew Disposal Unit Chessington w.e.f. 26th April 1944. This Headquarters Posting Notice 1G/2141/44 dated 25th April 1944 refers.

                    I have the honour to be,
                        Sir,
                    Your obedient Servant,
                        E.M. RICE A.V.M.
                        Air Officer Commanding,
                        No. 1 Group R.A.F.

The Under Secretary of State,
Air Ministry (S.D.& R)
Kingsway,
London W.C.2.

OPPOSITE AND LEFT These letters dating from April 1944 from the CO of 101 Squadron to the station commander at RAF Ludford Magna, and from the AOC 1 Group to the Air Ministry, shed some light on the official treatment of an LMF case, an Australian NCO air gunner, who was later regraded as a 'Waverer'. Unlike many such cases this one had a happier outcome. On appeal after his repatriation to Australia, the gunner succeeded in having his reduction from the rank of sergeant overturned, the restoration of his right to wear the air gunner's brevet, and his personnel record amended to read 'unfit for further flying duties' instead of the damning 'services no longer required'. The identity of the gunner has been redacted by the author, although the original documents are freely available and in the public domain. (National Archives of Australia)

Wg Cdr 'Rod' Rodley to Flg Off Alex Thorne on the merits of the Lancaster: 'Well, what do you think of her?' 'Lovely,' replied Thorne, an opinion he was to find universal among Lancaster crews.

Chapter Five

The aircraft

Within three years of the outbreak of war, Bomber Command had swapped its small twin-engine bombers like the Hampden and Blenheim, which carried comparatively light bomb loads, to four-engine heavies like the Halifax and Lancaster capable of carrying far greater loads over longer distances. The exception was the twin-engine Mosquito – the 'wooden wonder' – that could carry a 4,000lb Cookie to Berlin and return to its base within four hours.

OPPOSITE Majesty and might: the Avro Lancaster has come to symbolise the RAF's strategic air offensive in the Second World War. This is 619 Squadron's Mk III, PG-H/LM449, flying from its base at Coningsby in Lincolnshire. *(IWM/Getty Images)*

Although the Avro Lancaster flew the highest number of sorties of any of its contemporaries and equipped the majority of Bomber Command's heavy squadrons by the war's end, it was but one of 14 different types of bomber aircraft used at various times by the wartime Command. The Lancaster and the Halifax were at the forefront of the strategic night offensive, ably supported by the Mosquito, but the early marks of Halifax and Stirling were not such good performers. In the day bomber role, the Blenheim light bomber single-handedly bore the brunt of the early daylight offensive until the arrival in 1941 of the first of a trio of replacement US bombers, the Douglas Boston, Lockheed Vega Ventura and North American Mitchell. Although faster and better armed, these aircraft continued to suffer the same savage losses as those of the Blenheim at the hands of flak and fighters. This was not so much the result of poor aircraft design and armament, as through a blind adherence to daylight bombing in the face of increasingly effective enemy defences.

As the war progressed, new types of bomber aircraft entered service, gradually replacing those that had served the RAF from the outbreak of war. With their arrival the definition and classification of what constituted a light, medium or heavy bomber aircraft changed. In 1940, the twin-engine Wellington and Hampden were classed as medium bombers, while the Armstrong-Whitworth Whitley was classed as a heavy. The Whitley could fly 1,630 miles with a 3,750lb bomb load at a cruising speed

of 165mph. When it was eventually phased out of front-line service in 1942, successors to the appellation of heavy bomber were the four-engine Stirling, Halifax and Lancaster. Indisputably the best of the new breed of heavies, the Lancaster began to enter squadron service in January 1942 and could carry a 14,000lb bomb load up to 1,660 miles at a cruising speed of 216mph at 20,000ft.

Of the same period, the powerful twin-engine de Havilland Mosquito B XVI was classed as a light bomber, yet it was capable of carrying a 4,000lb bomb load 1,370 miles at 400mph at 28,000ft. By comparison, its predecessor in 1940 was the underpowered single-engine Fairey Battle, which could carry a 1,000lb bomb load, 1,000 miles at 200mph at 15,000ft.

These comparisons are perhaps not entirely fair because they illustrate successive generations of aircraft design, and the Air Ministry planners and aircraft designers of the early 1930s could not have foreseen the demands of the air offensive to come. However, they do serve to show how the exigencies of war acted as a powerful accelerant to bomber design.

Armstrong-Whitworth Whitley

Characterised by its distinctive nose-down flying attitude in level flight, Armstrong-Whitworth designer John Lloyd's ungainly looking twin-engine AW 38 (later named Whitley) was, in 1937, the first of the modern generation of monoplane heavy bombers to enter squadron service with the RAF. It also became the first to fly offensive night operations over Germany in the Second World War and could carry a greater bomb load than its contemporary the Vickers Wellington. The Whitley Mk V became the main production version, of which a total of 1,445 were eventually built to equip 15 squadrons.

Alongside the Wellington and the Hampden, the Whitley was in the vanguard and bore the brunt of Bomber Command's early night offensive against Germany. Whitleys flew on the RAF's first bombing raid against Berlin on 25/26 August 1940 and later against some of the longer-range targets in Czechoslovakia and Italy. Its last bombing operation was on 29/30 April

1942 against Ostend, but the type continued to see service with bomber OTUs and Coastal Command. Despite a slow cruising speed and an inability to carry anything larger than the standard 1,000lb bomb in its small main bomb bay, the Whitley soldiered on as a heavy bomber with Bomber Command's 4 Group until the last squadron relinquished its Mk Vs for the four-engine Halifax in the spring of 1942.

Avro Lancaster

The four-engine Lancaster probably did more than any other British aircraft of the Second World War to take the fight to Germany. Lancasters spearheaded Bomber Command's night offensive and flew thousands of sorties against targets the length and breadth of enemy-occupied Europe. By the end of 1942, 17 heavy bomber squadrons had converted to the Lancaster; by the war's end the type equipped 52 out of Bomber Command's 97 front-line squadrons, with both Pathfinder and main force groups.

Contrary to popular belief the Lancaster did not come about as the result of the failure of the twin-engine Manchester. The Ministry of Aircraft Production decided to go ahead with the four-Merlin Manchester III (later known as the Lancaster) months before the Vulture engine showed signs of trouble. The outcome was arguably the most successful Allied heavy bomber of the Second World War.

The first production Lancasters entered front-line service with 44 (Rhodesia) Squadron at Waddington on Christmas Eve 1941 and their first operation was a raid against Essen on 10/11 March 1942. The following month Lancasters of 44 and 97 Squadrons staged a spectacular

SPECIFICATION – ARMSTRONG-WHITWORTH WHITLEY	
Type	twin-engine five-man mid-wing heavy night bomber.
Powerplant	Mk I, 2 × 795hp Armstrong Siddeley Tiger IX 14-cylinder air-cooled radial engines; Mk II and III, 845hp Tiger VIII; Mk IV, two Rolls-Royce Merlin IV 12-cylinder liquid-cooled two-stage supercharged in-line engines; Mk V, 1,145hp Merlin X.
Dimensions	span 84ft 0in, length 69ft 3in (Mk V 70ft 6in), height 15ft 0in, wing area 1,137sq ft.
Weights	Mk II and III, empty 15,475lb, loaded 22,900lb; Mk V, empty 19,350lb, loaded 33,500lb.
Performance	Mk II and III, max speed 209mph at 16,400ft, service ceiling 23,000ft, range 1,315 miles; Mk V, max speed 230mph at 16,400ft, service ceiling 26,000ft, range 1,500 miles.
Armament, defensive	1 × .303in Browning MG in Nash and Thompson nose turret, 4 × .303in Browning MGs in Nash and Thompson tail turret.
Armament, offensive	max bomb load 7,000lb.
Production	1,811 (excl. prototypes).

BELOW Among the most famous combat aircraft of all time, the Lancaster was unique in being the only Allied bomber capable of lifting the 22,000lb Grand Slam earthquake bomb. This is 617 Squadron's B Mk I (Special) YZ-J/PD119 pictured in April 1945 with the giant Grand Slam weapon in place beneath the fuselage. Note the daylight camouflage scheme of light earth/light green with ocean grey undersides and a white flash on the tail fin. *(Library and Archives Canada PL44697)*

SPECIFICATION – AVRO LANCASTER

Type	four-engine seven or eight-man mid-wing monoplane heavy night bomber.
Power plant	Mk I and III, 4 × 1,460hp Rolls-Royce Merlin XX, 22, 38 or 224, 12-cylinder liquid-cooled, supercharged in-line engines; Mk II, 4 × 1,650hp Bristol Hercules VI 14-cylinder air-cooled two-row radial engines.
Dimensions	span 102ft 0in, length 69ft 6in, height 20ft 4in, wing area 1,297sq ft.
Weights	empty 36,457lb, loaded 68,000lb. With 22,000lb bomb, 72,000lb.
Performance	287mph at 11,500ft, cruising speed 210mph at 12,000ft, service ceiling 24,500ft (without bomb load), range with 14,000lb bomb load 1,660 miles.
Armament, defensive	2 × .303in Browning MGs each in Frazer-Nash nose and dorsal turrets, 4 in Frazer-Nash tail turret; some aircraft had 2 × Browning MGs in downward-firing ventral turret.
Armament, offensive	max bomb load 14,000lb. Special aircraft, either 1 × 22,000lb or 12,000lb deep-penetration bombs, 1 × 9,500lb Upkeep bouncing mine.
Production	7,373.

BELOW Unloved, unreliable and under-powered, the twin-engine Avro Manchester failed to live up to expectations after it entered service with Bomber Command in November 1940. The mechanical unreliability of its Rolls-Royce Vulture engines meant that many Manchesters spent more time on the ground than in the air, leading to some squadrons becoming the butt of jokes – 97 Squadron was dubbed 'the 97th Regiment of Foot'. This is 83 Squadron's Mk Ia, OL-N/R5833, seen at Scampton on 8 April 1942.

daylight low-level deep-penetration raid against Augsburg near Munich. Specially converted Lancasters of 617 Squadron attacked the Ruhr dams in May 1943 and went on to achieve lasting fame with further precision bombing operations. As a weight-lifter the Lancaster's capabilities were unmatched. Over short ranges it could carry a bomb load of 14,000lb and it was the only heavy bomber of the Second World War capable of lifting the 12,000lb Tallboy and 22,000lb Grand Slam bombs.

Few changes were made to the basic Lancaster design through the war and of more than 7,000 delivered during this period almost half were lost on operations. Eleven VCs were awarded to Lancaster crewmembers.

Avro Manchester

Designed to Air Ministry specification P13/36 for a medium bomber, the Manchester was built around two 1,760hp Rolls-Royce Vulture engines and offered a good range and load-carrying performance. At the end of 1937 an initial order for 200 Manchesters was placed with Avro, although the first prototype did not fly until July 1939. No 207 Squadron became the first to receive the new bomber in November 1940 and

deliveries continued to 5 Group squadrons throughout 1941 and into early 1942. The underdeveloped Vulture engine led to frequent engine failures and, combined with a troublesome hydraulic system and poor handling at fully loaded weight, the Manchester became an operational liability. Thus, from early in 1942, efforts were made to phase the type out of service for eventual replacement by the Lancaster and Halifax. The last operational use of the Manchester was on the 1,000-bomber raid against Bremen on 25/26 June 1942, after which the type was withdrawn. Many continued to see use as training aircraft until late 1943 with some of Bomber Command's HCUs.

Boeing B-17 Flying Fortress

More popularly known for its key role in the USAAF's daylight bomber offensive against Germany, 20 of the B-17C version were delivered to the RAF in May 1941 as the Fortress Mk I. They were used operationally by 90 Squadron on high-altitude daylight bombing operations, but serious technical problems and several losses caused the RAF to conclude that the type was unsuitable for Bomber Command's purpose. Further

SPECIFICATION – AVRO MANCHESTER	
Type	twin-engine seven-man mid-wing monoplane heavy night bomber.
Powerplant	2 × 1,770hp Rolls-Royce Vulture I 24-cylinder liquid-cooled 'X' engines.
Dimensions	span 90ft 1in, length 68ft 10in, height 19ft 6in, wing area 1,131sq ft.
Weights	empty 29,432lb, loaded 50,000lb.
Performance	max speed 264mph at 17,000ft, cruising speed loaded 205mph, service ceiling 19,300ft, range with 8,100lb bomb load 1,630 miles.
Armament, defensive	2 × .303in Browning MGs each in Frazer-Nash nose and dorsal turrets, 4 in Frazer-Nash tail turret.
Armament, offensive	max bomb load 10,350lb.
Production	200.

SPECIFICATION – B-17G/FORTRESS Mk III	
Type	four-engine ten-man mid-wing monoplane heavy bomber.
Powerplant	4 × 1,200hp Wright Cyclone R-1820-97 air-cooled radial engines.
Dimensions	span 103ft 9in, length 74ft 9in, height 19ft 1in, wing area 1,420sq ft.
Weights	empty 36,135lb, loaded 72,000lb.
Performance	max speed 302mph at 25,000ft, cruising speed 160mph, service ceiling 35,600ft, max range 3,400 miles.
Armament, defensive	12 × .50in Browning MGs, 2 each in chin, dorsal, ventral and tail turrets, 1 each in the cheek and beam positions.
Armament, offensive	max bomb load 7,600lb.

LEFT Some 20 B-17C Flying Fortress bombers were delivered to the RAF in May 1941 and were trialled by 90 Squadron, but without success. Later marks of B-17 gave good service with 100 (BS) Group and in Coastal Command. Here, 90 Squadron's Fortress Mk I, WP-F/ AN530 is airborne from Polebrook in July 1941.

SPECIFICATION – BLENHEIM Mk IV

Type	twin-engine three-man mid-wing monoplane light bomber.
Powerplant	2 × Bristol Mercury XV 9-cylinder air-cooled radial engines.
Dimensions	span 56ft 4in, length 42ft 9in, height 12ft 9in, wing area 469sq ft.
Weights	Empty 9,700lb, loaded 13,500lb.
Performance	max speed 266mph at 11,000ft, cruising speed 225mph, service ceiling 22,500ft, range 1,450 miles with full bomb load.
Armament, defensive	1 × fixed .303in Browning MG in port wing, 2 × .303in Browning MGs in Frazer-Nash under-nose mounting, 2 × Browning MGs in Bristol dorsal turret.
Armament, offensive	max bomb load 1,000lb, but additionally up to 350lb of light bombs on external racks.

BELOW The Bristol Blenheim Mk IV bore the brunt of the RAF's daylight operations early in the war until it was gradually replaced by the American Boston, Mitchell and Ventura from 1942. This is 40 Squadron's BL-V/R3612, which was lost on a night raid against invasion barges at Ostend on 8/9 September 1940.

supplies to the RAF of the Fortress E, F and G models under 'Lend-Lease' were diverted to Coastal Command for long-range maritime reconnaissance. The last production Fortress was the B-17G, of which 85 were delivered to Bomber Command's 100 (BS) Group as the Fortress Mk III in January 1944, and were used by 214 and 223 Squadrons in the radio countermeasures role.

Bristol Blenheim

As the first RAF aircraft to fly over German territory within hours of the Second World War being declared, and the first to make a bombing attack on a German target, the Bristol Blenheim quickly carved for itself a place in history. In common with other RAF bombers of the expansion period, the Blenheim was ordered straight off the drawing board, with the first two production aircraft serving as prototypes.

A development of the Bristol Type 142, 'Britain First', the first Blenheim Mk I was delivered to 114 Squadron in March 1937 and was hailed as one of the fastest bombers in the world. By the end of 1938 another 15 bomber squadrons in 2 Group had re-equipped with the type, although by September 1939 they were in the process of converting to the much-improved long-nosed Mk IV version. Blenheim squadrons were based in France in early 1940 as part of the Air Component of the BEF and suffered heavy losses due to their light defensive armament and suicidal low-level attacks against the advancing German Army.

During 1941 and 1942 the Blenheim squadrons of 2 Group continued to carry out low-level daylight bombing raids against targets in occupied Europe, and suffered grievous losses in the process. In the daring raid on Bremen by Blenheims of 105 and 107 Squadrons on 4 July 1941, the leader Wg Cdr Hughie Edwards was awarded the VC. By early in 1942 the Blenheim was slowly being replaced in 2 Group by the Boston, Ventura and Mitchell, the last aircraft being withdrawn from 18 Squadron in October 1942. Of the 1,012 Blenheims used by 2 Group between 1939 and 1942, 403 were lost on operations, 86 were damaged beyond repair and 96 were destroyed in flying accidents.

SPECIFICATION – B-24-J LIBERATOR Mk VI	
Type	four-engine ten-man shoulder-wing monoplane heavy bomber.
Powerplant	4 × 1,200hp Pratt & Whitney R-1830-65 air-cooled radial engines.
Dimensions	span 110ft, length 67ft 2in, height 18ft, wing area 1,048sq ft.
Weights	empty 36,500lb, loaded 56,000lb.
Performance	max speed 300mph at 28,000ft, range 2,100 miles, service ceiling 30,000ft.
Armament, defensive	10 × .50in MGs, two each in nose, dorsal, ventral and tail turrets, one each in beam position.
Armament, offensive	max bomb load 8,800lb.

ABOVE American B-24 Liberators were used in small numbers by 100 (BS) Group in the radio-countermeasures role. Its bomb racks were removed which, together with its roomy fuselage, made it well suited to accommodating bulky radar and jamming equipment. This anonymous 223 Squadron crew at Oulton, Norfolk, stand with their Liberator Mk IV, 6G-C. *(M.W.G. Thomas)*

Consolidated B-24 Liberator

Better known for its role alongside the B-17 Flying Fortress in the USAAF's daylight bomber offensive, the B-24 Liberator was also chosen by the RAF as an electronic warfare platform for its 100 (BS) Group. Its capacious fuselage lent itself to accommodating the racks of bulky radio-countermeasures (RCM) equipment. Two units, 223 Squadron and 1699 Flight, operated some 33 Liberators, mainly the B-24H and J versions, in the RCM and training roles from early 1944 until the war's end.

De Havilland Mosquito

Nicknamed the 'Wooden Wonder' by virtue of its largely wooden construction and superior performance (and 'Freeman's Folly' by its detractors after Air Marshal Sir Wilfred Freeman, who championed the design), the Mosquito became one of the most versatile and successful combat aircraft of the Second World War. It saw service in most theatres of operations and in a variety of different roles, most notably in north-west Europe with Bomber, Fighter and Coastal Commands. Although the Mossie made an important contribution in the pathfinding role with Bomber

BELOW De Havilland's 'Wooden Wonder' – the Mosquito – was probably the most successful and versatile Allied bomber of the war. Operating with Bomber Command's Light Night Striking Force, Mosquitoes could fly to Berlin and back twice in one night, with each aircraft carrying a 4,000lb Blockbuster bomb. B Mk XVI, 8K-K/ML963, served with the LNSF's 571 Squadron from Oakington in late 1944.

SPECIFICATION – DE HAVILLAND MOSQUITO	
Type	twin-engine two-man mid-wing monoplane bomber.
Powerplant	Mk I and IV, 2 × 1,460hp Rolls-Royce Merlin 21, 22 or 25 12-cylinder liquid-cooled supercharged in-line engines; Mk IX and XVI, 2 ×1,680hp Merlin 72 and 73 or 1,710hp Merlin 76 and 77 engines.
Dimensions	span 54ft 2in, length 40ft 6in, height 12ft 6in, wing area 454sq ft.
Weights	Mk IV, empty 13,400lb, loaded 21,462lb; Mk IX, empty 14,570lb, loaded 22,780lb.
Performance	Mk IV, max speed 380mph at 17,000ft, service ceiling 29,100ft, range 2,100 miles; Mk XVI, max speed 415mph at 28,000ft, service ceiling 37,000ft, range with max bomb load 1,485 miles.
Armament, defensive	none.
Armament, offensive	Mk IV, max bomb load 2,000lb; Mk IX and XVI, max bomb load 4,000lb, plus 2 × 500lb bombs under wings.
Production	7,781, of which 1,690 were completed as unarmed bombers.

Command, it was with the squadrons of the Light Night Striking Force (LNSF) that it achieved the most dramatic results.

The maiden flight of the first prototype was made in November 1940 and 105 Squadron became the first RAF bomber squadron to receive the aircraft one year later. Initial deliveries were of the PR Mk I, but the first B Mk IV arrived on the squadron in May 1942. A second 2 Group squadron, No 139, became operational on the Mosquito in November and for several months these two units flew specialised low-level precision attacks in daylight against high-prestige targets. When 2 Group became part of 2nd Tactical Air Force

on 1 June 1943, these operations ceased and the two Mosquito squadrons were transferred to 8 (PFF) Group, serving alongside 109 Squadron in the Pathfinder role. They continued to mount nuisance raids and 'spoofs' to divert attention from the main force targets and re-equipped progressively with the B Mk IX and XVI.

In early 1944, the LNSF was formed in 8 (PFF) Group, initially with 139, 627 and 692 Squadrons, although 627 soon left to join 5 Group's marker force. Later, 128, 571 and 608 Squadrons joined the LNSF and participated in the force's frequent nocturnal rovings over Germany, guided to their targets by Oboe-equipped PFF Mosquitoes, and bombed with a precision seldom achieved by the main force heavies. Between January and May 1945, the LNSF Mosquitoes dropped 1,459 4,000lb 'Cookies' on Berlin alone, and 1,500 on other targets.

The famous dam buster squadron, No 617, used a variety of different marks of Mosquito (Mk IV, IX, XVI, XX and 25) for low-level target marking, while Mossies were also used by the bomber and fighter squadrons of 100 (BS) Group for RCM and intruder work. A specially modified Mosquito, the B Mk IV (Special), was fitted with a bulged bomb bay to enable it to carry a 4,000lb 'Cookie' HC bomb all the way to Berlin. Later marks of Mossie were factory-fitted with the new bulged bomb bays and 100-gallon drop tanks, the definitive version being the B Mk XVI, which also boasted a pressurised cockpit cabin giving an operational ceiling of 37,000ft and a maximum speed of 408mph loaded.

Bomber Command statistics for the Mosquito at the end of the war showed a total of 39,795 sorties flown for the loss of 254 – at 0.6% this was the lowest loss rate for any bomber aircraft operated by the Command.

Douglas A-20 Boston

Rugged, versatile and dependable, this American twin-engine design was used principally by the USAAF, US Navy, RAF and Soviet Air Force in the attack bomber, night intruder and night-fighter roles. The DB-7B model, identical to the USAAF's A20-A, was ordered by the RAF as a replacement for the Blenheim and in the guise of the Boston Mk III it eventually equipped three squadrons in

SPECIFICATION – DOUGLAS A-20 BOSTON	
Type	twin-engine four-man mid-wing monoplane day bomber.
Powerplant	2 × 1,600hp Wright Cyclone GR-2600-23 air-cooled radial engines.
Dimensions	span 61ft 4in, length 48ft 0in, height 15ft 10in, wing area 465sq ft.
Weights	empty 16,650lb, loaded 21,700lb.
Performance	max speed 304mph at 13,000ft, cruising speed 200mph at 15,000ft, service ceiling 24,250ft, max range 1,240 miles with 2,000lb bomb load.
Armament, defensive	4 × .303in Browning fixed MGs in nose, 2 × .303in Browning hand-operated MGs in dorsal turret, 1 × .303in Browning ventral MG.
Armament, offensive	max bomb load 2,000lb.
Production	132 Boston Mk III and Mk IIIa used by 2 Group.

2 Group, Nos 88, 107 and 226. Although faster than the Blenheim, better armed, with a nose-wheel tricycle undercarriage and clean aerodynamic form, its range was not as good.

The first Boston entered service with 88 Squadron in July 1941, followed in early 1942 by Nos 107 and 226. Some 182 Bostons were used by the RAF on daylight bombing operations until the last aircraft was withdrawn in August 1943, to be replaced by the Mitchell.

In all, 30 Bostons were lost on operations; 8 were written off as the result of battle damage, and 10 were lost through flying accidents.

Fairey Battle

By the time the Second World War had started in September 1939, the single-engine two-man Fairey Battle was already

ABOVE Regarded by its pilots as a delight to fly, the Douglas Boston was faster and better armed than the Blenheim it replaced. It equipped three squadrons in 2 Group between July 1941 and August 1943. This is 107 Squadron's OM-D/AL754 that flew in the famous daylight raid on the Philips Works at Eindhoven on 6 December 1941.

obsolete as a bomber. It had been designed in the mid-1930s as a monoplane replacement for the Hawker biplane bombers and featured state-of-the-art construction for its day with light alloy and stressed skin. The prototype first flew in March 1936, ten months after an initial order for 155 aircraft had been placed for an unenthusiastic RAF. But the pressing need to expand the air force and a political wish to keep defence contractors busy meant that this unsatisfactory aircraft with its performance shortcomings was foisted on the RAF. No 63

LEFT Already obsolete as a light bomber when the Second World War began, the Fairey Battle equipped 17 bomber squadrons in September 1939, but suffered grievous losses in the Battle of France that soon followed. This is Mk I, 63-M/K7650, that belonged to 63 Squadron and was based at Benson, Oxfordshire, in late 1939.

SPECIFICATION – FAIREY BATTLE

Type	single-engine two-man low-wing monoplane light bomber.
Powerplant	1 × 1,030hp Rolls-Royce Merlin I 12-cylinder liquid-cooled in-line supercharged engine (also Merlin II, III and V).
Dimensions	span 54ft 0in, length 42ft 4in, height 15ft 6in, wing area 433sq ft.
Weights	empty 6,647lb, loaded 10,792lb.
Performance	max speed 257mph at 15,000ft, 210mph at sea level, service ceiling 23,500ft, range at 200mph, 1,000 miles.
Armament, defensive	1 × fixed Browning .303in MG in starboard wing, 1 × Vickers K GO MG in rear cockpit.
Armament, offensive	max bomb load 1,000lb.
Production	2,200.

Squadron was the first to receive its Battles in May 1937 and within two years there were 17 squadrons so equipped.

On the outbreak of war, ten Battle squadrons of 1 Group moved to France as the bomber element of the Advanced Air Striking Force, but suffered grievous losses due largely to their poor performance and ineffective armament. On 20 September 1939 a Battle gunner of 226 Squadron claimed the first German aircraft shot down in the Second World War, and on 11 May

SPECIFICATION – HANDLEY PAGE HALIFAX

Type	four-engine seven or eight-man mid-wing monoplane heavy night bomber.
Powerplant	Mk I, 4 × 1,145hp Rolls-Royce Merlin X 12-cylinder liquid-cooled supercharged in-line engines; Mk II and V, 1,280hp Merlin XX; Mk III and VII, 1,650hp Bristol Hercules XVI 14-cylinder air-cooled sleeve-valve supercharged radial engines; Mk VI, 1,800hp Hercules 100.
Dimensions	early production aircraft, span 98ft 10in, length 70ft 1in, height 20ft 9in, wing area 1,250sq ft; late production aircraft, span 104ft 2in, length 71ft 7in, height 20ft 9in, wing area 1,275sq ft.
Weights	Mk I, empty 36,000lb, loaded 60,000lb; Mk III, empty 38,240lb, loaded 65,000lb; Mk VI, empty 38,900lb, loaded 68,000lb.
Performance	Mk I, max speed 280mph at 16,500ft, service ceiling 19,100ft, range with 8,000lb bomb load 1,060 miles; Mk III, max speed 282mph at 13,500ft, service ceiling 18,600ft, range with max bomb load 1,030 miles.
Armament, defensive	Mk III, 1 × Vickers K GO MG in nose, 4 × .303in Browning MGs each in Boulton Paul dorsal and tail turrets.
Armament, offensive	max bomb load 13,000lb.
Production	6,135.

The RAF's Battle squadrons were finally withdrawn to England in June 1940. Eight squadrons continued to use the aircraft for bombing French and Belgian Channel ports from airfields in England before the type was eventually withdrawn from Bomber Command's front-line inventory in the autumn. Those Battles that had survived were transferred to training and target-towing duties.

Handley Page Halifax

Designed to Air Ministry specification P13/36, the Halifax became the second of the four-engine heavies to enter service with Bomber Command. The first Merlin-engine Mk I was delivered to 35 Squadron in November 1940 but it was not until 10 March 1941 that the first operation was flown by six Halifaxes when Le Havre was bombed. The British public had to wait until July to learn of the new bomber's existence, following a successful daylight attack on the battleship *Scharnhorst* at La Pallice in Brittany. However, increasingly effective enemy defences soon led to the Halifax being confined to night bomber operations.

By early in 1942, four of 4 Group's heavy bomber squadrons had converted to the Halifax and re-equipment continued apace until by 1944 it became the exclusive mount of 4 Group and 6 (RCAF) Group, and was also used in small numbers by 100 (BS) Group in the RCM role. The Halifax flew on virtually all the main raids of the night offensive between 1942 and 1945, and the last occasion when Bomber Command Halifaxes operated in strength against the enemy was in the attack on coastal gun batteries at Wangerooge on 25 April 1945.

The earlier Merlin-engine marks of Halifax – the Mk I, II and V – suffered heavier losses than the Lancaster on account of their inferior speed and operational ceiling. They also suffered from an incurable rudder lock-over problem, which could lead to an unrecoverable and therefore fatal deep stall developing. When the first examples of the much-improved Hercules-engine Mk III entered service in November 1943, the small triangular tail fins were replaced by new and larger rectangular ones, which cured the lock-over problem once

LEFT The Halifax became the exclusive equipment of 4 and 6 (RCAF) Groups for most of the latter part of the war. This 77 Squadron B Mk II Series 1 (Special), KN-X/JB911, beats up the 'drome at Elvington in July 1943.

and for all. The performance of the Halifax was now good enough for it to hold its own against the Lancaster and, although it could carry up to 13,000lb of bombs, the heaviest single weapon it could lift was the 8,000-pounder.

A longer-range Halifax with an extended wingspan, designated the Mk VI, was fitted with Hercules 100 engines and a redesigned fuel system, and issued to several squadrons in 4 Group to supplement the Mk IIIs in the closing months of the war. Airframes built as Mk VIs, but fitted with the Hercules XVI, were designated Mk VII and entered service with three squadrons in 6 (RCAF) Group from June 1944.

A total of 6,179 Halifaxes had been built by the time production ceased, with Bomber Command's squadrons flying 82,773 operational Halifax sorties during the Second World War for the loss of 1,833 aircraft.

Handley Page Hampden

Faster than the Whitley or Wellington, the Hampden was a joy to fly and possessed a good range and a respectable bomb load. In company with the Wellington it was classed as a medium bomber, and with the Whitley it formed the backbone of Bomber Command.

Built to Air Ministry Specification B9/32 for a twin-engine day bomber, the Hampden was

BELOW Faster than the Whitley or Wellington, the Hampden possessed near-fighter handling and was a joy to fly. However, its narrow fuselage made for cramped conditions inside and gave rise to the nickname of 'the flying suitcase'. These three Hampden Mk Is (GL-T/L4201 nearest the camera) are from 14 OTU based at RAF Cottesmore in Rutland. They still carry the unit code letters ('GL') of 5 Group's 185 Squadron, which disbanded and merged with 14 OTU on 8 April 1940.

SPECIFICATION – HANDLEY PAGE HAMPDEN

Type	twin-engine four-man mid-wing monoplane medium bomber.
Powerplant	2 × 1,000hp Bristol Pegasus XVIII 9-cylinder air-cooled radial engines.
Dimensions	span 65ft 6in, length 52ft 7in, height 14ft 3in, wing area 551sq ft.
Weights	empty 17,468lb, loaded 26,700lb.
Performance	max speed 289mph at 16,000ft, cruising speed 212mph at 11,000ft, service ceiling 24,800ft, range 925 miles with full bomb load.
Armament, defensive	2 × .50in fixed MGs on top of nose, 2 × .303in MGs in nose on flexible mounts, 2 × .303in MGs in Boulton Paul dorsal turret, tunnel gun position with 2 × .303in manually trained MGs.
Armament, offensive	max bomb load 2,500lb.
Production	1,451.

developed in parallel with the Vickers Wellington and made its maiden flight on 21 June 1936. The twin Bristol Pegasus radial engine monoplane boasted a number of novel design features, the most prominent of which was its narrow but deep flat-sided forward fuselage – no more than 3ft wide at its broadest point – and a slender twin-boom tail.

An order for 180 Hampdens was placed two months after the prototype had flown and deliveries to the squadrons of 5 Group commenced in August 1938, with 49 Squadron at Scampton being the first to convert on to the new bomber. In September 1939 ten squadrons of Hampdens were equipped and ready. Aircraft from 44, 49 and 83 Squadrons were

dispatched in daylight on 4 September to seek out and attack German shipping in the Schillig Roads, but before long and in common with the RAF's other medium and heavy bombers, the Hampden was confined to night operations.

No 5 Group's Hampden squadrons became increasingly committed to bombing German land targets and were involved in attacks on German invasion barges in the Channel ports during the summer and autumn of 1940. They continued to fly operations against a variety of enemy targets through 1941 and early 1942, but it was inevitable that with the Manchester and Lancaster beginning to come on stream in 1942 the Hampden should be withdrawn from front-line bomber operations. The last Hampden sortie in Bomber Command was flown on 14/15 September 1942 by 408 Squadron against Wilhelmshaven.

Hampdens flew a total of 16,541 bombing sorties and dropped 9,115lb of bombs for the loss of 413 aircraft, and a further 194 to other causes.

Lockheed Vega Ventura

A military development of the Lockheed Lodestar civil transport, the twin-engine Ventura was intended for the RAF as a successor to the Hudson, to which it bore a striking similarity. As well as the bulbous twin .303in Boulton Paul dorsal turret, it featured a stepped underside to the rear fuselage to accommodate a gun position armed with two

RIGHT Known to RAF bomber crews as the 'Pig' because of its ungainly appearance, the Lockheed Ventura equipped three RAF bomber squadrons. Although well armed it still suffered heavy casualties. This is Ventura Mk I YH-Y/ AE660 of 21 Squadron at RAF Methwold in Norfolk, pictured on 27 February 1943.

.303in guns. At 2,500lb its bomb-carrying capability was disappointing and it was not long before 2 Group crews realised that the Ventura light bomber did little more than the Hudson, except consume more fuel. Only three squadrons were equipped with the Ventura Mk I and II from May 1942 (Nos 21, 464 and 487 Squadrons), but due to its low speed and insufficient armament to withstand a determined fighter attack the type suffered heavy casualties on daylight bomber operations over north-west Europe and was withdrawn by late 1943. Of the 136 Venturas that saw service with 2 Group, 31 were lost on operations, 9 written off through battle damage, and 8 destroyed in flying accidents.

North American B-25 Mitchell

The third of the trio of American twin-engine designs intended as replacements for the Blenheim, the Mitchell Mk II (equivalent to the USAAF's B-25C and D) was used by four squadrons of 2 Group (Nos 98, 180, 226 and 320) between September 1942 and the end of the war. A five-man light bomber with a nose-wheel undercarriage and a range of more than 900 miles, the Mitchell could carry a 4,000lb bomb load. In May 1944, the heavier Mk III arrived on the squadrons but it proved to be much less popular with its crews. In total, 85 Mitchell Mk Is were lost on operations, 26 written off due to battle damage, and 22 lost in flying accidents.

Short Stirling

Of the eight heavy bomber types in service with the principal combatant nations during the Second World War, the RAF's Short Stirling was unique in several respects: it was the tallest at 22ft 9in, the longest at 87ft 3in and the slowest at a maximum speed of 260mph; at 99ft 1in it had the shortest wingspan, at 44,000lb the greatest empty weight, and the shortest range with a maximum payload, at 740 miles.

Of the three British 'heavies' the Stirling was the only one to be designed from the outset to take four engines, and the only one to have full

SPECIFICATION – LOCKHEED VEGA VENTURA	
Type	twin-engine four-man mid-wing monoplane light bomber.
Powerplant	2 × 2,000hp Pratt & Whitney Twin Wasp R-2800-31 air-cooled radial engines.
Dimensions	span 65ft 6in, length 52ft 7in, height 14ft 3in, wing area 551sq ft.
Weights	empty 17,468lb, loaded 26,700lb.
Performance	max speed 289mph at 16,000ft, cruising speed 212mph at 11,000ft, service ceiling 24,800ft, range 925 miles with full bomb load.
Armament, defensive	2 × .50in fixed MGs on top of nose, 2 × .303in MGs in nose on flexible mounts, 2 × .303in MGs in Boulton Paul dorsal turret, tunnel gun position with 2 × .303in manually trained MGs.
Armament, offensive	max bomb load 2,500lb.

SPECIFICATION – NORTH AMERICAN B-25 MITCHELL Mk II	
Type	twin-engine five-man mid-wing monoplane light bomber.
Powerplant	2 × 1,700hp Wright Cyclone GR-2600-13 air-cooled radial engines.
Dimensions	span 67ft 6½in, length 54ft 1in, height 15ft 9½in, wing area 610sq ft.
Weights	empty 16,000lb, loaded 26,000lb, max 30,000lb.
Performance	max speed 294mph at 15,000ft, cruising speed 237mph at 10,000ft, service ceiling 26,700ft. Range with 4,000lb bomb load 925 miles at 15,000ft.
Armament, defensive	2 × .50in MGs each in dorsal and ventral Bendix turrets, 1 × .303in MG in one of four ball-and-socket mountings in nose.
Armament, offensive	max bomb load 4,000lb.

BELOW Armed with six .50in machine guns in four positions, the Mitchell could also carry a 4,000lb bomb load. Four squadrons in 2 Group operated the Mitchell. This is 320 (Dutch) Squadron's Mitchell Mk II, NO-S.

SPECIFICATION – SHORT STIRLING

Type	four-engine seven or eight-man mid-wing monoplane heavy night bomber.
Powerplant	Mk I, 4 × 1,590hp Bristol Hercules XI 14-cylinder air-cooled sleeve-valve radial engines; Mk III, 1,650hp Hercules XVI.
Dimensions	span 99ft 1in, length 87ft 3in, height 22ft 9in, wing area 1,460sq ft.
Weights	Mk III, empty 43,200lb, loaded 70,000lb.
Performance	Mk III, max speed 260mph at 14,500ft, cruising speed 200mph at 10,000ft, range 2,010 miles with 3,500lb bomb load, 740 miles with 14,000lb bomb load.
Armament, defensive	Mk III, 2 × .303in Browning MGs each in Frazer-Nash nose and dorsal turrets, 4 × Browning .303in MGs in Frazer-Nash tail turret.
Armament, offensive	max bomb load 14,000lb.
Production	2,369.

dual control. It was introduced into RAF service in August 1940 with 7 Squadron and by the time the type was eventually withdrawn in July 1946, a total of 2,371 had been built, all of which were flown by the RAF. At the zenith of its operational career with Bomber Command in 1943, 12 squadrons in 3 Group were equipped with the Stirling, but with the introduction of the Halifax and Lancaster to most main force

and Pathfinder squadrons by the end of that year, the Stirling quickly became the poorer relation in the RAF's trio of four-engine heavies, principally for its inferior altitude performance and high attrition rate. It was therefore relegated to second-line duties and lightly defended short-range targets in France during the run-up to D-Day, with 149 Squadron flying the final Bomber Command Stirling sortie against Le Havre on 8 September 1944.

Vickers-Armstrong Wellington

The twin-engine Wellington became one of the outstanding bomber aircraft of the Second World War and was renowned for the amount of battle damage it could soak up. This was due largely to its unique geodetic construction that had been specially designed by Dr Barnes Wallis of 'bouncing bomb' fame. The first prototype flew in June 1936 and in October 1938 the first production aircraft entered service with Bomber Command's 99 Squadron. At the outbreak of war, eight operational bomber squadrons in 3 Group were equipped with the Wellington. 'Wimpys' flew the first bombing raid of the war against the German fleet at Wilhelmshaven on 4 September 1939, although from December the same year they were switched to night operations and became the RAF's principal night bomber until sufficient numbers of the Stirling, Halifax and Lancaster had reached the squadrons in 1942.

BELOW The Stirling was the first four-engine heavy bomber to enter service with the RAF in August 1940. These two early production aircraft are seen when W7427 (background) and N6069 (foreground) were serving with 26 Conversion Flight and 1651 Conversion Unit respectively. They had been relegated from front-line squadrons for aircrew training.

ABOVE Thanks largely to its unique geodetic construction, the Wellington was able to withstand an enormous amount of battle damage and still make it home. The Mk X aircraft in this photograph were powered by Bristol Hercules radial engines instead of the Pegasus that was used in earlier marks of the bomber. These 'Wimpys' belong to 300 (Polish) Squadron and are seen at RAF Hemswell in June 1943.

The Wellington was the first RAF bomber to drop the 4,000lb 'Blockbuster'.

The main production versions that saw service principally with Bomber Command's 1 and 3 Groups were the Mk I, Ia and Ic (Bristol Pegasus X and XVIII), the Mk II (Rolls-Royce Merlin X, 400 built), Mk III (Bristol Hercules XI, 1,519 built), the Mk IV (Pratt & Whitney Twin Wasp, 221 built), and the Mk X (Bristol Hercules VI, 3,804 built). Total Wellington production reached 11,460 aircraft, with many examples seeing service with Coastal Command and overseas, as trainers at bomber OTUs and as engine and armament test-beds.

SPECIFICATION – VICKERS-ARMSTRONG WELLINGTON	
Type	twin-engine five-man mid-wing monoplane medium night bomber.
Powerplant	Mk I, 2 × 1,000hp Bristol Pegasus X and XVIII air-cooled radial engines; Mk II, 1,145hp Rolls-Royce Merlin X in-line liquid-cooled engines; Mk III, 1,500hp Bristol Hercules XI sleeve-valve radials; Mk X, 1,675hp Bristol Hercules VI/XVI radials.
Dimensions	span 86ft 2in, length 64ft 7in, height 17ft 5in, wing area 840sq ft.
Weights	Mk Ic, empty 18,556lb, loaded 28,500lb; Mk X, empty 22,474lb, loaded 36,500lb.
Performance	Mk Ic, max speed 235mph at 15,500ft, service ceiling 18,000ft; Mk III, max speed 255mph at 12,500ft, service ceiling 18,000ft. Range with 4,500lb bomb load 1,540 miles.
Armament, defensive	Mk Ic, 2 × .303in Browning MGs in Frazer-Nash nose and tail turrets, 2 × manually operated Browning .303in MGs in beam positions.
Armament, offensive	max bomb load 4,500lb.
Mk III, defensive	2 × Browning .303in MGs in Frazer-Nash nose turret, 4 in Frazer-Nash rear turret, 2 × manually operated Browning .303in MGs in beam positions.
offensive	max bomb load 4,500lb.
Production	11,460.

'I went out to my Halifax to see this huge bomb strung up in the bomb bay and it was frighteningly big! It resembled two pillar boxes stuck together, so of course, the bomb doors were fully open and I didn't relish taking off at all.'

Michael Renaut, Halifax pilot, 76 Squadron, 1942, describing the 8,000lb HC 'Blockbuster'.

Chapter Six

Bombs and bullets

With an arsenal ranging from the diminutive but nasty 4lb stick incendiary to the 22,000lb Grand Slam 'earthquake' bomb, Bomber Command's squadrons had a wide range of highly destructive ordnance at their disposal. To protect them from attack by enemy fighters, the vulnerable bombers were defended by ingenious power-assisted multi-gun turrets.

OPPOSITE A 4,000lb HC 'Cookie' is wheeled towards this 75 (New Zealand) Squadron Wellington Mk III at Feltwell for hoisting into its bomb bay. The Wellington was the first aircraft to drop this type of bomb.

ABOVE Bomb loads great . . . A 12,000lb Tallboy ballistic bomb is craned off its cradle in the bomb dump at Bardney, before being carefully lowered on to the Type H bomb trolley. The Type H was similar in construction to the Type E, but differed in that it was fitted with a winch mechanism for raising the bomb into the aircraft.

BELOW . . . and small. Armourers assisted by the station armaments officer manhandle a bomb trolley loaded with four 250lb GP bombs under the open bomb bay of a 105 Squadron Mosquito B IV Series II (DZ367 GB-J) at Marham on 10 December 1942. (The Series II Mossies had flame-damped exhausts and long nacelles, but pilots considered them slower than the first series off the production line.)

In the years that followed the First World War, very little money was made available by the British government for armament research and development purposes. It was not until 1935, when the possibility of another war looked increasingly likely, that the government began to turn its attention towards developing new bomb designs for the RAF. But when Bomber Command eventually went to war in 1939 it found itself equipped with a very limited and inadequate arsenal of high-explosive general purpose (GP) bombs. It quickly became apparent that the GP range of bombs were poor performers with their low charge-to-weight ratio of 34% and many simply failed to detonate on impact. The GP range was gradually replaced over a period of three years by the newly developed medium-capacity (MC) range of weapons, which proved very effective. As the war gathered pace, so new and heavier bombs were designed to meet the needs of the growing offensive, finding their apotheosis in the specialist Tallboy and Grand Slam 'earthquake' bombs designed by Dr Barnes Wallis, who was also co-designer of the Vickers Wellington.

By early 1942, Bomber Command was in the process of changing over from small twin-engine bombers like the Hampden and Blenheim, which carried comparatively light bomb loads, to heavy four-engine bombers like the Halifax and Lancaster, capable of carrying far greater loads over longer distances. In 1939 the heaviest bombs that could be carried as part of a load were 500-pounders; by the war's end it was common for a bomber to carry individual high-explosive MC and HC bombs weighing between 2,000 and 4,000lb each.

The three principal types of bomb that Bomber Command employed in its offensive against Germany (apart from the specialist weapons) were the incendiary (or fire bomb) filled with either thermite pellets or a mixture of phosphorus and rubberised benzol; the high-capacity (blast) bomb; and the medium-capacity (for general bombardment) bomb, the latter two being filled with one of several high-explosive (HE) charges then available, which included RDX, Minol, Amatol, Amatex and Torpex. Used together, HE and incendiary produced devastating results when the blast bombs blew apart buildings and the incendiaries then set fire

to the scattered contents. At the beginning of the war HE bombs were considered the best weapons to use, with incendiaries employed in small quantities as a harassment measure, but in the final years of the war Bomber Command dropped mixed loads comprising a much higher ratio of incendiary to HE.

In 1940, bomb loads included no more than 6% by weight of incendiaries, but as the bomber offensive gathered momentum and the intensity of attacks grew ever greater, the value of incendiaries for fire-raising became appreciated. In fact, one of the great success stories of the war for the RAF was the small hexagonal stick-shaped 4lb incendiary bomb, of which Bomber Command dropped nearly 80 million during the course of the Second World War. By mid-1942 incendiaries comprised up to 40% of a bomb load and later during the Battles of the Ruhr and Berlin in 1943–44 they could account for up to 66%. It was from this point in the war that the combination of high-explosive blast bombs like the 4,000lb HC, used in conjunction with incendiaries, flattened many of Germany's urban centres and caused the terrible and uncontrollable firestorms that devastated the cities of Hamburg, Dresden, Kassel and Darmstadt.

The second of the three principal types of bomb was the high-capacity range of weapons that were essentially modernised versions of those used with some effect by the newly formed RAF against German targets towards the end of the First World War. The HC came in three sizes, all of which were cylindrical in shape, their thin steel casings packed with high explosive. With their high charge-to-weight ratio of more than 70%, the HC blast bombs had a devastating effect against most targets. The first of the 'Blockbuster' 4,000lb HC bombs appeared in the spring of 1941 and from then on, supplemented with incendiaries, they became the standard area load for Bomber Command's heavy bombers.

The HC family of weapons that followed the 'Blockbuster' were the massively destructive 8,000lb and 12,000lb HC bombs. Contrary to popular myth the 8,000lb HC was not made up from two regular 4,000lb HC weapons, but of sections specifically designed for the purpose and weighing approximately 4,000lb each. With the development of a new and powerful high-explosive filling called Minol, the blast effect of these awesome weapons was further increased and their incendiary side effects enhanced, making them a most successful range of bombs.

The third type of bomb was the medium capacity (MC), developed between 1940 and 1943 to supersede the unreliable and ineffective CP series with which the RAF was equipped at the outbreak of war. Based on the German SC range of bombs, the British MCs came in three sizes – 500, 1,000 and 4,000lb. All had a charge-to-weight ratio of 50%, were designed with

ABOVE Enough bombs and their handling crews to arm 20 Lancasters and send them to Berlin. This is a typical fire-raising area load of 4,000lb HC blast bombs to blow open buildings and small bomb containers, each loaded with 106 × 4lb incendiaries, to set alight the contents.
(Getty Images)

streamlined steel casings with pointed noses, and clip-on or bolt-on tail units. The MC range was sufficiently robust to withstand the impact stresses and subsequent penetration of most structures, except for reinforced concrete. The 500-pounder

was mainly for tactical bombing and was used to great effect in low-level attacks against the Philips radio and valve factory in Eindhoven in December 1942, the breaching of the walls of the Amiens prison in February 1944 and one month later against the Gestapo headquarters in Copenhagen. The 1,000 and 4,000-pounders were for general bombardment purposes. The 4,000-pounder was used mainly for high-level attacks, although Mosquitoes of 8 (PFF) Group used them effectively at low level in 1944–45. The 500 and 1,000-pounder MC bombs outperformed all the other general bombardment bombs used by the RAF and, following their introduction in 1943, the 1,000-pounder became Bomber Command's first choice, with 17,500 being dropped in 1943, 203,000 in 1944 and 36,000 in 1945.

Fusing

Two types of bomb fusing were employed: bomb pistols and bomb fuses. The former was relatively simple and provided detonation by the direct action of a mechanical pistol, while the latter contained its own integral striker and detonator mechanism. Fuses could also be more complex and often incorporated barometric, clockwork, pyrotechnic or hydrostatic processes, which provided a variety of options including airburst and underwater use. Where penetration of the target was desired, the bomb was fused with a slight time delay, for example, of 0.04 or 0.025 seconds.

Bombs could be fitted with either nose or tail fuses, or both. Those intended for instantaneous detonation were usually fused at the nose end, but with a standby fuse in the tail end just in case the nose fuse failed. Delayed-action bombs were only ever fused at the tail end.

Bomb-handling equipment

Due to continual increases in the variety of weapons available and the bomb loads carried, for much of the war bomb-handling equipment on RAF bomber stations lagged a stage behind the operational requirements. Bomb dumps were located on airfield perimeters and could store up to 200 tons of weapons at any one time. Bombs were 'picked' to order

Cluster incendiary projectiles and small bomb containers wait on bomb trolleys for loading at Tholthorpe in late 1944. The North Yorkshire base was home to 420 (Snowy Owl) and 425 (Alouette) Squadrons and their Halifax Mk IIIs. In the background is 425's NR134 'Overseas Zombie', a veteran of 434 (Bluenose) and 426 (Thunderbird) Squadrons, before she passed to the Alouettes. *(Marcel Baillargeon)*

and loaded on to bomb trolleys which were then towed by David Brown or Fordson tractors to aircraft awaiting bombing-up on the dispersals. All HE bombs were handled in the bomb dumps simply by rolling, but the large MC bombs like the Blockbuster and Tallboy had to be dealt with by crane. Incendiary bombs were delivered from ordnance factories to bomb dumps in packs, where they were laboriously transferred by hand into small bomb containers and stored on end in Nissen huts until required. Pistols and fuses were fitted to bombs on the dispersals prior to hoisting the weapons into the bomb bays.

All bomb trolleys (except the Type H) had a low rectangular chassis with small pneumatic tyres at each corner, and adjustable chocks on which to locate the bombs. In 1942 there were two standard bomb trolleys in use, the Type B, which was able to carry four 500lb bombs, and the Type D for one 4,000lb HC bomb. The Type B was slowly replaced with the Type C capable of carrying up to 6,000lb, and the Type F with a maximum load of 8,000lb. Towards the end of 1943 the steerable Type E trolley was introduced for HC bombs up to 12,000lb, and in 1944 the Type H entered service for the large MC bombs, equipped with a cradle capable of being winched up to enable the bomb to be hoisted into the aircraft.

BELOW Armourers wheel an early 4,000lb HC Cookie under the open bomb bay of 76 Squadron's Halifax B Mk II, L9530/MP-L, at Middleton St George in September 1941. Owing to problems with accommodating the bulky Cookie, the largest HE bomb carried operationally by the Halifax after 1942 was the 2,000-pounder. *(Crown Copyright/Air Historical Branch RAF)*

RIGHT A comparison of extremes: the corporal in the foreground holds a 40lb GP bomb, while supported in the cradle of a Type H bomb trolley behind him is the largest bomb in the RAF's wartime arsenal, the 22,000lb (10-ton) Grand Slam. Visible are the chains for securing the weapon to the cradle (tightened using turnbuckles) and two of the four winches used for raising the bomb into position underneath the specially modified Lancaster B Mk I (Special).

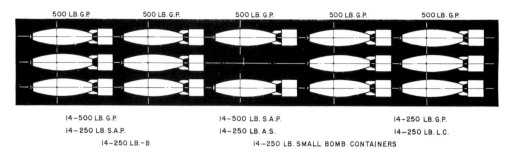

500 LB. G.P.   500 LB. G.P.   500 LB. G.P.   500 LB. G.P.   500 LB. G.P.

14–500 LB. G.P.   14–500 LB. S.A.P.   14–250 LB. G.P.
14–250 LB. S.A.P.   14–250 LB. A.S.   14–250 LB. L.C.
          14–250 LB.–B   14–250 LB. SMALL BOMB CONTAINERS

ANY ONE OF THE ABOVE LOADINGS MAY BE USED

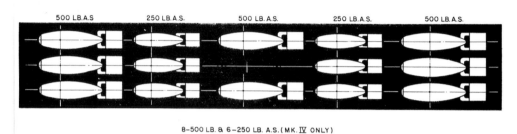

500 LB. A.S   250 LB. A.S.   500 LB. A.S.   250 LB. A.S.   500 LB. A.S.

8–500 LB. & 6–250 LB. A.S. (MK. IV ONLY)

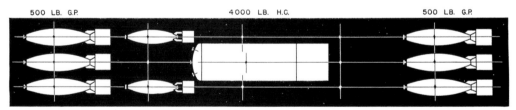

250 LB. A.S.   500 LB. A.S.   250 LB. S.A.P.   500 LB. A.S.   250 LB. S.A.P.

6–500 LB. & 3–250 LB. A.S. (MK. I, II & III) AND 5–250 LB. S.A.P.

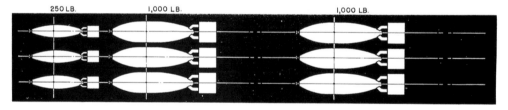

250 LB.   1,000 LB.   1,000 LB.

6–1,000 LB. & 3–250 LB. G.P.

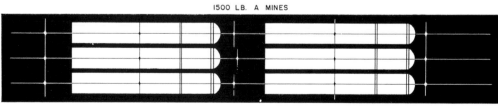

500 LB. G.P.   4000 LB. H.C.   500 LB. G.P.

1–4000 LB. H.C. -- 6–500 LB. G.P. & 2-250 LB. G.P. BOMBS

1500 LB. A MINES

6–1500 LB. A MINES OR 6–2000 LB. H.C. BOMBS

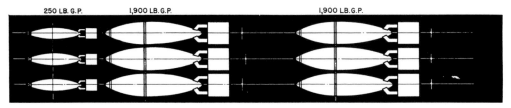

6-1900 LB. & 3-250 LB. G.P.

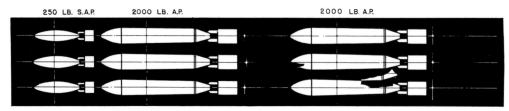

6-2000 LB. A.P. & 3-250 LB. S.A.P.

High-explosive bombs

40lb, 250lb, 500lb, 1,000lb, 1,900lb and 4,000lb GP

During the first two years of war GP bombs, which were really the products of pre-war thinking, formed the greater part of the RAF's armoury. All GP bombs suffered from the same shortcomings of too much metal and too little explosive and their effectiveness was questionable across the entire range, the 1,900 and 4,000-pounders being particularly suspect. They began to be superseded by the superior MC range from the end of 1941 onwards, although in the summer of 1944 many 250lb and 500lb GP bombs were resurrected to make up for the serious shortage of MC bombs. The 4,000-pounder saw limited use between May 1942 and November 1943 after which it was deleted from Bomber Command's inventory owing to fusing problems.

500lb, 1,000lb and 4,000lb MC

Introduced at the end of 1941, the 500lb MC contained about twice the HE content of the GP bombs then in use. Stocks were always inadequate of the 1,000-pounder, which was a very effective weapon following its introduction in the spring of 1943. During 1944 the shortage reached crisis point and stocks had to be rationed with the greatest of care. Intended originally for use in low-level bombing operations, the 4,000lb MC introduced in

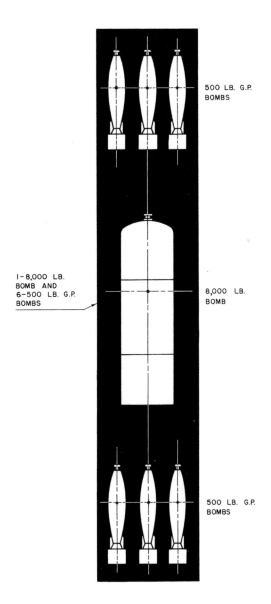

January 1943 never became widely used by Bomber Command, partly because only one could be carried by Lancaster aircraft and none by Halifaxes. During the autumn of 1944, the weapon was used by Mosquito aircraft for high-altitude night bombing.

American bombs

During 1944 large quantities of American bombs were used. These were the ANM 44, 58 and 64 (500lb) and ANM 59 and 64 (1,000lb). The 58 and 59 were semi armour-piercing bombs (SAPs) while the others were equivalent to the British MC range. These bombs were quicker and easier to fuse and tail than their British-made equivalents, and gave good service, but the American box-type tails drastically reduced the number that could be carried in British aircraft.

2,000lb AP

This weapon saw very limited use against the German battlecruisers *Scharnhorst* and *Gneisenau* at Brest in 1942, and against underground oil storage plants in France in 1944. The results were disappointing and faulty fusing led to a large number of duds.

SAP bombs

Few SAP bombs were used between 1942 and 1945 because suitable targets were seldom available, but with the grave shortage of HE bombs experienced in the summer of 1944 some SAP bombs were used against V-1 flying bomb sites in France.

2,000lb, 4,000lb, 8,000lb and 12,000lb HC

Initial use with a parachute attachment in early 1942 rendered the 2,000lb HC virtually unaimable. A request from Bomber Command for a fitted ballistic tail resulted in new supplies arriving in August the same year. The 4,000-pounder was formally introduced into

BELOW The three longitudinal cells of the Stirling's main bomb bay meant it was not able to carry anything larger than a 2,000lb bomb. Here armourers load 250lb GP (foreground) and a single 2,000lb HC into a 15 Squadron Stirling.

service in January 1942, although more than 400 had been dropped on German targets in the previous nine months. It was followed later by the two larger weapons, of which the 12,000-pounder was used mainly for special precision targets. In the event of a take-off crash, all of these bombs were liable to detonate owing to the delicate nose pistols.

Specialist HE bombs

'Upkeep'

This was the famous bouncing bomb designed by Dr Barnes Wallis and used with success by 617 Squadron against the Ruhr dams in May 1943. It was essentially

ABOVE Aircrew ride atop this 4,000lb Cookie loaded on a Type E trolley, which was fitted with a pair of steerable wheels at each end to assist armourers in positioning the heavy bomb beneath the aircraft. The Light Night Striking Force Mossie in the background is 692 Squadron's B IV Series II, DZ637/P3-C, modified by Vickers in June 1943 to carry the 4,000-pounder. Flying with 627 Squadron on 1 February 1945, DZ637 was shot down over Steigen and its crew were killed.

an air-dropped rotating cylindrical 9,150lb mine filled with 6,600lb of high-explosive Torpex and fitted with a hydrostatic fuse. It was used by one squadron only and on one occasion operationally. 'Upkeep' was designed to be dropped from a Lancaster using a special bomb-release installation

LEFT A fully armed 'Upkeep' mine is spun and dropped from a specially adapted Lancaster B Mk I (Type 464 Provisioning) in a live trial off the Kent coast at Reculver on 13 May 1943, three days before the dams raid. Minus its mid-upper turret and bomb doors, the dam buster Lanc looks very different from the standard version.

beneath the belly of the aircraft. The weapon bounced across the surface of the water in the reservoir, skipping anti-torpedo nets, before striking the inner face of the dam wall and sliding beneath the water where it exploded and breached the structure.

'Johnnie Walker'

Supplies of this air-dropped oscillating 500lb mine became available during 1943 but were not used operationally until 15 September 1944

when the *Tirpitz* was attacked by 27 Lancasters in a shuttle-bombing operation launched from northern Russia as the battleship lay in Kaa Fjord, Norway. Twenty aircraft were loaded with the 12,000lb Tallboy, while the rest carried several 'Johnnie Walker' mines. This was the only occasion on which the weapon was deployed operationally.

12,000lb 'Tallboy' and 22,000lb 'Grand Slam' MC

These so-called 'earthquake' bombs designed by Dr Barnes Wallis marked a major advance in bomb design and ballistics. They penetrated deep into the ground before detonation and the resulting shockwaves destroyed the target at its foundations, rather than relying on surface destruction, which required a direct hit. Becoming available in the summer of 1944, these weapons were used to devastating effect against key targets that included the *Tirpitz*, U-boat pens and viaducts. The *coup de grâce* was delivered against the *Tirpitz* on 12 November 1944 by 30 Tallboy-armed

LEFT The Bielefeld Viaduct was attacked twice by 617 Squadron with 18 Tallboys on 22 February and again on 14 March 1945. In the second raid, 13 Tallboys and the Grand Slam were dropped, the viaduct collapsing through the earthquake effect of the latter.

Lancasters of 9 and 617 Squadrons. At least two direct hits were recorded before a massive internal explosion caused the battleship to capsize and turn turtle.

Incendiary bombs (IB)

4lb, 30lb, 30lb J-Type, 250lb IB

Dropped from small bomb containers (SBC) the 4lb magnesium incendiary bomb (IB) was the mainstay of Bomber Command throughout the war. However, it suffered badly from a lack of aimability which meant that incendiary attacks could become widely dispersed downwind from the target, and friendly aircraft in the stream were susceptible to damage from showers of loose bombs over the target area.

Various marks of the 30lb aimable phosphorus-filled IB were used from 1941 to late 1944 when use of this range was abandoned in preference of the 4-pounder, although by this time over 3 million had been dropped.

Operational trials of the 30lb J-Type conducted between April and August 1944 showed that it was only half as effective per ton as the 4lb IB, so it was not adopted. The J-Type produced a spectacular 2ft-wide jet of flame out to a distance of 15ft for one minute and more than 400,000 were used in bombing attacks.

Using a light casing originally designed for being filled with chemical warfare agents, the 250lb IB was first used in 1940 and saw several years of service in the IB role before later being converted for use as a target marker filled with coloured pyrotechnic substances. The 500lb IB was a scaled-up version of the 250-pounder, filled with liquid phosphorus and designed mainly for special low-level missions by Mosquitoes.

Probably the least well-known weapon in the IB range, the 2,700-pounder was a 4,000lb HC bomb case filled with incendiary substance, which first saw use in 1944 for low-level attacks on special targets by Mosquitoes.

Cluster projectiles

CP 500lb, CP 750lb, CP 1,000lb

In May 1943, at the instigation of Bomber Harris, a requirement was raised with the Air Ministry for a cluster delivery device for IBs to replace the incendiaries released from SBCs that could not be aimed individually with the Mk XIV bombsight. This device was known as the cluster projectile (CP) and its benefits included improved bombing accuracy,

BELOW On the 4 Group base at Snaith in late 1944, Sqn Ldr Ian Roxborough and crew sit on a bomb trolley carrying a load of cluster projectiles (500lb, No 14), each packed with 106 × 4lb incendiaries. *(Andy Thomas collection)*

prevention of trail-back of incendiary attacks and protecting friendly aircraft from damage by showers of IBs (which, until the advent of the CP, had been scattered from SBCs). The first 500lb CPs (106 × 4lb incendiaries) were used towards the end of 1943 in the Battle of Berlin, followed in summer 1944 by the CP 750lb and the CP 1,000lb in the autumn. Two further CPs were introduced towards the end of the war – the so-called Cluster Nose Ejection (CNE) projectiles.

Air-dropped sea mines

A Mk I-IV 1,500lb and 1,850lb, A Mk V 1,000lb, A Mk VI 2,000lb and A Mk VII 1,000lb mines

Introduced in April 1940, the A Mk I-IV mine was robustly designed to withstand delivery from an aircraft flying at 200mph and from heights of between 100 and 15,000ft. It contained approximately 750lb of explosive and incorporated a number of triggering options. Together with the A Mk V and VII,

it became the predominant air-dropped mine to be used throughout the war. The A Mk I-IV was superseded by the A Mk VI 2,000-pounder in 1944.

The A Mk V 1,000lb mine was a smaller version of the A Mk I-IV and contained between 625 and 675lb of explosive. It was introduced during 1940–41 and was deployed predominantly in the magnetic mode. The A Mk VII 1,000lb mine was an upgraded version of the A Mk V mine and was introduced in 1944.

Guns and power-operated turrets

Of all the air arms of the combatant nations in the Second World War, it was the RAF and the USAAF that made the greatest use of power-assisted multi-gun turrets to defend their bomber aircraft. Although British manufacturers pioneered their development and first use operationally, it was the Americans who ultimately produced the better-armed and -armoured designs.

Experimental designs for power-assisted enclosed gun turrets had been worked on during the 1930s, mainly by Boulton Paul Aircraft Ltd, the Bristol Aeroplane Company and independent design engineers Archibald Frazer-Nash and Grafton Thompson. Although the Boulton Paul and Bristol-designed turrets saw use in Bomber Command aircraft in the Second World War, the designs for hydraulic gun control systems by Frazer-Nash and Thompson were adopted on a far larger scale in the .303in Browning-armed power-assisted turrets.

Much time and money was spent on the design and development of these gun turrets with great hopes pinned on their effectiveness against enemy fighters. Yet despite them, Bomber Command suffered such heavy losses in the early daylight raids that its heavy bombers were soon restricted to night operations. This situation persisted until after D-Day when the Command began a partial return to daylight operations with its heavy bombers, and by which time long-range escort fighters could be provided in sufficient numbers to protect the bomber streams.

As already stated, Nash and Thompson and Frazer-Nash designs became the most widely

BELOW A Mk V 1,000lb sea mines await their turn to be loaded into a 3 Group Stirling.

used of the war. The turrets themselves were manufactured at the Parnall Aircraft Company factory at Yate in Gloucestershire (acquired by Frazer-Nash and Thompson), while design and development was undertaken at Tolworth in Surrey. Their turrets were fitted to the Avro Manchester and Lancaster, Short Stirling, Vickers-Armstrong Wellington and Armstrong-Whitworth Whitley, and their use in service exceeded 50,000 examples. Boulton Paul turrets were also widely used for the Handley Page Halifax. Bristol turrets were fitted to the Blenheim IV, while small numbers of Preston Green mid-under turrets were used in the Halifax III, and the Rose Brothers' twin .50in tail gun turret in the Lancaster.

It was the tail and mid-upper turrets that were most used in combat and where the gunners needed to remain for the entire trip. The nose turret was mainly used for observation purposes, although sometimes it could be used to engage overshooting enemy fighters and was therefore not manned continuously. In roomy aircraft like the Stirling there was ample space in the front end of the fuselage to accommodate the turret and its gunner, but in the Wellington and Lancaster where space was at a premium the nose gunner's feet often dangled down over the bomb-aimer in the compartment below.

Gunners in the remote tail turrets had the coldest and most dangerous position of all, seated for hours on end on a hard seat inside a turret with no heating. To compound their discomfort the turret Perspex often misted over and then froze up completely, causing the gunner to smash out the sighting section to give a better view of approaching enemy fighters. Tail turrets were also the most vulnerable since the night-fighter's favoured attacking position was from astern and slightly below. However, the lot of the air gunner – and that of the 'tail-end Charlie' in particular – gradually improved as the war progressed, with more effective heated clothing to wear and extra armour protection fitted to the turret.

The turret itself was a minor marvel of hydraulic and mechanical engineering. Each turret was mounted on a pair of concentric circular metal rings, the inner one turned by a hydraulic rotation motor which derived its power from an engine-driven pump, thereby traversing

the turret. Nash and Thompson, Frazer-Nash and Bristol turrets were fully hydraulic and reliant on huge lengths of copper piping transmitting high-pressure fluid from the aircraft power source to the turret. Those of Boulton Paul were electro-hydraulic which meant that their hydraulic power unit was self-contained inside the turret and electrically driven.

The elevation or depression of the guns, and the traversal of the whole turret, was achieved hydraulically by operation of a pair of control handles mounted close together on a common control column, or on each side of the turret outboard of the guns. The guns themselves were fired by hydraulic units and electrical solenoids in hydraulic and electrically operated turrets respectively, operated by triggers or push-buttons on the turret control handle. Sighting was almost exclusively with the Mk III Reflector Sight, although the Mk IIC Gyro Sight was also used in conjunction with Automatic Gun Laying (Turret) (AGL(T))-equipped turrets from the autumn of 1944.

Ammunition was belt-fed to each turret along metal tracks from ammunition tanks contained in the aircraft fuselage, which meant that the gunner could fight his turret without having to reload magazines or drums of ammunition. The belt-feed system was not without its drawbacks, however, mainly in the form of belt breakages which led to gun stoppages that were not easy to rectify in the air.

ABOVE This is a restored example of an FN20 rear turret from a Vickers Wellington at the Imperial War Museum, Duxford. It was derived from the FN4/FN4A design and became the standard rear turret for the Lancaster. *(Alan Wilson/ Wikimedia Commons)*

Guns

Three models of machine gun were used operationally during the Second World War by aircraft of Bomber Command for defensive purposes. These were the Vickers .303in gas-operated Mk I No 1, the Browning .303in and the Browning .50in.

Vickers gas-operated .303in

Designed to replace the Lewis gun in the rear cockpits of day bombers, the Vickers gas-operated .303in gun was looked upon as a stop-gap until hand-held guns were finally phased out of service. Known in RAF parlance as the VGO, the design was based on a French light infantry machine gun in use at the end of the First World War and first entered RAF service in 1937. It used a drum magazine and was as reliable as the Browning .303in gun, but much easier to maintain.

At the outbreak of war in 1939, the VGO was used singly in the front turret of the Whitley, in the nose of the Hampden, the rear cockpit of the Battle and in the side gun hatches of the Wellington. However, with the gradual withdrawal of these types from front-line use and their replacement by aircraft fitted with Browning gun turrets, by 1943 the VGO was almost obsolete in RAF service – but this was not the end of the story. Its self-contained design, which needed no belt boxes, ensured its continued

use up to the war's end in the glazed nose position of all the later marks of Halifax.

Browning .303in

The Browning .303in was one of the two most important guns used by the RAF in the Second World War, and became the standard bomber armament for defence in multi-gun power-assisted turrets when they were introduced. The other weapon was the Hispano 20mm gun, which was the subject of extensive pre-war development trials by Boulton Paul, but which was finally considered too large to fit any existing gun turret. However, it did see extensive and highly effective service with Fighter Command.

Paradoxically the .303in gun remained the principal defensive armament for the bomber from its adoption in 1934 until the end of the war, despite its comparatively short range and hitting power. The reasons for this lie in the early days of the war when more heavily armed turrets had actually been designed, but were shelved when it became clear that maximum aircraft production was essential if the RAF was to pose a credible threat to Germany. Any interruption of the production lines caused through the introduction of new or modernised equipment was therefore not desirable. When Bomber Command was forced to switch to night operations, the comparatively short range of the .303in machine gun was not considered a pressing issue, and many believed that a battery of four Brownings blazing away from a turret would be sufficient deterrent to any night-fighter looking for an easy kill.

When German fighters became armoured against rifle-calibre bullets, the RAF's .303in gun turrets became largely ineffective and little use was made of the bombers' defensive armament. G.T. Wallace, a technical officer with the Directorate of Armament Development, had this to say on their effectiveness: '... 90 per cent of Lancaster sorties were made without contact with enemy fighters, but of the 10 per cent that were intercepted approximately half were shot down despite their armament.'

Browning .50in

Towards the end of the war when the Luftwaffe began to increase further still the armour

BELOW The Vickers GO gun is clear to see in the Perspex nose cone of 432 (Leaside) Squadron's high-scoring Halifax B Mk VII, 'Willie the Wolf' (NP707/QO-W), at East Moor, Yorkshire, in 1944. *(Phil Gallant)*

protection fitted to its fighters, several designs for turrets using twin 13.5mm or .50in guns were produced for potential use in Bomber Command aircraft, but only one entered service operationally. This was the Rose Brothers' .50in Browning turret, of which several hundred saw operational use and then only in the closing months of the war, although air gunners appreciated the extra firepower it brought to bear. Most were fitted to Lancasters in 1 and 5 Groups. The Model M2 version of the 'fifty-cal' was the standard defensive armament fitted on most American warplanes of the Second World War.

The Nash and Thompson FN82 and Boulton Paul D turret designs also incorporated twin .50in Brownings, which would have seen widespread use by Bomber Command had the war continued longer.

The American experience on daylight bombing raids showed that turrets fitted with heavier .50in machine guns made little difference to the survivability of a heavy bomber aircraft in combat when pitted against a fast, manoeuvrable and heavily armed fighter aircraft. That said, the US 8th Air Force's gunners gave good accounts of themselves.

Hispano 20mm cannon

Fitted as a fixed gun to Mosquito aircraft in 100 (BS) Group, this weapon gave satisfactory service. It was also intended for use in the Bristol Type B.17 mid-upper turret under development, but which was too late to see war service.

Power-assisted gun turrets

Boulton Paul

Type A Mk VIII nose turret

Mid-upper used with low profile fairing and fitted to the Halifax from the B Mk II Series Ia onwards.
Power system: BP electro-hydraulic.
Armament: 4 × Browning .303in Mk II guns.
Ammunition: 600rpg from boxes in turret.
Sighting: Mk IIIa reflector sight.

Type C Mk I nose turret

A nose turret used in Halifax B Mk I and II only, it caused problems with control of the aircraft when the turret was traversed in flight.

ABOVE From the Halifax B Mk II Series 1a onwards the four-gun Boulton Paul Type A Mk VII low-profile turret replaced the drag-inducing bulbous Boulton Paul Type C Mk II installation.

Power system: BP electro-hydraulic.
Armament: 2 × Browning .303in Mk II guns.
Ammunition: 1,000rpg.
Sighting: Mk IIIa reflector sight.

Type C Mk II dorsal turret

Mid-upper fitted to the Halifax B Mk II only. It reduced the speed of the aircraft in flight and was dispensed with altogether on the later Mk II Series I (Special).
(Specification same as Type C Mk I)

BELOW An armourer pulls through the twin Brownings in the Boulton Paul Type C Mk I front turret of a Halifax B Mk II of 35 Squadron at Linton-on-Ouse in 1942.

Type E Mk I-III tail turret

Fitted to all Halifax B Mk I, II, III and V, this tail gun turret was one of the most successful turrets ever produced and proved popular with gunners. In common with the Type A design, the Type E had the facility for high-speed rotation and elevation for rapid tracking of targets.
Power system: BP electro-hydraulic.
Armament: 4 × Browning .303in Mk II guns.
Ammunition: 2,500rpg.
Sighting: Mk III reflector sight.

Type K ventral turret

Only 27 examples of this under turret were manufactured. Adverse reports from the squadrons led to their removal from the early Halifax B Mk I.

Bristol

Bl Mk IE, II, IIIA, IV dorsal turret

This mid-upper turret was specifically designed for and fitted to the Blenheim Mk IV. When not in use the cupola could be partially retracted to reduce drag, but the turret design quickly became outdated.
Power system: Bristol hydraulic.
Armament: 1 × Vickers .303in GO (Mk IE, II); 2 × Vickers .303in GO (Mk IIIA); 2 × Browning .303in Mk II (Mk IV).
Ammunition: 400rpg.
Sighting: Mk III, Mk IIIA reflector sights.

Frazer-Nash

Nash and Thompson FN4A tail turret

Designed originally for the Whitley Mk IV and V, the FN4 was a milestone in bomber defensive armament, offering a rate of fire of 80 rounds per second from its four Brownings. The FN4 was also fitted to the Manchester Mk I and Ia, the early Stirling Mk I, and the Wellington Mk III.
Power system: Frazer-Nash (FN) hydraulic.
Armament: 4 × Browning .303in Mk II.
Ammunition: 1,000rpg stored in turret.
Sighting: Mk IIIa reflector sight.
Armour: none.

Nash and Thompson FN5 nose and tail turret

Designed originally for the Wellington Mk I, the FN5 was also selected as the front turret for the Stirling (FN5), Manchester and Lancaster (FN5A). The FN5 was the most widely used of the Parnall turrets.
Power system: Nash and Thompson (N&T) hydraulic.
Armament: 2 × Browning .303in Mk II.
Ammunition: 1,000rpg (nose), 2,000rpg (tail in Wellington only).
Sighting: Mk III reflector sight.
Armour: none.

Nash and Thompson FN7 dorsal turret

Designed originally for the Blackburn Botha, the egg-shaped FN7 was not popular with gunners due in part to its cramped layout and difficult escape route. Its asymmetric shape put a heavy strain on the rotation motor and made it difficult to follow a target accurately. It was fitted as a mid-upper turret to more than 700 Stirling Mk Is and over 200 Manchesters.

Power system: FN hydraulic from electrically driven pump.
Armament: 2 × Browning .303in Mk II.
Ammunition: 500rpg from boxes in turret.
Sighting: Mk IIIa reflector sight.
Armour: none.

Nash and Thompson FN16 nose turret

Adapted from the FN11 design used in the Sunderland flying boat, the FN16 was redesigned especially for the Whitley as a single-gun nose turret. It offered gunners an excellent field of view and was probably unique among gun turrets in being virtually draught-free and waterproof.
Power system: N&T hydraulic.
Armament: 1 × Vickers .303in GO Type K.
Ammunition: 5 × 50-round drums.
Sighting: Norman Vane (early models), Mk IIIa reflector sight.
Armour: none.

Nash and Thompson FN17 ventral turret

This power-operated under turret was designed to provide the Whitley with 360-degree protection to its underbelly against attack from fighters. The reality was somewhat different. Poor visibility for the gunner, a marked drag effect on the aircraft's performance when extended, and the tendency to extend unintentionally during flight led to its withdrawal. The FN17 was not fitted to any Whitleys after the Mk IV.
Power system: hydraulic.
Armament: 2 × Browning .303in.
Ammunition: 500rpg
Sighting: Mk IIIa reflector sight
Armour: none

Nash and Thompson FN20 tail turret

This rear defence turret was fitted to the Stirling, Whitley, Wellington, Manchester and Lancaster and was popular with gunners. It was also the most important in the Parnall range, being the standard tail defence turret of the Lancaster. The FN20 was essentially a redesigned FN4, the main improvements being in the provision of an armoured shield, a clear vision panel and greatly improved ammunition supply.
Power system: hydraulic.

Armament: 4 × Browning .303in Mk II.
Ammunition: 2,500rpg; 1,900 in fuselage boxes, 600 in feed tracks.
Sighting: Mk III reflector sight or GGS Mk IIc.
Armour: 9mm plates when fitted.

Nash and Thompson FN21 ventral turret

The FN21 was fitted to the Manchester and like the FN17 it was largely a failure. When extended it slowed the aircraft by 15mph, weighed a quarter of a ton and was not liked by gunners. Its one saving grace was that it gave the gunner a good field of view but nevertheless it was soon withdrawn from operational use and replaced by the mid-upper FN7.
Power system: N&T hydraulic.
Armament: 2 × Browning .303in.
Ammunition: from boxes on top of the turret.
Sighting: Mk IIIa reflector sight.

Nash and Thompson FN25 ventral turret

The specification for the cylindrical FN25 under defence turret designed for and fitted to the Wellington Mk I was almost identical to the FN17 fitted to the early marks of Whitley. The same unwelcome characteristics that plagued the FN17 (poor visibility and drag penalty) alas applied to the FN25 and it was soon consigned to the scrap heap. Unused turrets were later converted to take the anti-submarine Leigh Light.
Power system: N&T hydraulic.
Armament: 2 × Browning .303in.
Ammunition: 500rpg.
Sighting: Mk IIIa reflector sight.

ABOVE A 96th Bomb Group B-17 Flying Fortress crew mingle with Lancaster crews of 622 Squadron at Mildenhall in the spring of 1944. The Lancaster is fitted with the Nash and Thompson FN5A nose turret. Note the silver-coloured Window-ejecting chute beneath the nose. *(US National Archives)*

ABOVE Frazer-Nash FN50 mid-upper turret fitted to a Short Stirling of 75 (NZ) Squadron in 1943. Note the raised collar fairing ('taboo track') around the base of the turret and the 'taboo' arms to stop a gunner from shooting off his own tail or damaging other parts of the airframe. The FN50 was also fitted to the Lancaster. *(Alan Alexander/New Zealand Bomber Command Association)*

Parnall FN50 dorsal turret

Based on the mechanism for the FN5 nose turret, the FN50 was a replacement for the disliked FN7 turret fitted to the Manchester and early marks of Stirling. Roomy, comfortable and with an excellent all-round field of vision, the twin-Browning FN50 was fitted to the Stirling Mk I Series III and Mk III, but was used exclusively as the mid-upper turret for the Lancaster Mk I, II and III. A metal fairing was installed around the base of the turret to prevent damage to the fuselage.
Power system: N&T hydraulic.
Armament: 2 × Browning .303in.
Ammunition: 1,000rpg, from boxes on each side of the gunner.
Sighting: Mk IIIa reflector sight.
Armour: 7mm plate to front aspect, from the turret ring down.

Nash and Thompson FN54 under-nose rear-firing mounting

Developed in response to a need to protect the Blenheim Mk IV against fighter attack from behind and below, the FN54 was a rear-firing twin-Browning turret fitted beneath the nose of the aircraft and manually operated by the bomb-aimer with a pair of control handles and a periscopic sight. In the event of an emergency the whole turret assembly could be jettisoned to allow the gunner to escape from the aircraft.
Power system: manual.
Armament: 2 × Browning .303in.
Ammunition: 1,000rpg, stored in a box behind the turret.
Sighting: periscopic reflector sight.

Nash and Thompson FN64 ventral turret

Early production Lancasters were fitted with this rear-firing under turret, but its use was discontinued until reintroduced in mid-1944 by a handful of 1 Group squadrons in place of the H2S housing. The gunner sat facing to the rear and sighted the twin-Browning guns by means of a periscopic sight. Apart from being hydraulically driven, the whole system was identical in practice to the FN54 used in the Blenheim Mk IV and the gunner suffered problems with sighting due to the turret's poor field of vision.
Power system: N&T hydraulic.
Armament: 2 × Browning .303in.
Ammunition: 500rpg, from boxes on either side of the gunner.
Sighting: periscopic reflector sight.

Nash and Thompson FN82 tail turret

Developed during 1943 and 1944 to replace the existing Nash and Thompson and Boulton Paul tail turrets, the FN82 was built to the same specification as the Boulton Paul Type D and was designed to take two .50in Mk 2 Browning guns, which were sighted using the highly effective Type IId gyro sight. The FN82 was adapted to take the AGL(T) blind firing system and promised to be a potent tail defence turret. Fitted to the Lancaster in small numbers, had the war continued longer it would undoubtedly have seen wider use than it actually did.
Power system: N&T hydraulic.
Armament: 2 × Browning .50in.
Ammunition: 500rpg, from boxes in mid-fuselage.
Sighting: Mk IIc gyro gunsight.
Armour: 9mm plates to gunner's front.

Nash and Thompson FN120 tail turret

A modified version of the FN20 for the Lancaster, produced in late 1944 and featuring an improved heating system, electric ammunition feed and gyro gunsight.

Nash and Thompson FN121 tail turret

A modified version of the FN120 fitted with AGL(T) and redesignated FN121. Initially fitted to Lancasters of 49 and 460 Squadrons the device first saw operational use in July 1944, although before the end of the war AGL(T) was taken away from 460 Squadron. By May 1945 it was fitted to Lancasters of 35, 49, 582 and 635 Squadrons in 5 and 8 (PFF) Groups.

Nash and Thompson FN150 dorsal turret

A modified version of the FN50 for the Lancaster, sharing the same design improvements as the FN120.

Bendix

Model A dorsal turret

Used only in the North American B-25 Mitchell, the Bendix Model A was electrically powered and provided effective all-round defence. However, it was not very comfortable for the gunner whose movements and field of vision were fairly restricted.
Power system: Amplidyne electrical.
Armament: 2 × M2 .50in Browning guns
Ammunition: 400rpg, from cans inside turret.
Sighting: Type N8 retiflector or Type N6A reflector.
Armour: armoured apron to gunner's front.

Preston Green

Preston Green ventral turret

Introduced in February 1944 as Mod 871, some Halifax III aircraft used the Preston Green Mk II under defence turret armed with a single .50in Browning Mk II gun (occasionally two weapons were fitted). The rear-facing turret provided valuable protection against attack from below by *Schräge Musik* night-fighters. The Preston Green was used mainly by Canadian Halifax squadrons in 6 (RCAF) Group as well as by some RAF Halifax squadrons in 4 Group. When H2S production increased during 1944 the turrets were removed and replaced by radar scanners, target identification presumably being deemed more important than the survival of a bomber and its crew.
Power system: manual.
Armament: 1 × .50in Browning Mk II.
Ammunition: 250 rounds, stored in box beside gunner.
Sighting: Mk III reflector sight.
Armour: none.

Rose Brothers

Rose Rice tail turret

The Rose Rice twin .50in Browning tail turret was the result of an unusual collaboration between Grp Capt A.E. Rice of 1 Group and Alfred Rose of Rose Brothers Engineering in

Gainsborough, Lincolnshire. It added greater firepower to the defence of the Lancaster with its hard-hitting .50in machine guns. The turrets were fitted only to Lancasters, mostly in 1 Group, and were first used operationally in June 1944 by 101 Squadron.
Power system: Nicholls hydraulic.
Armament: 2 × Browning .50in guns.
Ammunition: 335rpg, from boxes in turret base.
Sighting: Mk IIIa reflector sight.
Armour: none.

LEFT An AGL(T) 'Village Inn' installation fitted to a Nash and Thompson FN121 tail turret on a 635 (Pathfinder) Squadron Lancaster. The radar scanner housed inside the black dome moved in elevation with the four Brownings and detected approaching aircraft. It then fed direction and range data to the navigator who coordinated the gunner's response. Note how the central Perspex panel of the turret has been removed to give the gunner a clearer view when training his guns. *(Philip Jarrett)*

BELOW Few photographs exist of the Preston Green ventral turret and its .50in Browning machine gun. This example is fitted to a 425 (Alouette) Squadron Halifax B Mk III at Tholthorpe in late May 1944. *(Jean-Paul Corbeil via Pierre Lagacé)*

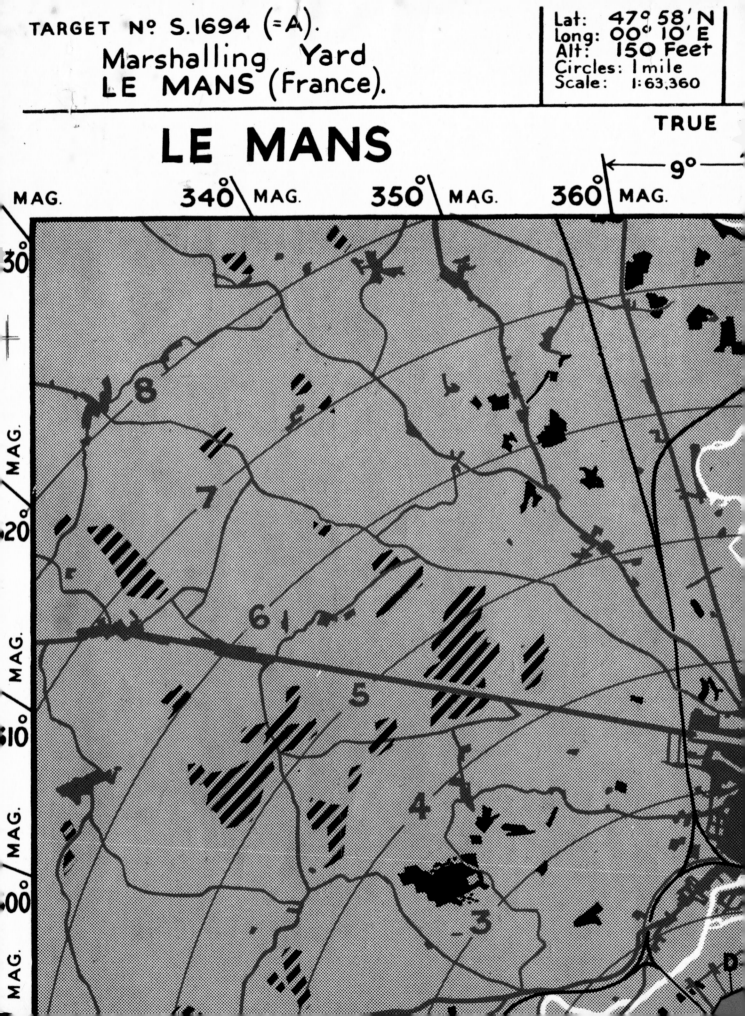

TARGET Nº S.1694 (=A).
Marshalling Yard
LE MANS (France).

Lat: 47° 58' N
Long: 00° 10' E
Alt: 150 Feet
Circles: 1 mile
Scale: 1:63,360

LE MANS

TRUE

9°

MAG. 340° MAG. 350° MAG. 360° MAG.

TES:−
Soc.Des Moteurs Gnome & Rhone. C=Le
D= Soc. Des Usines R
Co-ordinates are for Centre

NORTH
BEARINGS
10 MAG. 020° / MAG. 030°

Chapter Seven

Finding the target

New radio and radar aids like Gee and H2S made the job of the bomber navigator much easier, but high levels of navigation skill remained essential. Navigators continued to rely on conventional maps for plotting courses and map reading, as well as special tactical and intelligence charts. The introduction of complex electro-mechanical tachometric bomb-sighting equipment also brought hitherto unseen levels of accuracy in bomb-aiming.

OPPOSITE Detail of a target identification map (1:63,360 or 1 mile to the inch) showing the railway marshalling yard at Le Mans in France. The target detail on this series of maps was printed in magenta to make it stand out at night when viewed under an infrared light source by the navigator in his curtained-off compartment.

ABOVE The Gee R1355 Airborne Receiver had four different plug-in RF units, each covering a different frequency range to minimise interference from enemy radio-countermeasures. This is an RF Unit Type 25 in the cockpit of a de Havilland Mosquito. The indicator unit with its CRT screen can be seen to the right of the receiver unit, located behind the pilot's seat armour plate, where it could be viewed by the navigator.

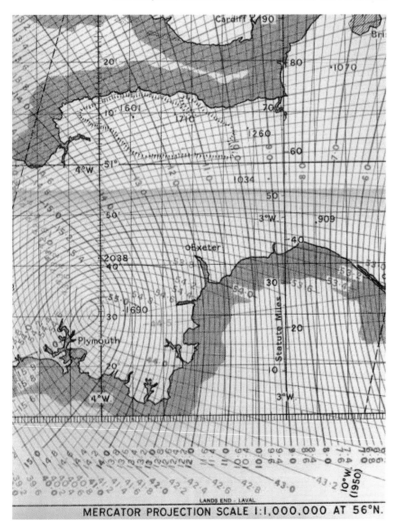

MERCATOR PROJECTION SCALE 1:1,000,000 AT 56°N.

Navigation and bombing aids

At the outbreak of the Second World War Bomber Command was dependent upon non-radar aids to safety and air navigation, such as position-fixing medium- and high-frequency direction-finding (MF and HF D/F) stations, which required the use of wireless equipment and a wireless operator. The 'Darky' system was another position-fixing procedure, but which used R/T (radio telephony) so that the pilot of an aircraft could speak to a ground station when over England and ask for his position. He would be given either his approximate position or courses to steer and distances from ground station to ground station until eventually he found his own airfield. Darky was intended for use by aircraft that were lost or in distress over Great Britain and was eventually superseded to a large extent by Gee.

From 1942, the new generation of radio and radar aids to navigation and bombing played an increasingly crucial part in Bomber Command's ability to find and then hit a target. It could confuse or jam the German Y (Listening) Service radar interception systems, but the only way it could completely deceive them when it came to the radar components of the system was to switch off all the transmitting equipment in its aircraft. However, Bomber Command's reliance on electronic navigational aids such as Gee and H2S to find its targets made this option virtually impossible. From late 1944, however, a partial solution came with the imposition of a total radio and radar silence on all bombers until the stream had crossed over the enemy coast.

Gee was the first of the three principal radio navigational aids to be developed and introduced into Bomber Command. It first saw use on 8/9 March 1942 in an attack on Essen when leading aircraft of the 211-strong force were fitted with the aid. Initially, Gee was a highly effective device that enabled bomber

LEFT Detail from a navigator's Gee lattice chart of an area over Belgium. The lattice lines are further apart than they would be if the aircraft were nearer to the two transmitter stations in England. With Gee, accuracy decreased with distance.

crews to reach the general area of a target within its range (about 350 miles) and for longer-distance targets it set them well on track, after which navigators could recompute courses with confidence. However, the Germans quickly discovered how to jam Gee and it soon became impossible to obtain fixes east of the Dutch coast. Nevertheless, navigators still used it to maintain an accurate track outbound over the North Sea; on the final leg of the journey home it was effective for homing to base. One of the great advantages of Gee was that it was passive, requiring only a receiver and no transmitter, so any aircraft that used it did not risk giving away its position to the enemy.

From three widely spaced ground transmitter stations situated on a baseline of about 200 miles in length, radiated sequential radio pulses laid down an invisible grid over the target. One of the Gee transmitters was known as the 'A' or Master station, while the other two were 'B' and 'C' or Slave stations. Each Slave transmission was locked on to a Master transmission. By measuring the differences in the time taken by the A and B and A and C signals to reach the aircraft, it could be located on two position lines – or Gee coordinates – and its ground position coincided with the point at which these coordinates (printed as a grid on special Gee charts) intersected. The data was displayed on a cathode ray tube (CRT) on the navigator's table in the aircraft and a good navigator could obtain a fix in less than a minute, with an accuracy of between half a mile and 5 miles, depending on his skill.

Because Gee depended upon transmissions from ground stations in England, its effective range was limited by the curvature of the earth to about 350 miles (the Ruhr was just included within this range limitation). The general rule of thumb for Gee was the greater the range, the lesser the accuracy.

Oboe was similar to Gee in that it depended upon transmissions from a pair of ground stations in England. Its accuracy was such that an Oboe-equipped aircraft flying at 28,000ft over the Ruhr could release its bombs within 120yd of the selected target. The drawback was that only one aircraft at a time could be controlled by a pair of Oboe transmitters every ten minutes, but later in the war this was partly solved by the use of multiple pulse frequencies.

Each Oboe ground station transmitted pulses and received them back from a suitably equipped aircraft, thus enabling the ground stations to measure the distance of the aircraft from them. One station (known as the Cat) controlled the track of the aircraft over the target, while the other station (the Mouse) calculated the point on that track when the bombs should be

BELOW Oboe was one of the RAF's most successful secret weapons of the Second World War and was introduced into service with the Pathfinder Force by 109 Squadron, enabling RAF Bomber Command to pinpoint unseen targets with a level of accuracy previously thought unattainable. This is 109 Squadron's Mosquito Mk IX, ML907, on completion of its 100th sortie in 1944. Pilot John Burt and navigator Ron Curtis pose for the camera with their groundcrew.

BOTTOM The principles of Oboe. *(Josh Hodgson)*

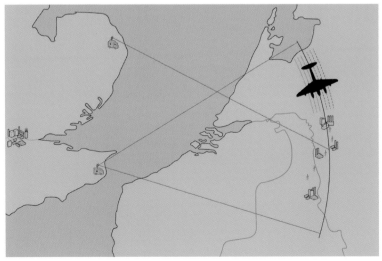

released. Oboe pulses travelled at a tangent to the earth's surface and for this reason its range was limited only by the height that could be reached by the controlled aircraft.

Because of the higher service ceiling of the Mosquito when compared to its contemporaries

BELOW H2S – officially the H2S Indicator Type 184 – was used by Bomber Command navigators for ground mapping and target identification. This is a trace on the PPI using a time exposure to capture a full 360-degree sweep of the H2S scanner and shows the Zuider Zee in the Netherlands. Water shows up as the dark areas, while the landmass is the lighter area. Coastlines showed up much better on screen than built-up areas like major cities.

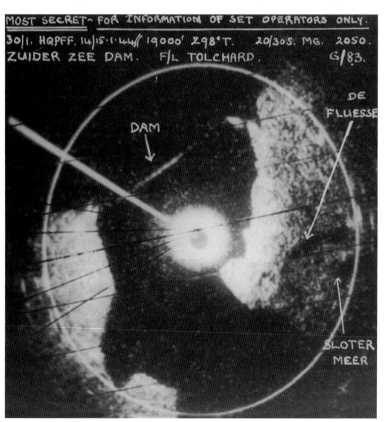

MOST SECRET~ FOR INFORMATION OF SET OPERATORS ONLY.
30/1. HQPFF. 14/15·1·44/ 19000' 298°T. 20/30S. MG. 2050.
ZUIDER ZEE DAM. F/L TOLCHARD. G/83.

DAM

DE FLUESSE

SLOTER MEER

in Bomber Command, it was invariably used with the Oboe system and for this reason – combined with the time and numbers limitations already described – it was used almost exclusively by the Pathfinder Force. Towards the end of the war the device was also used by Lancasters and Mosquitoes acting as Oboe leaders in formation bombing, where other aircraft in the formation bombed on a visual cue from their leader.

H2S was the only one of the three wartime navigational aids which was self-contained in the bomber and not limited in any way by range or altitude. Radar transmissions from a downward-looking rotating radar transmitter, fitted in the belly of the aircraft, scanned the terrain below and the echoes that 'bounced' back to receiving equipment in the aircraft were displayed on a television-type screen in the navigator's compartment, painting a radar impression of the ground over which the aircraft was flying. The contrast between land and water was particularly clear, less so built-up areas. Over large urban areas like Berlin and its suburbs it was virtually impossible to identify anything on the screen.

In conditions of total darkness and complete cloud cover, a blind bombing run could be made with a good degree of accuracy using H2S, and the bombs dropped blindly, but this method was not as accurate as Oboe bombing. However, H2S was a blessing in disguise because it also worked against the interests of the bomber stream in two dangerous ways. From January 1944, H2S transmissions could be detected and the bombers homed on to by

BELOW The CV64 cavity magnetron was the widget at the heart of H2S radar.

German night-fighters fitted with a specialised search apparatus called 'Naxos'. The Germans also developed a highly sensitive ground-based detection device called 'Korfu', which enabled them to keep a constant plot of the bomber stream from take-off to landing. It was so sensitive that it could even detect H2S test transmissions from bomber aircraft parked on dispersal pans at their English airfields.

G-H was a combination of Gee and Oboe (or H, which was similar to Oboe but which functioned in reverse), performing much the same job as Oboe and at much the same range. Its big advantage was that it could be operated by some 100 aircraft at a time, but its drawback was that unlike Gee or H2S it could not be used simultaneously by the whole force.

An aircraft fitted with G-H transmitting and receiving equipment depended upon transmissions to and from a pair of ground stations. The ground position of an aircraft could be measured by plotting the point at which the two lines from the two ground stations intersected. Although the range of G-H was limited, unlike Gee its accuracy did not diminish with increasing distance. It was not until June 1944 that Bomber Command began to make extensive use of G-H for formation daylight bombing and an urgent requirement was made for all Lancaster aircraft of 3 Group to be equipped with the system. However, progress was slow and by October insufficient aircraft had been re-equipped. In order to make full use of the equipment, G-H crews were trained to undertake marking duties for night raids and act as formation leaders for daylight attacks.

Similar in operation to Gee, Loran was an American hyperbolic navigational aid designed originally for use over water and with a range of 1,400 miles. Codenamed 'Skywave Synchronised' or 'SS Loran', the device was first used operationally on 11/12 November 1944 against Hamburg, but its use was restricted and SS Loran was only fitted to aircraft of 5 and 8 (PFF) Groups, and the heavy aircraft of 100 (BS) Group. SS Loran suffered from a number of technical shortcomings and was very susceptible to enemy jamming, but its value to Bomber Command was never fully exploited. Had the war lasted longer, its potential as a long-range navigational aid might well have come into its own.

Maps and charts for air navigation

Although the new radio and radar aids made the job of the navigator that much easier, a high level of navigation skill was still needed and Bomber Command's navigators still had to rely on conventional charts for plotting courses and map reading. They also used maps specially produced with intelligence requirements in mind.

The maps they used came in three scales: large for intelligence and target identification (1:63,360 or 1in to the mile); medium for air map reading over strategically important regions on the Continent (1:500,000 or 1in to 7.89 miles and 1:250,000 or 1in to 3.95 miles – the latter being especially useful for the industrial centres of the Continent where important detail was abundant), and small (1:1,000,000 or 1in to 15.78 miles) where the scale provided a useful general picture of any large area and could be used for plotting. A specially prepared plotting chart was also produced for navigators over which was printed a grid of Gee lattice lines for accurate course plotting and position checking at any time during a flight.

The large- and medium-scale maps were printed to a very high standard in full colour on a good quality paper with particular attention paid to lettering and the amount of detail shown. Small-scale plotting maps were generally printed in black or red on white and only a few of the features of the ground were shown. Because they were intended for use at the rate of one map per sortie, they needed to

ABOVE G-H-equipped aircraft (G-H Leaders) could be identified by the two horizontal yellow bars on the rudders of their aircraft. Non-G-H aircraft would formate on the leader of their vic of three and drop their bombs when he released his. This is a 218 (Gold Coast) Squadron G-H Leader crew with their Lancaster. *(Steve Smith/218 Squadron Association)*

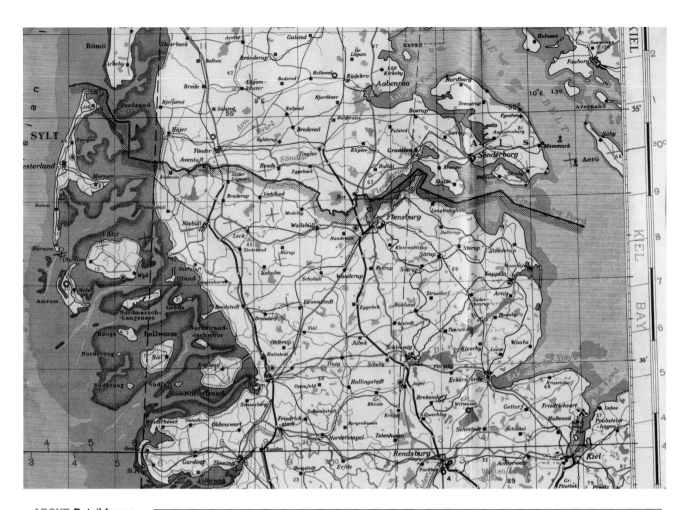

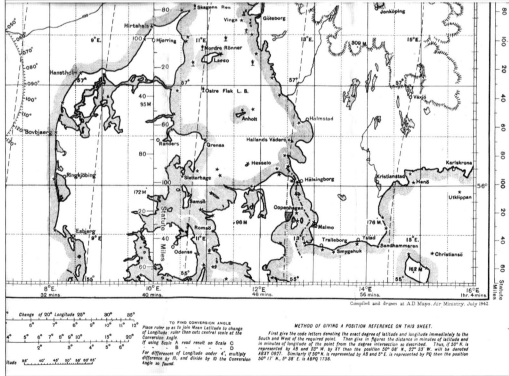

ABOVE Detail from a 1:500,000 (1in to 7.89 miles) air map, for use over important areas of the Continent.

RIGHT Detail from an RAF small-scale (1:1,000,000 and 1:2,000,000) aeronautical plotting series map on which a navigator would mark his route in pencil.

be cheap to produce and were printed on an inexpensive grade of paper.

Bombsights

For an aircraft loaded with bombs and navigated across land and sea to a target hundreds of miles distant, its crew needed some kind of sighting device to enable them to drop their bombs fairly and squarely on a target. Known as a bombsight, this device told the crew at which point – usually some distance from the target – their bombs should be released. As the Second World War progressed, the bombs in use became more complex, and so too did the problems associated with their sighting. New, more advanced bombsights were therefore designed and for the most part provided effective solutions.

Between 1939 and 1945 the RAF used two basic types of bombsight in its bomber aircraft: the vector sight and the tachometric sight. The first had been in existence since 1918, with modifications, and required the bomb-aimer to compute and then feed in data before the attack for the aircraft's speed, altitude, the ballistic performance of the bomb and estimated wind speed and direction. On a small reflecting screen in front of him, the bomb-aimer referred to a sighting cross made either from crossed wires or lines of light. As the aircraft made its bombing run, the right moment to release the bombs was when the centre of the sighting cross corresponded with the target beneath. The vector sight was simple and effective, but it was only as accurate as the data fed into it and only if the aircraft made a straight and level approach to the target. The reality was that data was not always accurate and a straight and level approach in the presence of flak and fighters was courting disaster for the bomber crew.

The tachometric sight was a very different device to the vector type in that it computed wind velocity and direction automatically. A motorised sighting telescope was focused on a stabilised glass screen mounted beneath it. Linked to a gyro-stabilised platform, the telescope enabled the bomb-aimer to view the target during the bombing run. Having programmed the analogue sighting computer with the aircraft's altitude and the bomb's ballistic performance, the bomb-aimer adjusted a pair of electric knobs connected to an electric motor to maintain the telescope's sighting graticule over the target, as viewed through the stabilised glass screen. Because the movement of the telescope relative to the platform was relayed to the sighting computer by the gyro stabilisation system, the computer in turn generated a stream of signals which were relayed to the pilot (or directed into the autopilot if it was engaged). These were displayed on a directional indicator on his instrument panel for corrections to be made in the aircraft's heading, thereby maintaining the sighting graticule accurately over the target. As the aircraft neared the target, the angle of the telescope on the bombsight progressively reached a vertical position. Once it had reached the release angle calculated by the sighting computer, a pair of electrical contacts closed to form a circuit and the bombs were released automatically.

The following are the principal bombsights used by Bomber Command during the Second World War, with the exception of the Dann sight, which was a one-off design for use only by 617 Squadron on the Ruhr dams raid.

Mk IX Course Setting Bombsight (CSBS)

From the outbreak of war, the Mk IX CSBS was in general use throughout Bomber Command. It was a pre-set vector sight used for night bombing of static targets when darkness prevented the target from being seen until the last minute. The sight was unsuitable for bombing while the aircraft was taking evasive action and its efficacy very much depended on the accuracy of wind computations.

In January 1942 a modified version, the Mk IXA incorporating the Fourth Vector (moving target attachment), was designated for use in all Halifaxes and Stirlings; Bostons and Mosquitoes were fitted with the CSBS Mk IXE* (without the Fourth Vector attachment), and all other aircraft were equipped with the CSBS Mk IXA* (also without the Fourth Vector attachment). Low-level attachments for the CSBS were issued to the light bomber squadrons of 2 Group in May 1942 to replace their hand-held low-level Mk I bombsight.

Mk XIV Stabilised Vector Sight

Introduced in the summer of 1942, initially to
the Halifax-equipped 35 (Pathfinder) Squadron,
the Mk XIV stabilised vector sight – sometimes
referred to as the 'area sight' – worked on
similar principles to the CSBS but was more fully
automatic, simpler to operate and better suited
to use under war conditions. Later versions
of the sight based on the T1 design would
serve RAF bomber squadrons well into the jet
age. Evasive action could be taken up to the
moment of bomb release and bombs could be
released even with the aircraft making a banking
turn to avoid flak or fighters, and even when
climbing or gliding. In February 1943 use of the
sighting head only was extended to Bostons,
Mitchells and Mosquitoes of 2 Group, in place
of their CSBS Mk IXE. By the middle of 1944

most operational heavy bomber aircraft in the
Command had been fitted with the Mk XIV sight.

A modified version of the sight known as the
Mk XIVA offered an increased height limitation
and was trialled in July 1943 by 8 (PFF) Group.
The Mk XIVA increased the operational height at
which the sight could be used, to 25,000ft, and
was first employed operationally in August 1944
by Mosquitoes of 8 (PFF) Group.

T1 bombsight

This American-built copy of the British Mk XIV
sight differed little from the original except in
minor details of construction, and by the end of
1943 it was in use by all operational Wellington
squadrons in the Command. By the spring of
1944 it was beginning to replace the Mk XIV
sighting head installations on OTU aircraft.

The T1A bombsight was the American-built
copy of the Mk XIVA, and first saw use in the
Command in July 1944 when Canadian-built
Lancaster X aircraft arrived from North America
ready-fitted with the sight. T1A sights were also
fitted in the Mosquito in January 1945 in place
of the Mk XIVA, which were then in short supply.

Mk II Stabilised Automatic Bombsight (SABS)

This precision tachometric bombsight was similar
to the American Norden sight used in USAAF
bomber aircraft. The Mk II SABS had been fitted
to aircraft of 97 and 207 Squadrons by February
1943, and 61, 83 and 106 Squadrons each had
three aircraft equipped with the sight. Although
it was more accurate than the Mk XIV stabilised
vector sight, the Mk II SABS was withdrawn
from use because the area bombing technique
used by the RAF on night raids did not require
a precision sight. In any case the need for a
straight-and-level approach to the target was
deemed a disadvantage at the height of the area
offensive. Thus the Mk II sight was withdrawn
from 5 Group's squadrons and replaced by the
Mk XIV sight, which was quite adequate for the
job of area bombing. From August 1943, only
617 Squadron was equipped with a modified
version, the Mk IIA SABS, for special precision-
bombing operations. By the war's end their
operational experience using this sight was such
that they could bomb a target from 20,000ft with
an average error of only 80yd.

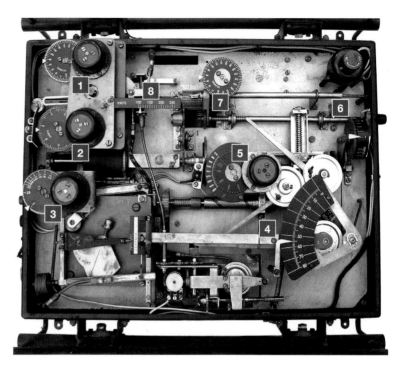

ABOVE AND RIGHT The Mk XIV sight was linked to the Mk XIV computer, which was designed to continuously calculate the point of impact for a bomb in the run-up to the target, even when the pilot was carrying out evasive manoeuvres or if the aircraft was flying straight and level for as little as 10 seconds. It could also be used to bomb both on the climb and in the glide. *(Martin Smith collection)*

Mk III Low-level (Angular Velocity) Bombsight

Designed for use at up to 1,000ft and developed primarily for the bombing of submarines at low level, the Mk III low-level bombsight was also very effective against land targets. It was introduced into service with Bostons of 2 Group in May 1943 and also saw use – but only once – by Lancasters of 617 Squadron in 1944. Because Coastal Command had absolute priority on the issue of this sight, Bomber Command's operational use of it during the war was minimal. A few examples were acquired by 627 Squadron and the Mosquitoes of 8 (PFF) Group.

Dann sight

This simple hand-held wooden bombsight was designed by Wg Cdr C.L. Dann at A&AEE Boscombe Down for use by bomb-aimers of 617 Squadron on the Ruhr dams raid in May 1943. In order to achieve an accurate release point for the Upkeep weapon, Dann used calculations based on the width between the sluice towers of the Möhne dam to make a simple triangular wooden sight. With a sighting peephole at the apex and two nails at the extremities of the base, the bomb-aimer held the sight by a wooden handle attached to the underside of the apex and looked through the

peephole. On the bombing run, when the twin towers of the dam coincided with the two nails, the bomb-aimer pressed the bomb-release mechanism.

However, the Dann sight had its drawbacks. Buffeting of the aircraft at low level by thermals meant that it was near impossible for a bomb-aimer to hold the sight steady with both hands and still maintain his balance in the bomb-aiming compartment. Some bomb-aimers dispensed with the Dann sight altogether and experimented with their own sighting devices, which included chinagraph pencil marks on the clear-vision panel and lengths of string attached to screws on each side of the panel to create a large triangle. Lying prone on the floor of the aircraft supported by their forearms, some bomb-aimers saw this as a more stable position to adopt during the bombing run.

1 Wind direction.
2 Wind speed.
3 Bomb terminal velocity (hundreds feet/sec).
4 Sighting angle.
5 Target height/sea level pressure.
6 Indicated height above target (when target height is set).
7 Course.
8 Indicated airspeed (knots).

LEFT An original example of the hand-held wooden Dann sight used by 617 Squadron's bomb-aimers in the famous dams raid on 16/17 May 1943. *(David Worrow)*

'All in D-Dog were ready when the first Mosquito's target indicator's hit the ground, causing a green suffused glow beneath the cloud. A minute later a "Wanganui" flare exploded into red and green stars, which hung above the cloud.'

Alex Thorne, Lancaster pilot and Master Bomber, 635 (Pathfinder) Squadron, 1944–45.

Chapter Eight

Bomber tactics

The tactics used by Bomber Command's crews can be divided roughly into three: those that helped find and mark the target (the Pathfinders), those that involved the use of electronic and radar devices to confound and destroy enemy defences (100 Group), and those employed by individual bomber aircraft as a means of finding their way to and from the target and evading enemy defences.

OPPOSITE Amid the fury of a developing attack, Lancasters release their bomb loads onto the Pathfinders' target markers. *(Piotr Forkasiewicz – www.peterfor.com)*

Leading the way: the Pathfinders

From its formation in the summer of 1942 the wartime exploits of Bomber Command's 8 (PFF) Group, better known as the Pathfinders, soon became synonymous with skill and bravery of the highest order to friend and foe alike.

Poor navigation and bombing accuracy in the opening years of the war had led Bomber Command's chiefs to the conclusion that specialist squadrons were needed to lead bombing raids. The Butt Report of August 1941, commissioned by Prime Minister Winston Churchill's scientific adviser Lord Cherwell, reached the alarming conclusion after analysing 4,065 night bombing photographs, that only one in four crews who claimed to have bombed a target in Germany were found to have been within 5 miles of it. Worse still, one-third of all crews dispatched could not claim to have even reached the target area. Added to these depressing revelations were the facts that Gee had not yet produced any great improvements in target finding and bombing accuracy, and aircrew losses continued to mount.

The idea of a specialist target-marking force was the brainchild of Grp Capt Syd Bufton, Director of Bomber Operations at the Air Ministry. Earlier in the war, Bufton had commanded 10 Squadron where he had pioneered attempts using his best crews to locate their targets with flares and then attract other crews to them by firing off Verey lights. He convinced his fellow staff officers at the Air Ministry of the very real need for a target-finding force for the whole of Bomber Command and the idea was put to Bomber Harris as soon as he assumed control in April 1942. Harris rejected it, vehemently opposing the concept of an elite group within Bomber Command. Arguments for and against the proposal rumbled on through the summer of 1942 but eventually Sir Charles Portal overruled Harris and ordered him to prepare the new force.

Four bomber squadrons, one taken from each of Bomber Command's heavy groups and used to form the new pathfinding force, moved to their new bases in Huntingdonshire and Cambridgeshire on 17 August 1942. These were 156 Squadron with Wellingtons from 1 Group, 7 Squadron with Stirlings from 3 Group, 35 Squadron with Halifaxes from 4 Group and 83 Squadron (Lancasters) from 5 Group. Lancasters and Mosquitoes gradually replaced the Wellingtons, Stirlings and Halifaxes on the Pathfinder squadrons.

The new force did not immediately have group status but instead worked under the direct control of Bomber Command HQ Plans Staff, with orders passing through the HQ of 3 Group. Grp Capt Basil Embry was initially suggested as the commander of the force but for unknown reasons he was not released from Fighter Command and the job went instead to Air Cdre Donald Bennett. The crews themselves were all volunteers and were generally recruited direct from the main force squadrons after completing their first tour, although a few were on their second or third tours of operations. Occasionally crews who had passed out of the training system with the highest marks on their courses were posted straight to a Pathfinder squadron. A Pathfinder tour was set at 45 operations and qualified aircrew were entitled to

BELOW No 627 Squadron's Flg Off Eric Arthur with the groundcrew of Mosquito B Mk XXV, AZ-V, at RAF Oakington. As a part of 8 (PFF) Group's Light Night Striking Force the squadron flew regular bombing sorties as well as pathfinder missions. *(www.627.co.uk)*

wear the coveted gilt eagle of the Pathfinders on their left breast pocket.

On 8 January 1943 the Pathfinder Force was re-designated as 8 (PFF) Group and in the steady expansion that followed, completed by January 1945, it grew to a total of 19 squadrons, of which 3 were permanently detached to 5 Group for its own target-marking force.

Operational duties

There were eight designated Pathfinder duties and all crews were expected to be able to fulfil the various tasks if and when required. The duties themselves were applied to the aircraft and not to the crews, although certain crews that excelled at a given duty were invariably selected for that particular task. Essentially, the Pathfinders were a team and the success of a raid depended very much upon the teamwork of the different duties.

1. When a new crew joined a PFF squadron it was sent to the target area as a 'Supporter' with the first group of the marker force to increase the number of aircraft over the target at the beginning of the raid.
2. 'Windowers' went in ahead of the marker force to drop Window and hopefully confuse enemy radar, thereby giving marker crews a better chance.
3. 'Backers-up' (later called 'Visual Centerers') were required to estimate the mean point of impact (MPI) of all the primary markers and then aim their target indicators (TIs) at this point with the aid of their Mk XIV bombsight.
4. 'Route Markers' dropped TIs at important turning points leading to the target to help the main force maintain a stream.
5. 'Blind Illuminators' used H2S to navigate to the target and then dropped flares blindly to help the 'Visual Markers' in 'Newhaven' attacks (see below).
6. 'Primary Visual Markers' aimed their TIs visually using the Mk XIV bombsight. This was the most difficult of all the PFF duties and only selected crews were allocated to this task.
7. 'Blind Markers' used either H2S or Oboe to drop their TIs and sky markers.
8. 'Re-centerers' arrived over the target halfway through a raid and marked it blindly using

H2S, the idea being to overshoot with their markers to compensate for the gradual creep-back in bombing from the main force as the raid progressed.

Two further duties introduced later in the war by the Pathfinder Force were 'Master Bomber' and 'Deputy Master Bomber', devised to reduce the multiplication of errors as an attack progressed. Their aircraft orbited high above the bomber stream over the target area and used VHF radio to correct marking errors and advise Backers-up where they should drop their TIs, or instruct the main force to ignore this fire or bomb that.

Bennett's Pathfinder Force operated at high altitude and could mark any target, for any size of bomber force, and in any weather conditions, but 5 Group operated its own independent target-marking force. For this task it used Mosquitoes and borrowed American Mustangs to mark for small bomber forces in clear weather conditions and at low level. This tactic was developed by Wg Cdr Leonard Cheshire (commanding 617 Squadron, November 1943–July 1944) and advocated by AVM Sir Ralph Cochrane (AOC 5 Group, 1943–45), but one to which Don Bennett could not subscribe because he feared for the safety of his crews at such low levels. It was not surprising, then, that a friendly rivalry should have persisted between 8 (PFF) and 5 Groups throughout the war.

Route and target marking

The Pathfinders used three methods of marking a target. These were codenamed 'Parramatta', 'Newhaven' and 'Wanganui'. Although the choice of codenames sounds obscure, the last two were named after the home towns of Bennett's confidential WAAF clerk and one of his air staff officers respectively, while Bennett himself chose the town of Parramatta in Australia for the former 'just to keep the balance with New Zealand'.

The first method was 'Parramatta', or blind ground marking, which fell into two categories: 'Parramatta' and 'Musical Parramatta'. In the former, crews using H2S performed the initial marking and dropped their TIs blind on the target, and then the Backers-up aimed TIs of a contrasting colour at the mean point of impact of all the original markers. The main force crews

visual marking using the Mk XIV bombsight, or 'Musical' marking using Oboe.

The second method was 'Newhaven', for which selected Pathfinder crews were needed, initially to identify the aiming point and then to mark it visually using the Mk XIV bombsight. Blind Illuminators (using H2S) were invariably sent in ahead of the Visual Markers to release bundles of flares at intervals in the target area to help the Visual Marker crews to see the ground.

The third, and arguably the least accurate of the three marking methods, was 'Wanganui', or sky marking. Flares were dropped blindly by marker crews and fused to burst above the expected height of the cloud found in the target area. The main force crews were instructed to release their bombs when bomb-aimers had a flare in their bombsights, and on a required course given at briefing, but it was difficult for them to aim accurately at a moving target which was prone to drift with the wind.

Deceiving the enemy: 100 (Bomber Support) Group

The continuing growth and successes of the German night-fighter force in 1943 led to the formation of a dedicated new bomber group in November that year. No 100 (Bomber Support – BS) Group was the last operational group to be formed in Bomber Command during the Second World War and was commanded by Air Cdre Edward B. Addison, a specialist in electronics and signals. It combined all the radio-countermeasures squadrons that already existed elsewhere in the Command as well as several Mosquito fighter squadrons that had been transferred from Fighter Command.

The group's role was clearly defined as giving direct intruder support to night bombing

ABOVE Pathfinder 'blind markers' use H2S or Oboe to drop target indicators on the coastal gun battery at St Pierre du Mont in Normandy during a raid in May 1944.

following were instructed to aim at the centre of the secondary markers and ignore the initial markers (if there were no secondaries burning). In the latter, 'Musical Parramatta', Oboe crews were responsible for the primary marking. Backers-up aimed visually at the primary markers which were dropped at intervals during the attack. The main force was instructed to bomb the primary markers and ignore the secondaries unless no Oboe TIs were visible. However, blind ground marking using H2S was never as accurate as

LEFT Photographs of 100 (BS) Group aircraft showing their radio-countermeasures apparatus are relatively rare, so this picture of 101 Squadron's SR-W/LL757 'Oor Wullie' on its dispersal at Ludford Magna is particularly unusual. The pair of 8ft 9½in-tall 'Airborne Cigar' Type 313 transmission masts on top of the fuselage can be clearly seen. 'Oor Wullie' failed to return from a sortie on 30 August 1944.

RIGHT Bundles of Window fall away from the bomb bay of 101 Squadron's Lancaster SR-B/NG128 over Duisburg during a daylight raid on 14 October 1944.

operations by attacking enemy night-fighter aircraft in the air or on the ground, and the use of airborne and ground-based radio-countermeasures (RCM) equipment to deceive or jam enemy radio navigation aids, radar systems and wireless signals. In so doing it was hoped to reduce Bomber Command's escalating losses that were reaching a new high during the Battle of Berlin that was being fought at this time.

To help them in their aim of confounding the enemy's defences, the aircraft of 100 (BS) Group were fitted with a variety of ingenious electronic and radar devices. Most were exclusive to the group, but some were in general use by main force and Pathfinder squadrons, like Window and Monica.

Jamming devices

There were two main types of jamming device, which numbered some 32 different pieces of equipment in total. The first type of device generated electronic 'noise' and was aimed at the enemy's early warning (EW), ground-controlled interception (GCI), gun-laying (GL) and airborne interception (AI) radars. The second produced audio interference, which disrupted the enemy's radio telephony (R/T) communication channels.

ABOVE Two units in 100 (BS) Group operated the American-built B-17 Flying Fortress in the radio-countermeasures role – 214 and 223 (BS) Squadrons. In this close-up of the rear fuselage of a 214 (BS) Squadron B-17G at Sculthorpe the 'Airborne Grocer' and 'Monica' antenna installations can be clearly seen, as well as the rear gunner inside his F-type tail turret. *(L. Budge)*

Window – the single most important RCM device of the war introduced by the RAF was used by all heavy bomber groups including 100 (BS) Group. Window was strips of metallised paper cut to a particular length and dropped from bomber aircraft in clumps to produce spurious responses on enemy EW, GCI, GL and AI radar screens. It was first used over Hamburg on 24/25 July 1943.

Airborne Cigar (ABC) – designed to disrupt enemy R/T control channels on spot frequencies.

Carpet – designed to jam enemy GCI and GL *Würzburg* radars in the 300–600 MHz waveband.

Jostle – designed for continuous wave jamming of German R/T transmissions, but fitted only to 100 (BS) Group's B-17 and B-24 aircraft.

Mandrel – designed in both ground and airborne forms to jam enemy early warning radar, it first entered service in December 1942.

Piperack – an American-developed device designed to jam enemy AI radars. Also known as Dina.

Shiver – designed to jam enemy GCI and GL *Würzburg* radars by transmitting a continuous squittering signal.

Tinsel – a microphone assembly fitted in the engine nacelle and connected to a transmitter, which could be tuned to the enemy's R/T frequency by a German-speaking crewmember and switched on, flooding it with engine noise.

Tuba – designed to jam enemy EW radars.

RIGHT This 420 Squadron Halifax is fitted with an antenna for the rearward-looking 'Boozer' early warning device, which alerted the crew that their aircraft was being 'painted' by ground-based *Würzburg* radar or by *FuG 202/212* transmissions from a night-fighter AI radar. *(Bert Parker Collection)*

BELOW The end of a Messerschmitt Bf 110 night-fighter of II./NJG 1, destroyed over Germany near Hangelar airfield on 4 November 1944 by a Mosquito night intruder of 85 Squadron from 100 (BS) Group.

Homing and warning devices

As the war progressed, so too did the number of airborne radar and other transmitting devices in use by both sides. It was inevitable, therefore, that both would soon develop homing receivers to give a bearing on a transmission source. Warning devices were also invented to alert crews to the presence of other aircraft in their corner of the sky. All 12 of these devices used by 100 (BS) Group (except for the tail warning radar Monica for use against enemy

interceptors) were passive – that is, they did not produce any signal themselves.

Boozer – a rearward-looking aerial fitted in the tail of a bomber introduced in 1943, it gave crews notice of when their aircraft was being monitored by ground-based *Würzburg* radar, and by *FuG 202/212* transmissions from a night-fighter AI radar.

Monica – an active tail warning device first used in 1943, it was fitted to aircraft of most heavy bomber squadrons to give warning of night-fighters stalking them from behind. It was largely withdrawn by 1944 when it was found that its transmissions could be homed on to by the German *FuG 227 Flensburg* airborne homing device.

Perfectos – designed to trigger enemy IFF sets and then produce a bearing on the transmission.

Serrate – designed to give a bearing on transmissions from enemy airborne interception (AI) radars, used by Mosquitoes of 100 (BS) Group and also by Fighter Command/Air Defence Great Britain.

Airborne interception radar

AI radar had a range of between 4 and 6 miles on average and was used in bomber support fighter aircraft like the Beaufighter and Mosquito to intercept German night-fighter aircraft preying on the bomber stream. There were four types of AI radar used by these aircraft: AI Mk IV, AI Mk VIII, AI Mk X and AI Mk XV.

Keys to survival

Safety in numbers: the bomber stream

When in the early years of the war bomber crews were briefed on the operation they were about to fly, they were given details of where the target was and individual captains were left to plan their own routes to and from it. At this stage in the war when the RAF's offensive was in its infancy and the enemy defences had yet to develop, it was very much a case of every man for himself. But with the advent of the German Kammhuber Line of defence in 1942, the approaches to Germany and its occupied territories were protected by a defensive early

warning network divided into radar-controlled fighter boxes. Its principal shortcoming was that its fighter boxes could only control one interception at a time, so Bomber Command's planners devised the bomber stream where as many aircraft as possible were funnelled over a given point in the shortest time possible to swamp the enemy defences. A force of some 600 aircraft could be spread over an area of sky 150 miles long, 6 miles wide and 2 miles deep.

This concentration of bombers, all flying in the same direction in darkness, was not achieved by pilots using visual contact to maintain formation. The reality was that each navigator was given route and timing points to follow at the pre-op briefing and instructed to follow them as best they could. With such a concentration of aircraft flying virtually blind in darkness, there was an ever-present risk of mid-air collisions. By the end of the war bomber streams had become four times as dense.

BELOW **By night it was altogether more dangerous when hundreds of aircraft flew alongside one another virtually unseen.** *(Piotr Forkasiewicz – www.peterfor.com)*

George Aylmore RAAF was a Lancaster wireless operator on 550 Squadron in 1944–45. He recalls:

For the most part you could well feel your aircraft was the only one in the air until you hit someone's slipstream. When this happened it felt as though the aircraft was standing on its wingtip, though probably it rolled about 60 degrees. While it always came as a bit of a shock, it was also comforting to know there was someone else about.

The Germans countered the bomber stream by deepening the Kammhuber Line and increasing the capacity of each box so that more night-fighters could be handled at once.

Evasive manoeuvres

If a prowling German night-fighter was spotted in time by a bomber crew, the standard fighter evasion manoeuvre developed by Bomber Command for the protection of its heavy bombers was put into action. It was known as the 'corkscrew' and the order to 'Corkscrew port [or starboard] go!' could be given to the pilot by any bomber crewmember who saw that a fighter attack was imminent. The constant changes in direction, speed and altitude of this manoeuvre proved highly effective in hampering accurate deflection shooting by the pursuing night-fighter. However, the physical exertion required of a pilot to 'corkscrew' a heavy bomber about the sky was immense and a successful manoeuvre often left him drenched in sweat and aching from the sheer physical effort.

Schräge Musik

The favoured position for a night-fighter to make its attack was from astern and slightly below in the bomber's blind spot, but the deadliest tactic was probably that called *Schräge Musik* by the Germans. A night-fighter would stealthily manoeuvre itself into position directly beneath a bomber, its presence hidden from the gunners by the wings. Using twin oblique upward-firing *Schräge Musik* MG 151 20mm cannon it would blast the bomb bay and fuel tanks with incendiary and HE shells. For the occupants

RIGHT For a stalking night-fighter this was the ideal position from which to attack a heavy bomber at night – from slightly behind and underneath. This is 78 Squadron's Halifax EY-B/W1245, which failed to return on 12 August 1942.

of the bomber there was no getting away from this sudden and unseen attack and the result was invariably a fiery and explosive end for the aircraft and its crew who were none the wiser by whom or from where they had met their end.

Searchlights

To be coned in a searchlight beam could be a frightening experience for a bomber crew, particularly if the light illuminated the hapless bomber for the predations of night-fighters and flak gunners. Searchlights could sometimes be avoided by diving the bomber through an illuminated area, or else flying around it.

Spoofs and dog-legs

For bomber crews, the stream continued to provide them with relative safety in numbers, but thanks to developments in interception techniques by the Germans it became necessary to funnel bombers over the target in as little as 15 to 20 minutes by mid-1943. Because early identification of a target was important for enemy fighter controllers to direct free-ranging *Wilde Sau* (wild boar) fighters, the RAF sought to keep them guessing for as long as possible by mounting 'spoof' raids to targets in the opposite direction to the intended one, and by the main force flying elaborate dog-leg courses to their target, only turning towards the true objective at the last minute. Control of *Wilde Sau* fighters depended upon ground-to-air R/T communication, which could be electronically jammed or subjected to spoof counter-orders by German-speaking RAF controllers of 100 (BS) Group.

Despite the best efforts at protecting the RAF's bomber force, these different defensive tactics did not prevent the carnage of the Berlin raid of 24/25 March 1944 or the Nuremberg débâcle on 30/31 March, when 72 and 96 bombers respectively were lost, mostly to marauding night-fighters.

By the spring of 1944 the German night-fighter force was in the ascendancy after its temporary setbacks in 1942–43. A new command and control system, better ground and airborne radar equipment and improved aircraft armament meant that it remained a formidable defensive organisation up until the end of 1944. By this point in the war the RAF's use of RCM and spoof

tactics, combined with intruder and bomber support operations, had tipped the balance in favour of the bombers once again and there it remained until the end of the war.

Meteorology in Bomber Command

Weather forecasting

Weather forecasting was a vital procedure at Bomber Command for determining the state of weather at bomber bases, en route and in target areas, and to provide a weather forecast picture of enemy territory that was clear, accurate and detailed enough to allow operations to be planned with confidence.

Magnus Spence was the civilian Senior Meteorological Officer in charge at Bomber Command HQ. He was made a group captain on paper, but continued to work in civvies. However, this all changed shortly before D-Day when the Americans objected to a civilian briefing their high-ranking officers and having access to top secret information. Towards the end of 1944 the Meteorological Service in Bomber Command became fully militarised at Group and Command levels.

One of the outstanding contributions of the Bomber Command Meteorological Service was the development of upper wind forecasting. This culminated in the formation at Bomber Command HQ in December 1943 of a dedicated Upper Air Section. Alongside the Navigation Branch, this section played

ABOVE Photographs of night-fighters with *Schräge Musik* installations are rare, although this captured Ju 88G-6 pictured at the end of the war shows to good effect the upward angle of the twin MG 151/20 *Schräge Musik* cannon in the rear fuselage. Also visible are the *FuG 220* AI aerials and the teardrop blister housing on top of the cockpit for the *FuG 350 Naxos Z* antenna, which detected emissions from bomber H2S sets at up to 37 miles, guiding the night-fighter crew to the bomber stream.

a vital role in the successful application of Pathfinder methods and the special technique of concentrated bombing, which required accurate time-keeping, concentration of aircraft and correct timing over the target (see also Chapter 13, Operational research). On deep-penetration operations selected crews ('wind-finders') were tasked with reporting back to HQ the values of wind direction and velocity. These 'found winds' were plotted and examined by the Upper Air Forecasters before they were transmitted by W/T back to the aircraft at prearranged intervals so that navigators could amend the forecast winds.

From January 1942 weather reconnaissance (or 'PAMPA') flights were made over enemy territory by Mosquitoes of 1409 (Met) Flight (initially from Bircham Newton, and after the Flight's transfer to the Pathfinder group in April 1943, from Wyton and later Upwood). With the target for the coming night's operation selected at Bomber Harris's 09.00 briefing, there might be several 'PAMPA' flights made over enemy territory in the few hours before the first bombers took off. Their task was to obtain broad surveys of weather features and cloud distribution along the route to the target, which would help the Command meteorologist Spence produce an accurate weather forecast for the operation. 'PAMPA' flights were made in every kind of weather and the crews who flew them were singled out for the highest praise by Harris.

Diversions due to weather

A Central Flying Control Organisation was formed at Command HQ in early 1942, which worked in conjunction with the Command Meteorological Service concerning the weather forecasts at the time of take-off, and for bases at the time of return from an operation. Where inclement weather was expected to cause problems for returning bombers, provisional diversions to airfields outside a particular Group, or to USAAF bases, would be arranged before aircraft took off. Final decisions on diversion airfields could also be taken after aircraft had taken off.

A final decision as to how many aircraft from a specific Group could be accepted by the Group being used for diversions was made by the latter's air staff on the advice of the Group Forecaster, who had specific knowledge of local conditions. Diversions from one airfield to another within the same Group were organised by the Group Flying Control Officer, based on advice from the Group Meteorological Officer.

Fighting fog – FIDO

An important aid to the survival of wartime RAF bomber crews, weary at the end of a gruelling flight, was a device codenamed 'FIDO' – an acronym of Fog Investigation and Dispersal Operation. In the early years of the war bomber crews often returned home only to discover their airfields completely fogbound. Usually short of fuel and occasionally disabled by battle damage, the many crash-landings that resulted took a savage toll in valuable aircraft and crews.

After the personal intervention of Winston Churchill, this deadly hazard was largely overcome by the government's Petroleum Warfare Department and the result was the development of FIDO. Thousands of gallons of petrol were fed into long lines of burners installed on either side of runways. Flame jets at regular intervals along the length of the installations burned the fuel and the heat generated lifted the fog from the airfields, thereby allowing aircraft to take off and land in relative safety. At full burn, a typical FIDO system might consume 90,000 gallons of petrol per hour – enough to fill the fuel tanks of more than 40 Lancasters.

A countrywide FIDO system at 15 British

airfields covering most RAF and USAAF front-line commands was in place by the end of 1944. Ten Bomber Command airfields were equipped with the system: Carnaby (Emergency Diversion Airfield) and Melbourne, Yorkshire; Fiskerton, Ludford Magna, Metheringham and Sturgate, Lincolnshire; Graveley, Huntingdonshire; Downham Market and Foulsham, Norfolk; and Tuddenham, Suffolk. By the time of the Ardennes Offensive in the winter of 1944/45, FIDO had enabled more than 1,000 Allied aircraft and their crews to make safe landings despite dense fog over Britain and the Continent. However, the forecasting of fog remained one of the primary responsibilities of Bomber Command's Meteorological Officer.

BELOW On 16 November 1944, 1,188 RAF bomber aircraft and 1,243 of the US 8th AF escorted by 282 P-51 Mustangs attacked targets behind the German frontline in daylight. Visibility deteriorated seriously during the course of the day and orders were given to light FIDO at RAF Woodbridge at 11.35hrs to aid the returning aircraft. Over the next 7 hours some 85 fighters and bombers landed safely thanks to FIDO burning away the fog at a cost of 717,544 gallons of petrol – enough to fill the tanks of more than 330 Lancasters. This is a Lancaster of 35 (Pathfinder) Squadron landing at Graveley during a test burn of FIDO in late 1943.

'On the way out of the target the fighter attacks began. ... I saw the first orange ball of an exploding bomber as we were leaving the target area. Soon, every few minutes, an orange ball lit up the otherwise black sky.'

Walter Thompson,
Lancaster pilot, 83 Squadron, 1943.

Chapter Nine

Defending the Reich

The main reason behind Bomber Command's high losses was the Third Reich's formidable air defence network, the Kammhuber Line, built to protect the Fatherland from air attack in the West. Some 15,000 flak guns defended the Reich's airspace while at least 4,000 *Würzburg* radar sets were built to track the bombers and guide night-fighters in for the kill.

OPPOSITE Night-fighter ace Major Wilhelm Herget, Gruppenkommandeur of I./NJG 4, runs through cockpit checks in his Messerschmitt Bf 110 before a sortie in the spring of 1944. On the night of 20/21 December 1943 he was credited with the destruction of five Halifax and three Lancaster bombers within the space of 45 minutes. He finished the war with 73 victories (58 night, 15 day). *(BA 101I-492-3342-38)*

BELOW Defenders of
the Reich: Generalmajor
Josef Kammhuber,
architect of the German
air defence system
(centre), with night-
fighter ace pilots
Leutnant Hans Hahn
(left, 3./NJG 2) and
Oberfeldwebel Paul
Gildner (right, 1./NJG 1)
on 9 July 1941. Hahn
was a successful night
intruder pilot until his
death over England on
11 October that same
year flying a Ju 88C-4,
while Gildner died when
his damaged Bf 110
crashed near Gilze-
Rijen on 24 February
1943. Hahn and Gildner
were both holders of
the Knight's Cross and
were credited with 12
and 44 night victories
respectively. As with the
RAF bomber crews that
they came up against,
skill and experience were
no guarantors of survival
for German night-fighter
crews. (BA 183-R97856)

The Kammhuber Line

In 1940 Generalmajor Josef Kammhuber
was given the task of establishing the
Nachtverteidigung, or night defence, of Germany.
He devised an integrated radar early warning and
air defence network, dubbed the 'Kammhuber
Line' by the RAF, which was organised in a
coastal belt around the northern and western
approaches to Germany, from Denmark to
northern France, for protection against air attack.

Kammhuber's belt was made up of three
layers: an outer *Freya* early warning radar zone,
with overlapping coverage; a manually directed
searchlight belt, *Helle Nachtjagd* (illuminated night-
fighting), where night-fighters (initially the obsolete
non radar-equipped Messerschmitt Bf 109 D,
later replaced by the more capable *Lichtenstein* AI
radar-equipped twin-engine Bf 110) were guided
on to the bombers by searchlight illumination; and
finally a combined night-fighting zone (*Kombinierte
Nachtjagd*) using flak, searchlights and night-
fighter aircraft concentrated around industrial
centres like the Ruhr, and major cities such as
Berlin, Hamburg and Stuttgart.

In due course the *Helle Nachtjagd* and
Kombinierte Nachtjagd systems were overtaken
by changes in tactics and abandoned. In
early 1942 the *Bürgermeisters* of German
cities decided that with the introduction of
new radar equipment Kammhuber no longer
needed searchlights in his defensive line. Hitler
supported their relocation with the flak units

around major urban centres. Kammhuber
objected strongly to this decision, but in the end
he conceded that it forced night-fighter crews
to place their trust in the ground controllers to
guide them to their targets. Once the crews had
got used to the new system it proved far more
effective than *Helle Nachtjagd*.

At the grass roots of the Kammhuber Line
was a series of so-called *Himmelbett* ('Four-
poster bed') zones, which were subdivided into
a series of three-dimensional command areas
known as night-fighter boxes (a *Raum* or room),
numbered from 1 to 9. Each *Raum* was under
the operational control of a *Nachtjagd Raum
Führer*, who in turn reported to the *Nachtjagd
Gruppe*. Within each *Raum* were three circular
controlled zones, laid out side by side, with the
radius of each circle corresponding to the range
of its radar equipment – two Giant *Würzburgs*
and a single *Freya*. The ground radars guided a
single night-fighter on to a single bomber. Once
the night-fighter crew picked up the bomber on
their onboard radar (the *Lichtenstein*) the night-
fighter crew completed the contact on their own
and made their attack on the bomber. It was an
efficient system but was restricted by the limited
number of fighters operating in the boxes through
which the bomber stream was passing. It was
also a rigidly parochial system, which meant that
(for example) NJG 1 in Holland was not allowed
to intercept a raid on Hamburg or another north
German port unless bombers had strayed off
course and into their area; likewise, NJG 3 in
Denmark could not help defend the Ruhr. In fact,
within the command area of a *Geschwader* the
night-fighter crews of individual *Gruppen* seldom
operated more than 30 miles from their airfield.

Würzburg radar

The *Würzburg* radar was the lynchpin of
Kammhuber's early warning and night-
fighter defences. Originally designed as a
gun-laying and searchlight control radar, it was
adapted for ground control interception (GCI) to
work in conjunction with the night-fighter force.
The *Würzburgs* came in two sizes: the FuMG
39T(D) Small *Würzburg* D with a range of up to
21 miles; and the FuMG 65 *Würzburg-Riese* G
or Giant *Würzburg,* which could track aircraft up
to 42 miles away.

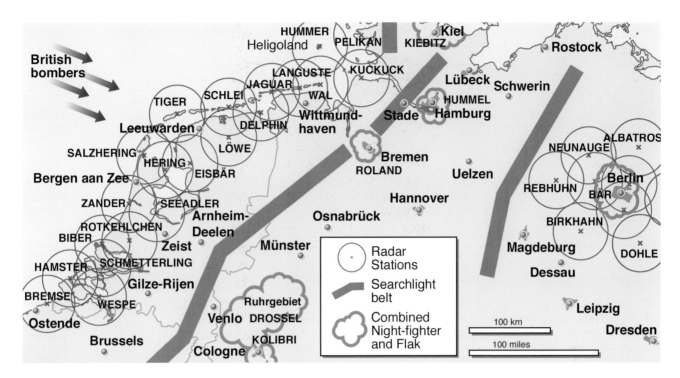

British bombers

HUMMER
Heligoland PELIKAN
Kiel
KIEBITZ
Rostock
LANGUSTE
JAGUAR
KUCKUCK
Lübeck Schwerin
TIGER SCHLEI
WAL
HUMMEL
Leeuwarden DELPHIN
Wittmund- Stade Hamburg
haven
LÖWE
Bremen ROLAND
SALZHERING
HERING
EISBÄR
Bergen aan Zee
ZANDER SEEADLER
Arnheim-
ROTKEHLCHEN Deelen
BIBER
Zeist Münster
HAMSTER SCHMETTERLING
Gilze-Rijen
BREMSE
WESPE
Ostende
Brussels
Cologne

ALBATROS
NEUNAUGE
Berlin
REBHUHN BÄR
BIRKHAHN
Magdeburg DOHLE
Dessau

Uelzen
Hannover
Osnabrück

Leipzig
Dresden

Ruhrgebiet
Venlo DROSSEL
KOLIBRI

⊗ Radar Stations
▬ Searchlight belt
☁ Combined Night-fighter and Flak

100 km
100 miles

ABOVE Schematic of the Kammhuber Line. Note the animal-themed codenames for the radar stations. *(Ian Moores)*

Under Kammhuber's leadership some 300 GCI stations were set up, but his rigid adherence to the *Seeburg-Lichtenstein-Verfahren* control system (of which more later) meant an over-reliance on night-fighter defences, which absorbed massive manufacturing and manning resources. For all its clever organisation, the weak link in the *Würzburg* and *Seeburg-Lichtenstein-Verfahren* chain was its lack of flexibility as we have already seen. Bomber Command soon recognised this and the fact that it could not provide defence in depth.

Once a bomber had passed through the belt, further night-fighter control was impossible. Bomber Harris's answer was the introduction of the bomber stream tactic in the spring of 1942 to swamp the German air defence system with large numbers of aircraft funnelled over a narrow corridor in a short space of time.

Later, when the countermeasure codenamed 'Window' was used by the RAF for the first time against the defences of Hamburg on 24 July 1943, most of the *Würzburg* network was thrown into a state of complete paralysis, rendering it useless for night ground-controlled interception. It was a huge setback for the Luftwaffe. This was one of the factors that led to the removal of Kammhuber from his command in September 1943 as General der Flieger.

BELOW With a range of 1.6 to 40km, the Small *Würzburg* D-type FuMG 39T(D) with its sheet metal 3m parabolic dish and rotating dipole antenna was used for flak fire control, gun laying, searchlight control and height finding, and as a standby in GCI. A tally of at least nine bombers is recorded on the dish itself, with the date of the victory painted next to a silhouette of the aircraft type. *(BA 101I-662-6660-27A)*

ABOVE A searchlight unit in action during May 1942. Note the victory markings on the light body. *(BA 101I-616-2514-36)*

BELOW FuMG 80 *Freya* was a mobile and motorised air search and fight GCI radar capable of tracking targets at ranges varying from 12 to 75 miles, depending on their height. *(US National Archives)*

New tactics

Recognising the seriousness of this situation, the Luftwaffe came up with a new tactic. Instead of controlled individual night-fighters operating in boxes, the entire night-fighter force would be used in large numbers along the routes followed by the bombers to and from the target. However, until the new SN-2 radar was developed for the fighters, a stop-gap measure was required.

This found expression in the *Wilde Sau* (wild boar) method where single-seat fighters like the Bf 109 and Focke Wulf Fw 190 were able to range freely over the target using searchlight illumination for target acquisition, operating above the height of the flak barrage. This tactic was developed by a former bomber pilot, Major Hajo Hermann.

By early January 1944 the arrival of SN-2 radar in large enough numbers enabled more than half the night-fighter force to be equipped with an AI radar that worked on a frequency that could not be jammed by Window. The so-called *Zahme Sau* (tame boar) method was where freelance twin-engine night-fighters like the Bf 110 and Ju 88 infiltrated the bomber stream and used their onboard radar to find quarry for themselves. With increasing numbers of long-range Ju 88s arriving on the *Geschwadern* and the adoption of upward-firing *Schräge Musik* cannons, the Luftwaffe gained the upper hand for a period of time, but not for long.

With the exception of the infamous Nuremberg raid of 30/31 March 1944 when over 200 night-fighters were committed to battle and accounted for most of the 95 RAF bombers lost that night, the tame boar method ultimately failed to yield the hoped-for results for a number of mainly technical reasons.

Tracking and snaring the bombers

The sequence of events for the interception of a bomber in 1942–43 using the *Himmelbett* system worked as follows.

FuMG 80 *Freya* air-search and early warning radars were sited around the coastline of enemy-occupied territory and gave continuous early warning radar coverage of aircraft flying at

10,000ft out to a range of 70–80 miles. *Freyas* secured early warning of the approach of a bomber force and passed the target information to the *Würzburg* units for interception. At the same time, flak guns were manned along the probable route of the bombers. (*Würzburgs* were also used for gun-laying and searchlight control and were arranged in strength at dozens of gun-defended areas.)

On the way towards their target, the bombers passed over the fixed areas (Rooms or *Räume*) of territory surrounding the GCI sites controlled by pairs of Giant *Würzburgs*, each circular zone within the *Raum* being contiguous with adjacent radar boxes in the defensive chain. Because the Giant *Würzburg*'s radar beam was too narrow to pick up the target bomber on its own, the assistance of an additional (*Freya*) system with its broader beam was used to acquire the target and inform the *Würzburg* crew where to look in the sky.

The three radars were grouped together in each control zone with one Giant *Würzburg* (codenamed 'Red') plotting and tracking the course of the bomber after vectoring by a *Freya* radar, while the second ('Blue') *Würzburg* was used to guide and track the night-fighter.

The *Seeburg* plotting table

Information coming from the pair of *Würzburgs* was collated and presented in the Luftwaffe ground control room on a *Seeburg Tisch* (*Seeburg* table), which formed the basis of the *Himmelbett* system. The apparatus was a light table with a frosted glass screen mounted on a raised wooden platform. On the screen the positions of friendly and enemy aircraft were shown using coloured spots of light – red for enemy, blue for friendly – projected on to the underside by light-pointers.

The primary object of the *Seeburg* plotting table was to convert the azimuth, elevation and range readings provided by tellers working inside the control cabin of each of the two Giant *Würzburgs* into a visual form that was convenient for manual control of an interception. The tellers gave instructions by telephone to the two plotters seated underneath the frosted glass screen of the *Seeburg* table, who in turn controlled the position of each light projector.

By this stage a night-fighter crew had been

ABOVE FuMG 65 *Würzburg-Riese* G (Giant *Würzburg*) had a 7.5m parabolic dish and a range of up to 50 miles in search mode and 31–37 miles in direction-finding mode. *(US National Archives)*

BELOW Information coming from the *Würzburgs* was collated on the *Seeburg Tisch*, named after its inventor. The *Jägerleitoffizier* (JLO) Fighter Control Officer in the centre of the picture reads off the positional data from the plot. *(Copyright unknown)*

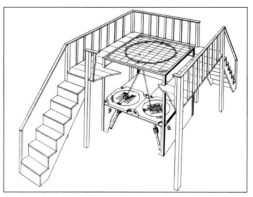

LEFT *Seeburg Tisch* schematic. *(TNA AIR 40/3023)*

scrambled and were at operational altitude orbiting a radio beacon in the controlled airspace of the box. A second fighter was crewed and ready to take off, while a third was held in reserve.

The position of the spots of light on the glass table-top map as viewed from above represented the relative positions of the fighter and bomber aircraft plotted. Their respective tracks were marked in coloured crayon on to the top surface of the glass screen. The *Jägerleitoffizier* (JLO) Fighter Control Officer in the gallery surrounding the plotting table read off the positional data and using R/T vectored the night-fighter pilot in his *Lichtenstein* radar-equipped aircraft into visual range of the bomber to make his attack. This was called the

Seeburg-Lichtenstein-Verfahren – the *Seeburg-Lichtenstein* system.

Himmelbett-Verfahren

In response to Bomber Command's changes in tactics in May 1942 when it introduced the bomber stream, the Germans increased the depth of the *Himmelbett* system. New sites were established in front of and behind the original belt, along with increases in the number of radar sets and supporting equipment, thereby enabling the tracking of two bombers and two night-fighters simultaneously. This became known as *Himmelbett-Verfahren* and in conjunction with the *Seeburg* system it remained in use from 1943 until the end of the war. Working with new radar equipment that was not disrupted by Mandrel or Window countermeasures, it was used mainly for intercepting bomber stragglers and in controlling night- and day-fighters using the 'Benito' ground-controlled system.

Askania-Gerät

The original manually operated *Seeburg* system was eventually upgraded with the automatic *Askania-Gerät* (*Askania* system), which used a series of motor drives to allow the spot of light to follow automatically the position of the *Würzburg* in azimuth, elevation and range to provide the same end data, but doing away with a total of 12 operating personnel for each GCI. This was particularly relevant when manpower became increasingly tight towards the end of the war.

Fighter and flak control

The *Seeburg* table was only able to provide local interception data, but the large wall-mounted transparent plotting map used in fighter and flak division control rooms covered a wider operational area to provide more of a strategic oversight. The vertical frosted-glass map was divided into white-marked grid squares representing the Luftwaffe's *Planquadrat* map reference system (*Gradnetz* or *Gradnetzmeldeverfahren*), which covered all of Europe and was in use on the Western Front until mid-1943 when it was superseded by the *Jägermeldenetz* system in the air defence

BELOW In the control room of a Luftwaffe night-fighter division the ghostly hands of the tellers behind the frosted glass panel plot the movement of a bomber stream over the northern Netherlands in 1944 on the gridded *Planquadrat* map reference system. (BA 101I-668-7167-30)

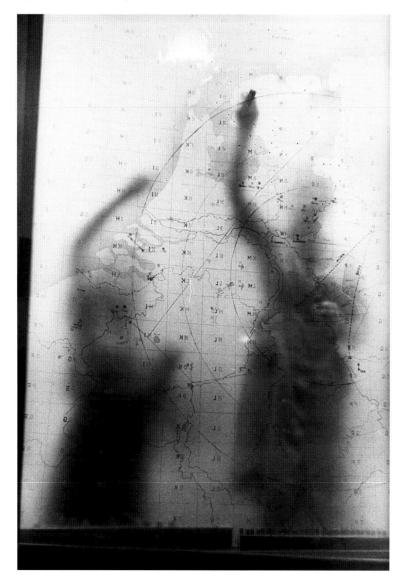

of Germany. Behind each grid square was a honeycomb structure into which coloured light bulbs could be plugged in/unplugged by tellers to indicate the position and movement of enemy and friendly aircraft.

Nachtjäger – the night-fighters

In the early years of the war the flak and searchlight units were Germany's first line of night defence against bombers. The use of fighters for night interception was not considered, and those few pilots who did attempt to find lone bombers in the dark experienced little or no success.

A first night-fighter wing, *Nachtjagdgeschwader 1*, was eventually formed in June 1940, but only after it became clear that flak on its own could not prevent British bombers from

ABOVE Messerschmitt Bf 110F-2 (3C+AR) flown by Oberleutnant Hans-Karl Kamp, Staffelkapitän of Nachtjagdgeschwader 4 (7./NJG 4) during the summer of 1942. The Bf 110F was armed with 2 × MG FF and 4 × MG 17 cannon and equipped six night-fighter *Geschwadern* from the summer of 1942 until late 1943. It had no AI radar fitted. *(BA 101I-360-2095-31)*

GERMAN NIGHT-FIGHTER SUCCESSES, 1940–45

Reich Air Defence and Western areas

Year	Night	Day
1940	42	–
1941	421	1
1942	687	4
1943	1,820	110
1944	2,335	100
1945	528	–
Total	5,833	215

RIGHT A section of the victory board for NJG 1 from 10 April to 24 June 1941, listing actions that resulted in the shooting down or destruction of almost 100 RAF bombers, mostly Wellingtons and Whitleys. Some 141 RAF bombers were shot down by night-fighters in this three-month period. *(BA 101I-355-1798-02A)*

RIGHT The tail fin from night-fighter ace Heinz Wolfgang Schnaufer's Messerschmitt Bf 110G-4 was sold at auction in England in 2015 for £90,000. It records some of his 121 victories (seen in this detail photograph), noting the date of each kill beneath stencilled motifs of twin- and four-engine bombers. *(Author)*

ABOVE Messerschmitt Bf 110 with *Lichtenstein* SN-2 AI radar.

BELOW The Junkers Ju 88 was probably the most versatile German combat aircraft of the Second World War. This is a Ju 88G-6 belonging to 7./NJG 2 equipped with SN-2, *Naxos* and *Flensburg* AI radar.

getting through into Germany. Kammhuber's proposal to further expand the night-fighter force was acted on with hesitancy by the German High Command, while his request for a centrally controlled fighter arm was brushed aside.

By mid-1943 five *Nachtjagdgeschwadern* were operating over north-west Europe. When the Battle of Berlin was in full spate in the autumn of 1943, *XII Fliegerkorps*, which controlled all night-fighter units, was disbanded and the air defence of the Reich was decentralised even further, subordinated to *Luftwaffen Befehlshaber Mitte* in September. Even so, the *Nachtjagdgeschwadern* continued to extract a heavy toll on RAF bombers by night, equipped mainly with the Bf 110 and Ju 88, although some units used the Dornier Do 217. Skilled pilots like Major Heinz Wolfgang Schnaufer (nicknamed 'The Ghost of St Trond', with 121 kills), Oberst Helmut Lent (102 kills)

and Major Heinrich Prinz zu Sayn-Wittgenstein (83 kills) became masters of their craft, downing several hundred Allied bombers between them.

It took several years for the night-fighter *Gruppen* to receive and benefit from specialised versions of existing aircraft types like the Messerschmitt Bf 110G-4 and the Junkers Ju 88C-6. It took longer still for newer high-performance aircraft with cutting-edge AI radar systems like *Lichtenstein* SN-2 and heavier armament to reach the units – the He 219 and Ju 88G-6b were only received in small numbers and the worsening fuel shortage late in the war meant that little more than a handful ever made it into combat.

In the spring of 1945 the German night-fighter force was still a potent adversary, but it was hobbled by a desperate lack of aviation fuel and the collapse of the ground control system, which kept many aircraft earth-bound. At the war's end it remained undefeated in battle.

Flak

At its peak the Flak branch of the Luftwaffe numbered some 1.25 million personnel, which constituted about half of the Luftwaffe's total manpower across all theatres, with 32% on the defence of the homeland from air attack. The 8.8cm Flak gun was central to the defence of the Reich.

In the early years of the war a Flak battery comprised four guns arranged in a square pattern with the command post, including the predictor, at the centre. From 1941 battery size

grew as the weight of fire needed to increase to match the growing numbers of Allied bombers. Six-, eight- and even twelve-gun batteries were developed (the latter were known as *Grossbatterien*) and all were controlled by one or two *Würzburg* radars and multiple predictors, which fed data to the gun crews for fuse/timer settings, gun-aiming and gun-firing.

Flak guns came in different sizes, light and heavy, depending on their use. Light Flak was typically heavy machine guns or 2cm cannon like the 2cm Flak 30/38, and a series of 3.7cm guns that included the 3.7cm Flak 18/36/37 and Flak 43. These guns were ideal for engaging low-flying and fast aircraft. As automatic weapons they could put up a tremendous volume of shot. Although medium-calibre guns, such as the 5cm Flak 41, were developed to fill the middle ground between light AA and the heavy weapons, they were not particularly successful and were produced in limited numbers.

'Heavy' referred to the 8.8cm Flak, the 10.5cm guns (10.5cm Flak 38 and 39) and the 12.8cm Flak 40. As single-shot weapons, the heavy guns individually could not lay down the volume of fire of the light AA guns, but they could reach up to progressively higher altitudes to engage high-flying bombers. The Flak 18/36/37 could achieve about 26,246ft (8,000m), the medium 5cm Flak 41 and the 12.8cm Flak 40 up to 35,022ft (10,675m) and the 10.5cm Flak 38 and 39 to 31,003ft (9,450m).

In the closing stages of the war, huge numbers of heavy flak guns and their crews were progressively drawn away to the east for use on the land front to try to hold back the Soviet advance. Between October 1944 and May 1945 the Luftwaffe transferred a total of 555 heavy and 175 medium/light batteries to the fighting fronts, effectively stripping entire areas within Germany of their air defences and laying them open to uncontested aerial attack.

Confounding the defenders

The struggle between bombers and fighters ebbed and flowed throughout the war, with constant developments in technology and tactics putting one side ahead of the other for a short while until a new radar device or weapon turned the tables again.

With radar at the heart of the process for intercepting a bomber, the device was open to jamming by Bomber Command's specialist countermeasures squadrons in 100 (BS) Group. Mandrel was used against *Freya*, while Window and Carpet were particularly effective in jamming *Würzburg*, interrupting flak and shutting down GCI. The radio communications between the night-fighter and ground controller, which was key to a successful interception, could also be compromised electronically through Airborne Cigar and Jostle, or by the German-speaking 'Spec Ops' (codenamed 'Corona') flying on board 100 (BS) Group aircraft. Electronic countermeasures were also effective in jamming night-fighter airborne radar sets, for example Airborne Grocer was used from May 1944 against SN-2 (see Chapter 8 for further information).

ABOVE A captured Ju 88G-1 with *FuG220 Lichtenstein* SN-2 AI radar attracts the interest of USAAF pilots at the end of the war. Note the solid nose and four MG 151/20 cannon in ventral gun tray. *(US National Archives)*

BELOW A curtain of flak lights up the night sky over a European town. *(BA 183-B14660)*

Eight monolithic Flak towers (*Flaktürme*) were built in Germany after 1940 to defend major cities against air attacks from bombers. There were three in Berlin, two in Hamburg and three in Vienna. Other cities also had their own towers, but not on the same huge scale as the big eight. The towers carried multiple Flak guns and doubled as public air-raid shelters with room for up to 10,000 civilians, including their own medical facilities.

Horst Kesner, who was a 16-year-old *Flakhilfer* in the Berlin Zoo Flak tower in 1943, recalled:

The people were crammed in every room and in every section, right up to the fourth floor where the military section began. They crowded into the passages so that we had to step over them as they slept on the floor.

I think we had up to 20,000 people on the worst night [of the Battle of Berlin]. In the morning, when the raid was over, it took hours to get everyone out.

With walls up to 11ft (3.5m) thick, each tower system consisted of two structures – a *Gefechsturm* or G-tower – the gun tower; and a neighbouring *Leit-turm* or L-tower, which was also known as the command or fire-control tower. The G-tower stood 128ft (39m) tall and 231ft (70.5m) square and featured dual-level gun platforms. The upper level was equipped with eight 12.8cm (5in) Flak 40 guns in pairs at each corner, while the lower platforms sported 2cm, 3cm and 3.7cm guns to deal with lower-flying aircraft. At 164ft (50m) tall, the L-tower was usually equipped with *Würzburg* fire-control radar and sixteen 2cm guns.

With a rate of fire of some 8,000 rounds per minute (although most of this was from the smaller-calibre weapons like the 2cm Flak 30) the *Flakturm* was a formidable platform from which to unleash a devastating curtain of anti-aircraft fire at overflying bombers. Capable of firing 20 rounds per minute, only the 12.8cm Flak 40 with its 27.9kg (62lb) shell travelling at

BELOW The fire and fury of a flak tower in action at night was a sight and sound to behold. On platforms at the four corners of the tower are eight 12.8cm (5in) Flak 40 guns belching deadly 5in rounds skywards. Radar-directed flak used fragmentation rounds and was accurate up to 30,000ft. Proximity fuses were generally not used. This vivid recreation of the Berlin Zoo *Flakturm* features in the video game *Sniper Elite* v2 by Rebellion Developments. *(Courtesy 505 Games, 2012)*

RIGHT This is one of several 3.7cm *Flak-Vierling* guns and their crews that occupied platforms on the lower levels of the Berlin Zoo *Flakturm*. In the background can be seen the *Leit-turm* command tower with *Würzburg-Riese* fire-control radar on the upper level, 16 April 1942. *(BA 183-G1230-0502-004)*

880m (2,887ft)/sec had the effective range to hit and destroy a bomber flying at 30,000ft.

Germany was not unique in this provision: for the defence of London and the ports of Felixstowe and Harwich, seven ack-ack platforms (called Maunsell forts) were built in the Thames Estuary; three more were built in the Mersey to defend Liverpool.

BELOW Built to defend the port city of Hamburg against Allied bombers, the *Flakturm IV* G-tower at Heiligengeistfeld in the suburb of Sankt Pauli is pictured at the end of the war. Note the pairs of 12.8cm Flak 40 guns at each corner. The tower could accommodate up to 15,000 civilians inside, and included a hospital with 95 beds. *Flakturm IV* has survived into the 21st century simply because demolition of its structure has proved impossible. It was converted for residential use in 1993.

'The intensified roaring; the thrust against our bodies; the shrinking flarepath; the vanishing buildings and woods. Though it was possible that we would come this way again, it was equally possible that never again would we leave the Elsham runways… .'

Don Charlwood, Lancaster navigator, 103 Squadron, 1942–43.

Chapter Ten

Target for tonight

━━━(●)━━━━━━━━━━━━━━━━

Planning and launching a maximum effort night-raid (codenamed 'Goodwood') required the combined resources of a bomber station's headquarters and operations staff, ground crews and aircrews. Feverish activity continued from daybreak to dusk when the first of several dozen bombers and their crews thundered off the runway, out into the darkness and towards Germany.

OPPOSITE Lancaster B Mk I, KM-A/R5729 of 44 Squadron awaits the arrival of its crew at Dunholme Lodge before taking off for Berlin on 2 January 1944. Joining 44 Squadron in 1942 she went on to complete more than 70 ops until shot down by a night-fighter on a sortie to Brunswick on 14/15 January 1944, with the loss of all her crew. The Lanc was seen from the ground attempting a forced landing in the village of Gieboldehausen in Lower Saxony, but it struck an electricity pylon causing it to crash and burn.

ABOVE In the winter snows of January 1945 armourers in the bomb dump at a 4 Group Halifax station in Yorkshire manhandle **Cluster Incendiary Projectile** containers on to a waiting bomb trolley. *(PhotoQuest/Getty Images)*

The description that follows is of a typical day and night for an RAF heavy bomber station during 1944, as station headquarters staff, ground- and aircrews, plan and launch a 'Goodwood' or maximum effort night raid to a target 'somewhere in Germany'.

After breakfast, aircrew report to their flight officers, and are told whether operations are planned for the coming night or if there will be a stand-down. From the moment that details of the target for the coming night come through on the telephone from group headquarters, to the point some 18 hours later when the last few aircraft land back at their home base, activity on a heavy bomber station to get their squadrons airborne is intense. Meanwhile, in station headquarters the group broadcast has come through on the telephone requiring a 'Goodwood' (maximum effort) and details of the target for tonight. The bomb load and H-Hour (the time of take-off) along with route details will follow shortly, but first of all the station intelligence officer notifies everyone who needs to know, from the station, squadron and flight commanders, through to flying control and the bomb dump.

Now that it is official that ops are planned, the crews go out to their dispersals to check on the serviceability of their aircraft – and if necessary fly air tests. The groundcrews busy themselves preparing the aircraft, tradesmen from the various sections check instruments, radar and electrical equipment, and the aircraft is fuelled, armed and bombed-up. The aircrews have lunch in their respective messes before the Tannoy announces the times for operational meals of bacon and eggs and the briefing.

CENTRE An RCAF armourer screws the fuse into the tail of a 250lb bomb on a dispersal at Croft in 1944. Bombs only became 'live' in the air after the bomb-aimer armed his load by operating switches on a panel in his compartment that electromechanically retracted arming pins from the bombs inside the bomb bay.

LEFT The fuel tanks of a 6 (RCAF) Group Halifax B Mk III are topped up from a Matador bowser while in the foreground a train of A Mk V 1,000lb sea mines awaits its turn to be loaded. *(M. Wright via Ken Merrick)*

Later in the afternoon, crews congregate outside the briefing room before finally entering. Once inside they sit on long wooden forms facing the end wall where a large map of Europe, shrouded from view by a blackout curtain, hangs on the wall above the raised platform from which the briefings are conducted. Once it has been ascertained by a roll-call of pilots' names that all crews are present, the whole assembly rises to its feet and stands smartly to attention when the platform party enters the room, comprising the station and squadron commanders, and the senior flight commanders. The briefing room doors are closed by an RAF policeman who then stands guard outside. Already present on the stage are the Station Intelligence Officer (SIO), the Met Officer, the Base Engineering Officer and the Flying Control Officer (FCO).

The SIO opens the briefing by unveiling the map to reveal the target for the night, with the route to be followed marked with red tape. Known flak and searchlight positions are also marked on this map by red and green celluloid overlays respectively. First, the SIO explains details of the target and why it has been chosen, followed by the signals, bombing and navigation leaders who explain the various routines for the night. Next comes the FCO who outlines engine start-up and marshalling times, and the runway to be used. Then the Met Officer gives a full briefing on wind speeds,

ABOVE A David Brown VIG 1 bomb tractor named 'Crasher' delivers a 4,000lb Cookie to a waiting Lancaster on dispersal at a 1 Group airfield. Judging from its pristine condition, this aircraft is a new arrival on the squadron.

RIGHT Engineering officer and erk check the port inner Merlin of 218 Squadron's Lancaster B Mk III, HA-Q/LM577 'Edith', on hard standing No 30 at RAF Chedburgh, Suffolk, in 1945. With 84 ops recorded in this photograph, 'Edith' survived the war only to be scrapped in 1947. In the background is C Flight's XH-D/PD229, a G-H leader. *(Steve Smith/218 Squadron Association)*

RIGHT On 10 September 1942, Halifax crews from 76 and 78 Squadrons at Middleton St George hang on the words of the briefing officer as he gives them the 'gen' about their target for the night: Düsseldorf. Losses were high, with 33 bombers failing to return from 479 dispatched. No 78 Squadron lost one aircraft. *(Hans Wild/LIFE/Getty Images)*

ABOVE Lancaster crews of 467 (Australian) Squadron engage in banter and a smoke outside the locker rooms at Binbrook in March 1943 before the transports arrive to take them out to the dispersals. Four of the gunners wear bright-yellow one-piece Taylor buoyant suits, which gave warmth, buoyancy in water (in case of ditching) and a certain amount of fire protection to the wearer. However, Taylorsuits were not universally popular because they often short-circuited and were known to have caused minor burns. *(Vincent Holyoak collection)*

maps for the night from the station map stores and mark on to them their proposed routes. The wireless operators draw their flimsies on which are printed radio frequencies and the colours of the day. Crews hurry to the parachute stores to collect 'chutes and Mae Wests, then make for the locker rooms where valuables are handed in and escape kits collected before changing into flying kit.

Amid the usual babble of conversation and the jumble of parachutes, helmets and flying boots, each man struggles into his unwieldy flying gear, the gunners usually taking the longest with their layers of electrically heated clothing and the bulky Taylorsuits. Sandwiches and flasks of coffee for the return journey together with slabs of chocolate and barley sugar sweets are handed out to each crew member from wrappings of newspaper.

Outside the locker room the buses arrive to take the crews on the short ride to their aircraft, dispersed around the perimeter of the airfield. A corporal stands at the open door shouting out the letters by which each aircraft is known. As space becomes available on a bus for that aircraft's crew, they climb on board and are taken out to their waiting aircraft.

Once on their respective dispersals, each pilot completes the formalities of signing the Form 700 for the groundcrew corporal after a careful check of the control surfaces, wheel tyres and undercarriage oleo legs. Then, after a last leak on the dewy beside the dispersal, he and the

cloud and the weather likely to be encountered over the target. The squadron wing commanders follow by speaking to the crews in detail about the operation before handing over to the station commander who then wishes everyone good luck and a safe return.

With the briefing over, pilots obtain their

RIGHT Going out to the kite. With parachutes and Mae Wests slung over shoulders and carried in hand, the crew of a 76 Squadron Halifax walk to their waiting aircraft to prepare for take-off, 22 October 1943.

rest of his crew board the aircraft: flight engineer, pilot, navigator, bomb-aimer and the wireless operator make their way up the fuselage to the nose, and the two gunners to their turrets. The pilot stows his 'chute and straps himself into his seat. Outside in the dark on the dispersal pan the groundcrew move the battery starter trolley into position under the port wing.

The flight engineer checks to see that all the fuel cocks below his instrument panel are in their correct positions, then leans forward to the pilot and declares he is ready for engine start-up. The engineer looks out of the cockpit window and down to the ground beneath, calling back that the groundcrew are ready with their battery cart to start the port inner. When the pilot switches on the ignition, the fitter down beneath the wing shouts 'Contact!' The engineer presses one of the four black starter buttons on his panel and the first of four engines coughs, splutters and finally roars into life. The same procedure is repeated until all four engines are running. The pilot checks the intercom to all crew positions, then opens up the engines and allows them to warm up to operating temperature.

Taxiing times for each individual aircraft were set at briefing and the time to taxi out for take-off has now arrived. The engineer stands behind the pilot, keeping watch on the array of dials on his engineer's panel and the bomb-aimer comes up from his station in the nose to assist the pilot at take-off. The rear hatch door is secured by the groundcrew before the wheel chocks are pulled away and the pilot gently opens the throttles. On doughnut tyres the big bomber trundles and sways forward, following the aircraft in front around the perimeter track in slow procession towards the duty runway for the night, and joining the queue at the end. The pilot goes through his final cockpit check and the navigator outlines the flight plan and climb instructions. A green Aldis light flashes from the control van signalling to the pilot that it is his turn to line up for take-off.

The pilot runs up the engines against the brakes, which are then released and the aircraft begins to accelerate down the runway. Although the throttles are almost fully open, to build as much speed as possible he purposely holds the bomber's nose down as she strains to leave

the ground, using the full length of the runway if necessary. The bomb-aimer eases the throttles through the gate for full take-off power and slams the clamp on to keep them from slipping back through vibration at the crucial moment. With both hands firmly grasping the control column, the pilot eases it back and the engine note changes as the bomber claws its way into the sky at little more than 100mph, leaving the

ABOVE The pilot of a Merlin-engine Halifax checks that the master fuel cocks on the bulkhead behind his right arm are 'on' before engine start.

BELOW About to take off on its 100th (and last) operational sortie, Flt Lt David Shaw (also on the last trip of his tour) is at the controls of 550 Squadron's ED905/BO-F for 'Freddie' as it thunders down North Killingholme's runway on 2 November 1944: destination Düsseldorf. A knot of well wishers wave him and his crew on their way. 'Freddie' survived the war only to be written off in a landing mishap on 20 August 1945.

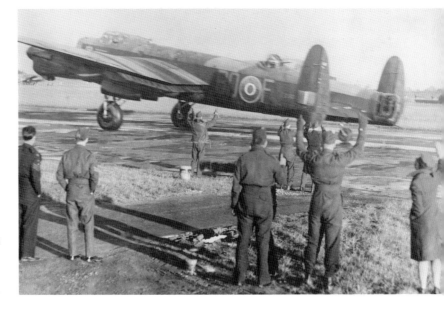

runway to slip away beneath. The wheel-brake lever is nipped to stop the wheels turning before the main gear retracts with a clunk. The red and green indicator lights go out on the pilot's instrument panel as each leg locks up and at last they are airborne.

BELOW The wireless operator tunes the dial on his R1155 receiver for broadcast winds, while further forward – in his 'snug' behind the pilot – the navigator glances up from his charts. The reel device in the foreground on top of the front spar is for the trailing aerial. (Alamy)

BELOW RIGHT Inside his curtained-off snug, the navigator rarely ventured out in the air. This is Flg Off Philip Ingleby hunched over the chart table inside his 619 Squadron Lancaster in February 1944. He was killed six months later on 7 August when the 617 Squadron Mosquito he was flying in suffered structural failure during a training exercise and crashed into the sea near Wainfleet, Lincolnshire.

The bomber continues in a shallow climb until the airspeed has built sufficiently for the pilot to adjust the fuel mixture and engine revolutions to normal. The engineer eases the throttles back as the heavy bomber continues to climb. The flaps are now fully retracted and the power eased off again to suit the rate of climb selected. The navigator gives the pilot a course to steer for the group's assembly point and with the reassuring red and green glow of navigation lights on the other aircraft in the sky all around them they fly in the climb towards the coast.

Once rendezvous has been made with the other aircraft of the group, navigation lights are turned out as the armada of bombers drones its way seawards at a speed of some 200mph – usually towards Cromer for bomber groups below the River Humber, Flamborough Head or Spurn Point for those to the north of this line – where they leave the shores of England behind.

The gunners now request permission to test-fire their guns over the sea as the bomber continues to climb towards the briefed height for crossing the enemy coast, now some ten minutes' flying time away. Continually scanning the sky for the first signs of enemy fighters, they swing their turrets from side to side. Behind the pilot, the flight engineer continues to monitor his instrument panel, checking fuel states, oil temperatures and pressures, and cross-feeding petrol when necessary. Meanwhile, the

wireless operator tunes his set to listen in to the broadcast winds which come through at regular intervals. These are an average taken at group headquarters from meteorological data received from selected aircraft on the raid, and then rebroadcast to all aircraft to enable them to navigate using the same wind speeds and directions. The navigator tunes the brilliance knob on his Gee set to get a comfortable picture, while down in the nose the bomb-aimer keeps a lookout for the enemy coast ahead, and the first puffs of flak coming up to greet them. Passing through the 5,000ft height band, the order comes from the pilot to switch on oxygen.

After the enemy coast has been crossed, the navigator gives the pilot a new course to steer that will take them to the target, with an estimated time of arrival. It is about 30 to 40 minutes' flying time from the Dutch coast to the Ruhr, but more than two hours to a more distant target like Berlin. The gently waving fingers of searchlights continue to probe the night sky as the bomber drones on its course to the target.

A strong 'Mandrel' screen keeps the Germans guessing where the bombers will finally strike and a special 'Window' force drops bundles of metal foil strips to swamp the enemy radar screens with false returns. The aim is to put the enemy fighter and flak controllers off their stroke. Aircraft of the Pathfinder Force are timed to drop coloured route and target markers just before the arrival of the main force. On a typical raid against a target in the Ruhr in late 1944 involving a main force drawn from three heavy bomber groups, plus Pathfinders, the whole raid is timed to last just 14 minutes with 553 bombers being streamed over the target during this time.

Ahead, the heavy flak opens up with a vengeance as the Pathfinders begin to mark the target with the aid of H2S – route markers in green and target markers in red. As the pilot turns on to the final leg to the target, the bomb-aimer goes down into the nose to check his bombsight and fusing panel; the engineer moves beyond the cockpit bulkhead to check the master fuel cocks; the wireless operator pushes bundles of Window down the flare chute at regular intervals to add to the confusion of enemy radar operators down

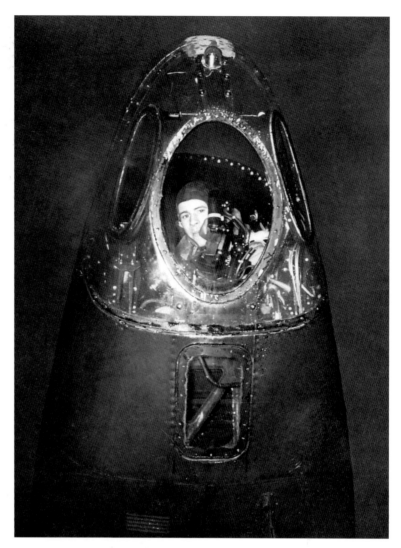

ABOVE Bomb-aimer's view: the optically flat and clear panel in the nose cone of a Halifax B Mk III of 425 (Alouette) Squadron in 1944. *(Pierre Lagacé)*

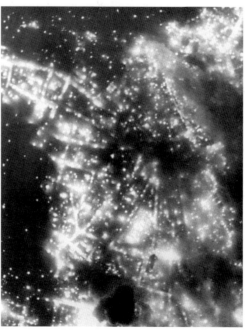

LEFT Looking into hell. A German city burns.

ABOVE Four miles below the bomber stream, on the streets of central Berlin civilians run to escape the fires on Jerusalemer Straße in the Mitte district in 1944. (BA 183-J30142)

RIGHT The calm, reassuring voice of the WAAF controller in the tower as a bomber entered the circuit was a welcome sound to the ears of returning crews. This is flying control in Tempsford tower in 1945. (Connie Annis via Ken Merrick)

BELOW Home is the airman (with apologies to Robert Louis Stevenson) as a 10 Squadron Halifax B Mk II touches down at Melbourne, Yorkshire.

below; the pilot calls up to the gunners to keep their eyes peeled for enemy fighters; and the navigator's voice comes over the intercom to give the pilot the ETA on target. Each member of the crew is busy as the procession of aircraft begins its final run-in to the target.

With the bomb doors now open, the pilot holds the bomber on a straight and level course for its bombing run. Beneath, the target area is a sea of flame, punctuated by the red and green target markers dropped by the Pathfinders. Dozens of searchlight beams grope the sky, hoping to latch on to a bomber during its most vulnerable phase of the operation, so that the flak batteries below can get a bead on it and then attempt to blast it from the sky. The crew can hear the occasional dull thud of a shell bursting close by, and perhaps the clattering on the fuselage as pieces of spent shrapnel hit it.

The bomb-aimer directs the pilot with calm instructions of 'Left, left, steady, right a bit. Hold it there, left a bit. Bombs gone!' The aircraft seems to rear up in the sky, relieved of her heavy cargo of bombs, but the pilot needs to fly straight and level for another 30 seconds to enable the aiming-point photograph to be taken. Without it their operation will not count towards their tour of 30 operations. With the enemy defences now well awakened and throwing all they can at the slowly moving bomber stream overhead, most crews see this as the longest 30 seconds of their lives. Before they can leave the target area, the bomb-aimer checks on his panel for signs of any bomb hang-ups, which could mean another run over the target, but if all is well the bomb doors are closed and they turn for home.

Vigilance is still required on the long haul back across blacked-out Europe to the enemy coast. Flak and searchlights are still active and German night-fighters loiter for the unwary crew who have let down their guard now that the tension of the bomb run has passed, or the one that has lost its way from the relative safety of the bomber stream. Some, even, have been shot down on the home straight by enemy intruders lurking in the circuit at their base as they prepare to land.

Once across the enemy coast and over the sea, the navigator picks up his Gee lattice line and they join the procession that will lead

LEFT In the early hours of 15 January 1944, this unidentified Lancaster crew have just returned from ops to Brunswick and are being debriefed by the squadron intelligence officer. Out of the 496 Lancasters and two Halifaxes dispatched, 38 Lancasters failed to return, representing an unsustainably high loss rate of 7.6% of the force. *Zahme Sau* night-fighters (see page 128) infiltrated the bomber stream and in a running battle were responsible for most of the losses. *(Popperfoto/ Getty Images)*

to home. In a short while, 50 miles from the English coast, the pilot calls up on VHF and identifies his aircraft. Once over England, the crew look out below for the Pundit beacon that flashes in Morse code the identification letters of their home airfield. A call is then made to the control tower asking for permission to join the circuit and land.

Once safely back on the ground, the engines are throttled back for the first time in more than six hours, the white-hot exhausts making a reassuring crackle, and the bomber is marshalled to its dispersal. The engines are finally shut down and the exhausted crew climb out of their aircraft and are taken by crew bus to the briefing room

where they are dropped off for interrogation by the station intelligence staff. They answer a lengthy questionnaire giving details of the operation they have just flown. A welcome mug of tea or coffee, laced with rum, and a much-needed cigarette help the crew to unwind before interrogation is completed and they return their flying kit to the stores and lockers before retiring to their billets for a well-earned sleep.

For the aircrews, the whole process starts again the following evening, but for the squadron ground staff responsible for aircraft servicing, fault rectification and battle damage assessment and repair, their work will begin in a few hours' time.

LEFT Aftermath. The 515ft-tall twin spires of the city's Cathedral Church of St Peter pierce the sky above the gutted streets of Cologne in this photograph taken on 24 April 1945. *(US National Archives)*

'So far as I could see, we should go on flying until we were killed and there wasn't any point in teasing oneself with the prospect of ultimate safety.'

Miles Tripp, Lancaster bomb-aimer, 218 Squadron, 1944–45.

Chapter Eleven

Failed to return

RAF Bomber Command experienced among the highest casualties of any fighting force on all sides in the Second World War. The only other combat arm that suffered more was the German U-boat service during the Battle of the Atlantic. Some 47,000 bomber aircrew were killed on operations and a further 8,000 died during training or in flying accidents.

OPPOSITE The fate of so many RAF bombers: a Luftwaffe Feldwebel stands guard over the wreckage of 77 Squadron's Halifax Mk II, JB847, in woodland at the village of Moyvillers near Estrées Saint Denis in northern France. Skippered by 23-year-old Flt Lt Julien Balley, the bomber was homeward-bound from Duisburg when it passed through a *Himmelbett* box and was shot down by a patrolling Bf 110 night-fighter flown by Ofw Kurt Karsten of 7./NJG 4 at 00.10hrs on 9 April 1943. All the crew were killed except for the bomb-aimer, Plt Off Roland Wilson, who managed to bale out. *(Interfoto/Alamy Stock photo)*

ABOVE Somewhere in Germany: the broken-off tail section of an unidentified Lancaster lies where it fell in a wooded gorge in the Eifel hills near Cochem on the River Mosel. The original photograph is dated 21 September 1942. *(BA Bild 146-1975-062-30)*

COPY.   No. 460 Squadron R.A.A.F.,
                              R.A.F. Station,
                              Breighton,
                              Bubwith,
                              E. Yorkshire.

REF. 460S/S.8/19/Air.   5th June, 1942.

Dear Mr. Bourke,

    It is with very deep regret that I have to confirm the sad news that your son, Flight Lieutenant Tom H. Bourke is missing as a result of operations.

    Your son was the Captain of an aircraft which left base on the night of the 29th May, 1942 to attack targets in the Gennevilliers area of Occupied France, but since take-off nothing has been heard of either the aircraft or the crew.

    I cannot stress too deeply how much I feel the loss of Tom, who was one of my finest Captains and one who also was fitting himself for the position of second in command of one of the Flights. He was exceedingly popular in the mess and with all with whom he came into contact during the execution of his duties, which were always carried out in a most efficient manner. I sincerely hope that he and the rest of the crew are safe although perhaps prisoners of war, as I could rely upon him to get out of a tight corner, and I know that this wish is shared by all his comrades.

    The personal items of Tom's kit have been collected and will be forwarded to you in the near future, that is, as soon as the estate has been settled, via the Central Depository, Colnbrook, Slough, Bucks.

    If there is anything I can do to help you or to relieve you in your present time of deepest anxiety please do not hesitate to communicate with me and I will do all that I possibly can.

    On behalf of Tom's friends and, on behalf of all the Officers and men of the Squadron, I extend to you our very heartfelt sympathy and trust that the good news will soon be forthcoming.

                    Yours sincerely,

                    A. Hubbard
                              W/Cr
                              Officer Commanding.

Mr. Bourke,
T & G Building,
King William Street,
ADELAIDE.

The sight of the telegram boy walking up the garden path followed by a rat-a-tat at the front door was dreaded by every Second World War household with a family member in the armed forces, for he was usually the bearer of bad news. For families with sons, husbands or fathers who were aircrew in Bomber Command the telegram message became seared into their memories – 'Regret to inform you that your son Flying Officer John Smith is reported to be missing as the result of air operations on 26 March 1944. Stop. Any further information received will be immediately conveyed to you. Stop. Letter will follow. Air Ministry.'

From that moment a family's life changed utterly, hoping against hope that their loved one was safe or, at best, that he'd become a prisoner of war. The uncertainty that came from not knowing – holding out for a shred of reassurance that everything would be all right – was often too much to bear. For the lucky survivors from a crew, a message might be relayed via the International Red Cross informing their families that they were PoWs, but for everyone else where there was no news, the pain continued. After a period of time the Air Ministry would write to say that in the absence of any further information their loved one's death had been 'presumed for official purposes'. Families were still desperate for answers and some closure, as we would call it today.

When an aircraft failed to return from operations there were at least four possible outcomes for those crewmembers who had been posted missing: they may have been shot down and killed, with their mortal remains recovered by the Germans and buried at a cemetery near to where they fell; some who survived became prisoners of war, while others evaded capture and went on the run from the Germans with the help of one of the escape lines in occupied

LEFT An official letter from the squadron commander followed an initial telegram that confirmed a son, brother, husband or father was missing as a result of operations. It was a difficult balance to strike between showing concern for the family while telling them about practical matters including the disposal of personal items.
(National Archives of Australia)

Europe, eventually making their way to safety; or they might simply have been lost without trace on land or over the sea, with no known grave. Later, their names along with 20,000 others who had no known graves would be inscribed on the imposing Commonwealth Air Forces Memorial to the missing at Runnymede in Surrey, overlooking the water meadows of the River Thames.

By the end of the war in Europe some 42,000 aircrew whose aircraft had crashed behind enemy lines were still listed as missing without a trace. The fate of aircraft and crews that crashed in the UK, whether on training flights or when setting off on or returning from operations, was easier to determine, although some high-ground crashes in places like the Scottish Highlands or the Lake District could lay undiscovered for some time.

'The Air Ministry regrets'

Official casualty notification

At the outbreak of war the Air Ministry's existing system for casualty notification was handled by the Casualty Branch, S7d (a branch of Secretarial Division S7), but it was quickly overwhelmed with the sudden increase in aircrew casualties. Its role was to collate and pass on information to the RAF and next of kin, but when compared to what came later it was an amateur activity relying on information gleaned from the

RIGHT Evader: air gunner Len Manning was on only his third op when his 57 Squadron Lancaster (JB318) was shot down by a night-fighter on a raid to the railway yards at Revigny-sur-Ornain on 18/19 July 1944. Here, he poses for the camera (second from left) with his rescuers Louisette Beaujard (second from right) and her mother (far left). *(Len Manning)*

RIGHT Ditcher: this Stirling was put down in the sea by its crew near the tiny island of Siø in the Danish South Funen archipelago between Tåsinge and Langeland. It is possibly 218 Squadron's HA-E/R9190, which made a successful crash-landing there while on a 'gardening' sortie in the area codenamed 'Geranium' (Swindemünde, Germany) on 11/12 October 1942. R9190 had only been on the squadron since 16 September.

LEFT After four months of anguished waiting for news, the wife of Mosquito navigator Flg Off Cecil Arrieta received this short letter from P4 (Cas) informing her that her husband was a prisoner of war. *(Michael Arrieta)*

> Tel. No.:
> GERRARD 9234, Ext.
> Correspondence on the subject of this letter should be addressed to
> THE UNDER-SECRETARY OF STATE,
> AIR MINISTRY (P.4 (Cas.)),
> and should quote the reference
> P.424893/2/P.4.P/W.B.5.
>
> Your Ref.
>
> AIR MINISTRY,
> 73-77, OXFORD STREET,
> LONDON, W.I.
>
> 21st February, 1945
>
> Madam,
>
> I am directed to inform you that the following message from your husband, 155919 Flying Officer C.M. Arrieta, D.F.M., was broadcast from Germany on February 16th.
>
> "My dearest Monica,
>
> I am in Stalag Luft 1. Please send chocolate and other things. Give my love to Michael.
>
> Love,
>
> Cecil."
>
> I am, Madam,
> Your obedient Servant,
>
> *E.F. Clark*
>
> for Director of Personal Services.
>
> Mrs. C.M. Arrieta,
> 71 Burnham Road,
> Fleetville,
> St. Albans,
> Herts.

LEFT London's Oxford Street of the 21st century is much changed from the scene of the 1940s. The building that once housed the offices of Air Ministry P4 (Cas) at Nos 73–77 has long since been swept away and replaced by this shiny steel and glass temple to retail.

BBC and the press. The Air Ministry recognised that the system was not fit for purpose and moved quickly to reform its procedures.

On 16 October 1939 a dedicated new casualty branch was formed, P4 (Cas), with sole concern for the management of officer casualties and the main responsibility for those of other ranks (in conjunction with the RAF record office in Gloucester). It was housed in London, initially at Adastral House on Kingsway, but was relocated in late 1942 to 73–77 Oxford Street, with offices situated above a large furniture department store.

The men and women who staffed P4 (Cas) had a difficult and at times unpleasant job to do that required tact and sensitivity. In essence, their task was to record details of new casualties, inform the next of kin and then deal with the paperwork for funerals and settlement of estates. P4 (Cas) had an 'open-door' policy for relatives of a man who was missing and who demanded to know more, which meant that individuals could write, telephone or visit the branch in person at any time.

Initially no consideration had been given to investigating the cases of missing aircrew whose numbers increased steeply as Bomber Command's offensive gathered pace – they were euphemistically referred to in the language of the day as 'failed to return'. To avoid the conflicting requirements of the regular administrative work of P4 (Cas) and that of the detailed and time-consuming investigations into missing aircrew, a new section was set up at the beginning of 1942 to manage these cases. This was the Missing Research Section (MRS) of P4 (Cas), which was led by Flt Lt A.P. Le M. Sinkinson, a middle-aged son of the Raj (his civil servant father was Financial Secretary to the Government of Bengal) who had initially served with the Army in France during the First World War.

Despite working with limited resources and a small staff, Sinkinson and the MRS soon held

BELOW This 158 Squadron air gunner, whose Halifax (HR753) was shot down by Bremen's flak en route to Berlin on 27 March 1943, appears dazed as his Luftwaffe captors fire questions at him. He has been taken to what looks like the headquarters of a flak division inside a *Flakturm* (Flak tower). Behind the officers on the right is a grid map showing fighter boxes of the Kammhuber Line. He is probably safer here than outside on the streets, where summary justice at the hands of the mob could spell a swift and brutal end. Five of the crew managed to bale out before HR753 crashed on to Bremen's central railway station.

a fine reputation for tracking down missing RAF aircrew. Their tasks included confirming the date and location of death, finding a grave, identifying an airman through his personal effects and tracing any eyewitnesses to the incident that led to his death.

ABOVE Stalag Luft III at Sagan in Poland achieved notoriety in 1944 when 53 recaptured RAF escapers were murdered by the Gestapo. It later became the setting for the film *The Great Escape* (1963) based on Paul Brickhill's best-selling book of the same name. Pictured in about 1942, the camp was run by the Luftwaffe for captured airmen until its liberation on 29 April 1945. *(Hulton Archive/Getty Images)*

'For you the war is over'

The prisoner of war experience

Some 10,541 Bomber Command aircrew (the equivalent of more than 1,500 RAF heavy bomber crews) became unwilling guests of the Third Reich in Germany during the Second World War. These prisoners of war (POWs) were incarcerated in more than 20 camps spread across Germany and Poland, the most famous being Stalag Luft III at Sagan in eastern Silesia (the *Great Escape* camp), and Oflag 4C inside the medieval Colditz castle near Leipzig – the supposedly secure camp for serial escapers. Stalag Luft camps were specifically intended for RAF aircrew and were administered by the Luftwaffe.

Durchgangslager der Luftwaffe (abbreviated to *Dulag Luft*) at Oberursel, some 8 miles north of Frankfurt-am-Main, was the main interrogation centre and transit camp for captured aircrew. At its peak it housed some 20,000 Allied

LEFT Light Night Striking Force aircrew Flg Offs Ken King and Cecil Arrieta of 128 Squadron were flying a sortie to Berlin on 30 September/1 October 1944 when their Mosquito (Mk XX, KB199) took a hit from flak. They struggled to make it to friendly territory but ran out of luck and crash-landed in countryside near Hamm. King was killed, but Arrieta (illustrated) survived with serious injuries. He was cared for by nuns until transferred to a POW camp two months later. *(Michael Arrieta)*

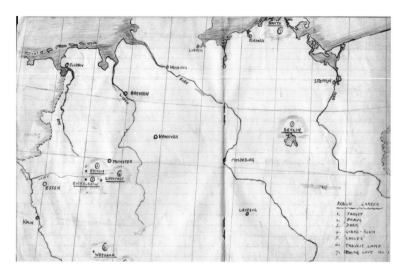

ABOVE A hand-drawn map from Cecil Arrieta's PoW journal showing the location of places and events – from their target Berlin, to the crew's crash-landing at Beckum, near Hamm, and Arrieta's eventual arrival in Stalag Luft I, Barth. *(Michael Arrieta)*

aircrew POWs. However, by autumn 1943 it was used only for interrogation and prisoners were no longer held there pending their move to a permanent camp. To cope with the large numbers of aircrew captured as the bomber offensive intensified, a new transit camp was built at Wetzlar, 37 miles north of Frankfurt. Between 1,000 and 2,000 airmen were kept there during any one month, although most only stayed for a few days before they were transferred to their permanent camps.

Initially, life in German POW war camps was tolerable, notwithstanding food shortages, lack of warmth in the winter and the terrible boredom of confinement miles from home. Treatment of prisoners was largely in accord with the terms of the Geneva Convention, but when the fortunes of war turned against Germany in 1943 the treatment of prisoners began to worsen. Towards the end of the war when the Russians were closing in from the east, the Germans decided to move occupants of certain camps further west to prevent their liberation by the Russians. Some 30,000 airmen prisoners were force-marched west across Poland and into Germany in a 500-mile 'long march' during January and February 1945, in freezing winter conditions with little in the way of food or warm clothing. Many froze to death or died from hunger, exhaustion and frostbite.

As the ragged columns of exhausted 'Kriegies' reached the western side of Germany, some met up with the advancing British and American armies, but others who were not so lucky were used as human shields by the Germans in attempts to save their own skins.

Missing Research and Enquiry Service (MRES)

Prior to 1944 all missing research enquiries had been undertaken from London, but with D-Day on 6 June 1944 came the gradual liberation of Europe, which meant search teams were able to operate in the field for the first time. As the Allied armies moved deeper into the Continent, setting free large areas of enemy-held territory, the Missing Research Section (MRS) came into its own.

In December 1944 the RAF and Dominion Air Forces' Missing Research and Enquiry Service (MRES) was created 'for the purpose of research and enquiry, in liberated territories and those occupied by Allied forces, into the circumstances of air crews reported missing of whom no previous trace has been found. The service will also endeavour to obtain additional information to supplement that already received.'

In the New Year eight MRSs were established across western Europe, but such was the scale of the task confronting the MRES that in July 1945 it was decided to expand the organisation even further. By April 1946 the eight MRSs had been superseded by four larger Missing Research and Enquiry Units (MREUs) that covered western and central Europe (later, a fifth MREU was created in Italy to conduct investigations in southern Europe and the Mediterranean).

Although the MREUs were attached for administrative purposes to RAF formations in the country or region in which they operated, the MRES remained under direction from London of the Air Ministry's Director of Personal Services and its work was coordinated by P4 (Cas).

Following the disbandment of the MRES on 30 September 1949 the casualty branch continued to be responsible for all aspects of research into those still listed as missing and a small number of Missing Research and Enquiry Liaison Staffs (MRELS) posts remained after this date.

CAUSE OF LOSSES

In late 1941, Bomber Command's Operational Research Section (ORS) estimated bomber aircraft losses to have been due to a number of factors. It was considered that all losses to fighters en route and losses to flak unaided by searchlights were attributable to ground-controlled radar.

	% of missing	% of total wastage (aircraft missing and written off)
Flak at target	30% (⅔ while held in searchlights)	20%
Flak en route	15% (½ while held in searchlights)	10%
Fighter at target	5% (½ while held in searchlights)	3%
Fighter en route	40% (¼ while held in searchlights)	26%
Not due to enemy action	10%	41% (inc. non-operational wastage)

(Source: 'Operational Research in Bomber Command', p. 388, Air Historical Branch, RAF.)

Finding the fallen

The task of tracing missing aircraft and their crews overseas was compounded by a number of factors. Navigation errors, equipment faults, changes in the weather or in wind direction, could all cause individual aircraft or entire bomber streams to stray off their flight plan and scatter over a wide area. Even with knowledge of the route and the objective, a simple search along the track of the aircraft might yield nothing and be a waste of time.

Much of the physical evidence recovered from bomber crash sites in Europe by the MRSs was fragmentary and had to be painstakingly pieced

BELOW Three dead crewmen from a Halifax of 78 Squadron have been laid out beside the wreckage of their aircraft. They were shot down by flak near Delmenhorst on their way to bomb Hamburg on 3 February 1943. All are without their flying boots and gloves. These may have been taken as souvenirs by the Germans, or if the aircraft had exploded in mid-air the men might have lost them during their fall to earth. Whatever the story, it is clear that the crew were not able to bale out.

RIGHT Relatives of missing aircrew received advice from the Air Ministry about what was being done to trace their loved ones.

ADVICE TO THE RELATIVE OF A MAN WHO IS MISSING

In view of the official notification that your relative is missing, you will naturally wish to hear what is being done to trace him.

The Service Departments make every endeavour to discover the fate of missing men, and draw upon all likely sources of information about them.

A man who is missing after an engagement may possibly be a prisoner of war. Continuous efforts are made to speed up the machinery whereby the names and camp addresses of prisoners of war can reach this country. The official means is by lists of names prepared by the enemy Government. These lists take some time to compile, especially if there is a long journey from the place of capture to a prisoners of war camp. Consequently "capture cards" filled in by the prisoners themselves soon after capture and sent home to their relatives are often the first news received in this country that a man is a prisoner of war. That is why you are asked in the accompanying letter to forward at once any card or letter you may receive, if it is the first news you have had.

Even if no news is received that a missing man is a prisoner of war, endeavours to trace him do not cease. Enquiries are pursued not only among those who were serving with him, but also through diplomatic channels and the International Red Cross Committee at Geneva.

The moment reliable news is obtained from any of these sources it is sent to the Service Department concerned. They will pass the news on to you at once, if they are satisfied that it is reliable. It would be cruel to raise false hopes, such as may well be raised if you listen to one other possible channel of news, namely, the enemy's broadcasts. These are listened to by official listeners, working continuously night and day. The few names of prisoners given by enemy announcers are carefully checked. They are often misleading, and this is not surprising, for the object of the inclusion of prisoners' names in these broadcasts is not to help the relatives of prisoners, but to induce British listeners to hear some tale which otherwise they could not be made to hear. The only advantage of listening to these broadcasts is an advantage to the enemy.

The official listeners can never miss any name included in an enemy broadcast. They pass every name on to the Service Department concerned. There every name is checked, and in every case where a name can be verified, the news is sent direct to the relatives.

There is, therefore, a complete official service designed to secure for you and to tell you all discoverable news about your relative. This official service is also a very human service, which well understands the anxiety of relatives and will spare no effort to relieve it.

(18997) 20217/M.595 20,000 7/43 K.H.K. **Gp. 8/8**

---

together. Aircraft crashes left very little in the way of identifiable wreckage and the bodies of crews often remained inside their aircraft where they fell. Surface wreckage strewn across the landscape was invariably gathered up by salvage teams and the aluminium recycled. Occasionally, if the bodies of individuals had been recovered, they were sometimes buried with full military honours by the Germans, but more often than not they were simply left inside the wreckage and covered over with earth, which is where they remained – lost and unidentified.

Bodies suffered severe trauma resulting from a high-speed crash into the ground and quite often the remains were mutilated and tangled together, making individual identification difficult. Forensic pathology was in its infancy in the 1940s and the capability to unravel the hidden secrets contained in DNA was 50 years in the future.

It was vital that the research teams carried out their work as thoroughly and as expeditiously as possible. Not only was it necessary to dig out wreckage and exhume human remains for examination, but it was also important to track down and interview local residents in good time before they either forgot the events or lost any interest in helping.

Dossiers were opened by MRES on all missing aircraft and every piece of information received, no matter how small or seemingly insignificant, was filed away for future reference. To this was added any information received from intelligence sources such as agents in the field, or from the various resistance organisations in occupied Europe. Each file was allocated a case number prefixed with the initial letter of the country over which the aircraft was presumed lost – F for France, G for Germany, etc.

Identifying missing aircrew

The MRES used a number of methods to help in identifying missing aircrew. These are the main ones they employed.

German *Totenlisten* – these casualty lists (*Totenlisten* means 'death lists') were compiled on a regular basis by the Germans and passed through to the Air Ministry via the International Red Cross. They were not always reliable and often contained errors of transcription. The Red Cross organisations in individual countries also sent casualty information to Britain.

Aircraft serial numbers and parts – aircraft

components, airframe and equipment part numbers, engine makers' plates and serial numbers could – and did – yield a great deal of information. Through liaison with the manufacturers and by careful cross-referencing of these details with documentary records it was possible to positively identify any aircraft type and its individual identity, and then by referring to squadron and Air Ministry casualty records link it to a particular crew who were flying in it when it went missing.

Pathology – following the exhumation of a casualty a basic physical description would be taken of the body including its condition – for example, if it was burned, or the absence of body parts; its height, build and hair colour were noted; a dental chart was completed (although it was only the Dominion air forces that kept accurate dental records); the presence and condition of fingers and hands were recorded, and the presence of any wounds that might point to a probable cause of death. Details of the type of soil in which the casualty was buried were also recorded, which might be compared with other information obtained from the body in order to establish a possible date of death.

Personal effects – these were obtained from

a body or the surrounding soil after exhumation and might include uniform fragments. The type and colour of cloth could often reveal whether the owner was RAF, Australian or South African Air Force (for example, Royal Australian Air Force uniforms were dark blue); rank insignia, aircrew trade badges, tunic and battledress buttons also told their own stories; identity tags ('dog tags'), wrist watches, items of jewellery like signet rings or bracelets (which were sometimes engraved with initials or inscriptions) could also disclose personal information.

Laundry labels – the humble laundry label sewn into clothing bearing the initials or name of an individual became one of the surest guides to the identity of its wearer. Many thousands of missing aircrew were identified thanks to this simple but conclusive means. Most aircrew had

BELOW In remembrance: Flt Lt Harold Hornibrook RAAF, his rear gunner Flt Sgt Graham McLeod RAAF and mid-upper Sgt Lawrence Chesson RAFVR were all killed when their 158 Squadron Halifax (HR979) was downed by a night-fighter near Berlin on 24 August 1943 – the first raid in the bomber Battle of Berlin. They were buried by the Germans in an unmarked collective grave in Zehdenick Cemetery 32 miles north of the German capital before their reburial in 1947 at the Berlin 1939–1945 War Cemetery. Four other crewmembers survived to become POWs. *(Shutterstock)*

The case of an Australian Wellington bomber shot down over Paris on 30 May 1942 during a raid on the Gnome-Rhône aero engine factory at Gennevilliers was investigated in 1946 by the RAF Missing Research and Enquiry Unit's No 3 Section based in the French capital.

No 460 (RAAF) Squadron's Wellington Mk IV, Z1388, was captained by 29-year-old Flt Lt Tom Bourke RAAF from Point Piper, Sydney. It was one of 77 aircraft briefed that night for the raid on Gennevilliers. On the bomber's first run over the target, the rear gunner, Sgt Gratley

Holborow, was wounded in the leg by shrapnel from flak. While Bourke was making a second run-in at 3,000ft, the Wellington took a direct hit. The aircraft exploded and split in half at about 02.30hrs with pieces falling about 300yd apart near Colombes on the Île Marante on the left bank of the River Seine.

Miraculously, Holborow was thrown clear from his turret by the explosion and parachuted to the ground. He was captured and became a POW. His four crewmates probably died instantly in the explosion and their bodies were later found by the Germans lying among the main wreckage. They had not been burned and were 'in fair condition' according to the MREU report. Official photographs taken of the bodies at the time bear this out.

The Germans kept a close guard of the site and placed the bodies of Flt Lt Tom Bourke, Plt Off W.M. Murphy, Sgt R.P. Davis and Sgt B.G.P. Balleine into simple wooden coffins before taking them for burial at Viroflay New Cemetery a few miles away near Versailles.

The four airmen were laid to rest in a dignified Christian burial ceremony with full honours on the Sunday evening following the raid. The committal was conducted by the Curé of Viroflay and the Germans supplied an honour guard of an officer and a detachment of soldiers. Wreaths were placed on the graves by the Germans, and on the same night some local inhabitants laid their own floral tributes despite orders to the contrary from the German authorities. Sadly, this respect shown to fallen foes was not always to be the case as the war progressed.

A letter from P4 (Cas) in London to the Department of Air in Melbourne, Australia, stated the following:

German Totenliste 81 reports that according to a statement made by Sgt Holborow, who is a prisoner of war, the four remaining members of the crew were killed on 30th

BELOW On 30 May 1942 a German photographer recorded the body of Flt Lt Tom Bourke RAAF where he fell on the Île Marante in the Parisian suburb of Colombes. *(Interfoto/Alamy Stock photo)*

LEFT The fully clothed body of one of Bourke's fellow Australian crewmembers is carefully placed inside a simple wooden coffin by Luftwaffe airmen. *(Interfoto/Alamy Stock photo)*

May 1942. In view of the evidence and the lapse of time, action has been taken to presume, for official purposes, that the death of these four occurred on that date.

The next of kin were informed in a letter dated 23 December, which must have been devastating news for them, particularly at Christmas. One can only imagine their grief.

After the war had ended, the MRES were instructed to investigate the burials in Viroflay New Communal Cemetery because it had not been possible to locate graves for wireless operator Sgt R.P. Davis or front gunner Sgt B.G.P. Balleine. An exhumation was carried out on Graves 36 and 37 by MRES's No 3 Section staff in order to ascertain individual identification.

Here is an extract from the report made on 26 June 1946 by the RAF MRES Search Officer, Flt Lt H.J. Prior. Of interest are the methods of identification – laundry label, personal name tag, Australian battledress (distinctive dark blue in contrast to the RAF's blue-grey), and wireless operator's brevet:

I was present at the exhumation at Viroflay and graves thirty-six (36) and thirty-nine (39) contained the bodies of two Australians. Also graves thirty-seven (37) and thirty-eight (38) contain two identified Australians, namely Bourke and Murphy from [the above] crew.

On the collar of the body in grave thirty-six (36) the name BALLEINE, B.G.P. was written in ink and clearly visible.

In grave thirty-nine (39) a black sock bearing the name Davis, R.P. written on a piece of tape was clearly visible. He was also a wireless operator and wearing Australian battledress.

FINDINGS: I am certain the four members of this crew are buried in the New Cemetery Viroflay and in the following graves:

MILITARY PLOT	ROW 14	
Grave 36	Aus 407280	Sgt Balleine, B.G.P.
Grave 37	Aus 407192	F/O Bourke, T.H.
Grave 38	Aus 404353	P/O Murphy, W.M.
Grave 39	Aus 407285	Sgt Davis, R.P.

their clothing laundered using facilities on the airfield. With the help of the laundry industry the MRES compiled a database of label designs and reference numbers against which scraps of labels bearing numbers that were recovered with human remains from crash or burial sites could be cross-referenced.

Intelligence sources – debriefing of aircrews after returning from a raid could sometimes give insights into the location and circumstances of the loss of a particular aircraft – for example, if it was seen to explode in mid-air, or seen to fall out of the sky and crash, or collide in mid-air with another aircraft.

Post war – if, after the war, a body was recovered by the MRES and positively identified, then the individual would be reclassified from 'missing in action' to 'killed in action' and the Commonwealth War Graves Commission (CWGC) informed. Action would then be taken to reinter the body in a CWGC cemetery near to where they fell and an official headstone would be commissioned.

As a point of interest, British policy was to bury their fallen in the country where they died, but the Americans took a different approach to their missing servicemen. The families of casualties could claim the bodies of their loved ones for repatriation to the United States.

War crimes against downed aircrew

As the war progressed, Allied bombers rained ever greater death and destruction on Germany by day and by night, with the civilian population bearing the brunt. In the spring of 1944 Hitler decreed that enemy airmen shot down over Germany should no longer be protected by the Wehrmacht against angry civilians and he actively encouraged the killing of captured aircrew. With the exception of the head of the SS, Heinrich Himmler, and certain of his subordinates, there was a general reluctance among commanders of the regular armed forces to implement Hitler's orders against Allied airmen and other Allied prisoners of war, possibly for fear of what might happen to German POWs in Allied hands.

The Nazi state continued to push an extensive domestic propaganda campaign concerning 'Terrorfliegers' (as they called Allied bomber crews) and encouraged the populace to vent their anger against downed airmen. Hitler's propaganda minister, Josef Goebbels, published a front-page editorial in the 27 May 1944 issue of *Völkischer Beobachter*, stating that Anglo-American air attacks over Germany were no longer warfare, but murder – pure and simple – and that it was indefensible to use German police and soldiers to protect the lives of shot-down enemy pilots against the 'sorely tried population'. A few days later Martin Bormann, Hitler's closest associate, issued a memorandum admitting that British and American airmen had been lynched by the Germans: 'Several instances have occurred where members of crews of such aircraft, who have bailed out or who have made forced landings, were lynched on the spot immediately after capture by the populace, which was incensed to the highest degree.'

Certainly, from D-Day, 6 June 1944 onwards, as the tide of war turned against the Germans, aircrew shot down over Germany faced the ever-increasing possibility of abuse or death at the hands of baying mobs. This meting-out of summary violence was not altogether a surprise given the growing devastation of German cities, the de-housing of thousands of city dwellers and the resulting anger from relatives of those who had died through Allied bombing.

By the summer, confirmed reports of hangings, shootings and beatings to death of Allied airmen captured by angry civilians and police had grown so much that the US government cautioned the Germans through Switzerland that the atrocities must cease. Their reply was that the reports were exaggerated and in every case the people acted in self-defence.

The truth was that ordinary German citizens took the law into their own hands if they could capture downed aircrew, RAF or American, stringing them up from lamp posts, beating them to death or shooting them from close range, safe in the knowledge that they would never be brought to book by officialdom for their avenging brutality.

One such case of summary execution took place on 25 March 1945 and involved a Canadian Halifax crew. No 415 Squadron's Halifax Mk III, MZ907, captained by Flg Off J.R. McCollum RCAF, was shot down by flak over Münster, crashing near the small town of Dorsten-Wulfen. The pilot and rear gunner died at their posts, but the navigator and wireless operator were taken prisoner. However, the mid-upper gunner, bomb-aimer and flight engineer were rounded up by German soldiers and attacked by a hostile crowd led by a local Nazi Party official, SA-Haupttruppführer Ferdinand Assmann. The three airmen escaped briefly from their attackers but their freedom was short-lived because they were caught again and savagely beaten. Standing with their hands in the air they were mocked by another local Nazi Party official, SA-Sturmführer Otto Wunderlich, before he shot and killed them in cold blood. The Canadians were buried in a bomb crater in the cemetery at Wulfen, but reinterred at Groesbeek War Cemetery after the war. In due course details of the murders were uncovered by the Allies and the perpetrators tracked down. Assmann was arrested by the British in Bückeburg and is said to have hanged himself in prison. Wunderlich was also apprehended and he, too, took his own life in prison before he could be brought to trial.

In March 1945 one of Hitler's final directives was for all Allied bomber crews recently captured to be 'liquidated'. By the end of the war about one in every 20 captured RAF aircrew and one in every 80 Americans had been murdered 'in violation of the laws and usages of war' enshrined in the internationally recognised Lieber Code and the Hague Convention of 1907. Many of these crimes went unpunished, while others went undiscovered.

When the war was over, Allied military courts looked to bring justice to the chaotic world of postwar Europe with war crimes investigations and tribunals. Within months the showcase trials of prominent Nazi leaders were held in Nuremberg by an Allied war crimes court. However, out of the large number of trials held, only a very small percentage concerned prosecutions for aircrew lynchings and murders.

In 1948 the Allies handed responsibility for the prosecution of war criminals to the West German authorities, who proceeded to drop many of the cases as it was deemed not in the

LEFT War crime: Nazi Party official Hans Knab was responsible for ordering the killing of a wounded RAF bomber crewman after his Lancaster, ME864 from 57 Squadron, was shot down near Eutingen returning from a raid on Stuttgart on 28 July 1944. The injured flight engineer, Cyril Ludlow, was discovered by local police and taken to the town hall where he was murdered in cold blood by members of the SA on the orders of Kreisleiter Hans Knab (pictured).

spirit of reconciliation or of rebuilding the West German nation as a European bastion against Communism. Realpolitik had overtaken matters of justice and morality.

BELOW In June 1945 Allied Missing Research and Enquiry Teams from the RAF and the USAAF exhumed bodies from the graveyard at Eutingen. They discovered that one body (the one identified as Cyril Ludlow) had gunshot entrance and exit wounds in the head, which led to an investigation. Three of the surviving men accused of murdering Cyril Ludlow were traced, arrested and remanded; one committed suicide in his cell, while the other two were eventually acquitted through lack of evidence. Knab, however, had already been hanged for his involvement in the killings of Allied airmen elsewhere in Huchenfeld and Dillweißenstein. (www.ww2talk.com)

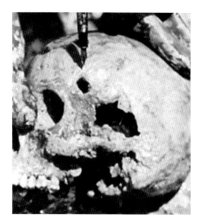

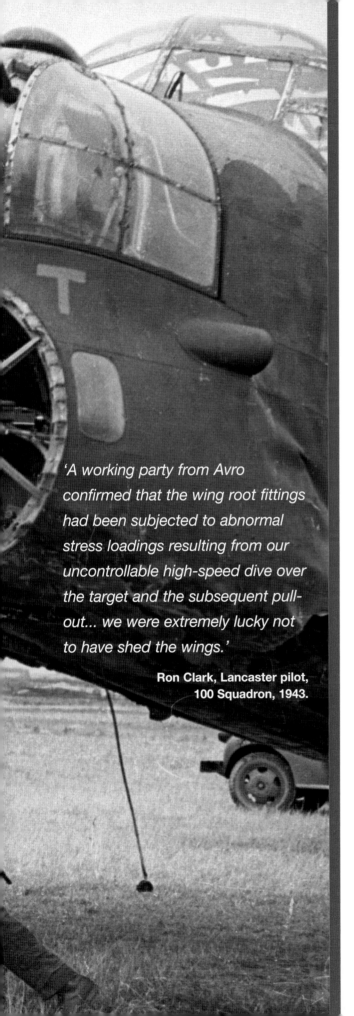

'A working party from Avro confirmed that the wing root fittings had been subjected to abnormal stress loadings resulting from our uncontrollable high-speed dive over the target and the subsequent pull-out... we were extremely lucky not to have shed the wings.'

Ron Clark, Lancaster pilot, 100 Squadron, 1943.

Chapter Twelve

'Ubendum, wemendum' – bomber repair and salvage

As the war progressed and Bomber Command's operational losses began to mount, particularly in 1943 and 1944, the need to return repaired aircraft to the squadrons as quickly as possible became essential. It was soon recognised that repairing battle-damaged bombers was a more efficient use of manufacturing resources than building new aircraft.

OPPOSITE Having suffered a wheels-up landing at Winthorpe on 18 September 1943, 1660 HCU's seriously battered Lancaster B Mk I, YW-T/R5845, is recovered by 58 MU personnel from Newark, who will take her to RAF Langar for repair. Amazingly, she was patched up and flew again in January 1944, seeing further service with 3 LFS, 90 Squadron, 1656 and 1657 CUs before finally retiring in September 1945.
(Leonard McCombe/Picture Post/Getty Images)

ABOVE Winged but not downed: this Whitley has suffered flak damage to its starboard outer wing and aileron, which could be repaired fairly easily and the aircraft returned again to service.

Before the Second World War there was no specialised aircraft repair organisation in Britain for RAF aircraft. Minor damage was often repairable by squadron ground staff on site, while major repairs and rebuilds were carried out by the manufacturers.

The rapid expansion of the RAF's front-line squadrons in the late 1930s, followed by the outbreak of war, saw the Air Ministry recognise the need for a separate repair organisation to allow manufacturers to get on with the vital job of building new aircraft. As attrition levels began to mount it was soon understood that valuable aircraft damaged in accidents or in combat should be either repaired or 'reduced to produce', thereby easing pressure on new production and enabling an aircraft's return to front-line service as quickly as possible.

The Civilian Repair Organisation (CRO) was formed by the Air Ministry in 1939 to coordinate the repair and overhaul of British military aircraft. In May 1940 control of the organisation was passed to Lord Beaverbrook's Ministry of Aircraft Production (MAP), which had been formed out of the Air Ministry's Development and Production organisation by the new premier, Winston Churchill. The CRO was supplemented by No 1 Metal and Produce Recovery Depot (MPRD) whose job was to collect aircraft and parts that were beyond repair, and scrap metal for reclamation.

As the war progressed it became a more efficient use of resources to harness industrial assets for repairs than to build new aircraft. The constant losses suffered by front-line bomber squadrons, particularly in the high-loss years of 1943 and 1944, meant there was unrelenting pressure on the CRO to return repaired aircraft to service. By using what spares and cannibalised parts were to hand, many bombers re-emerged as hybrids – some Lanc airframes acquired mixed Rolls-Royce-built and American Packard Merlins, while numerous other Lancs or Halifaxes became 'cut and shut' bombers, combining the wings and fuselage sections (and often much else) from more than one aircraft of the same type. In 1943, 55% of Lancasters supplied to the squadrons were hybrids, where new spares were combined with salvaged and repaired sections to produce complete airframes. Between 1942 and 1945 the materials used to repair 3,816 Lancasters would have made only 622 new-build aircraft, so the economics of 'make do and mend' made perfect sense and ensured that Bomber Harris's squadrons had enough aircraft to fight the war.

The average turnaround time taken for a Category B Lancaster (damaged beyond repair on site, but repairable at an RAF maintenance unit (MU) or contractor's works) to be reissued to a squadron was about six months, which the bomber groups considered to be too long. Repaired aircraft had to be to the latest modification standard when they were returned to use. Dozens of modification directives were issued monthly, which meant the standard could change almost daily as new ones were

---

ESTIMATED CAUSE OF DAMAGE TO NIGHT BOMBERS, FEBRUARY 1942–MAY 1945

Fighters
   1,728 (163 wrecked, 1,565 repairable)
Flak
   8,848 (151 wrecked, 8,697 repairable)
Not by enemy action
   3,159 (876 wrecked, 2,283 repairable)
From unknown causes
   43 (37 wrecked, 6 repairable)
Total damaged, night sorties
   13,778
(Source: Webster and Frankland, *The Strategic Air Offensive*, Vol IV)

introduced – requirements for the repositioning of equipment and strengthening of parts accounted for the issue of 800 modification leaflets by early 1944. It was clear how an aircraft could quickly become out of date by its modification standard during its time under repair, and consequently became unsuitable for operational use without further lengthy rectification. Special equipment like Gee and Oboe was sometimes fitted by the RAF on the bases, but from March 1944 H2S became a standard factory fitting for new aircraft and those under repair, which helped the situation.

However, when it came to engines the Air Ministry proved that repaired Merlins were statistically twice as unreliable as new engines, which suggested that the repair policy did not cover all items that required replacement. Because of the latter, a huge number of man hours were wasted owing to the need for more frequent engine changes.

Spares versus complete aircraft

In 1940 Churchill's crony Lord Beaverbrook had increased the production of complete aircraft at the expense of spares manufacture, but the former head of the Air Ministry's Development and Production organisation, Air Chief Marshal Wilfred Freeman, took the view that the production of spares in sufficient quantities was vital for the RAF and the aircraft and engine repair organisations. However, Beaverbrook's meddling in production planning

and his obsession with numbers and targets saw the MAP stagnate under his leadership. Eventually, Churchill was forced to concede that drastic reforms were needed at the MAP if the RAF was to continue to receive enough new and repaired aircraft for its many operational commitments, and Beaverbrook resigned in April 1941.

When Freeman eventually returned as the MAP's Chief Executive in October 1942, one of the first things he did was to ensure that resources were reorganised in favour of spares production. By 1944 some 18% of labour in British factories was for the manufacture of spare parts, which equated to more than 20 complete Lancasters and 110 Spitfires per month in that

ABOVE Avro workers repair a damaged Lancaster in the workshops at Langar. A surplus of certain sections often built up at repair depots. The centre section of the Lancaster was not as vulnerable as other parts and so a number of these were gratefully accepted back into the Avro production lines. *(Leonard McCombe/ Picture Post/Getty Images)*

LEFT Canadian-British press baron and politician Lord Beaverbrook was appointed Minister of Aircraft Production by Winston Churchill in May 1940. He was a controversial figure who was frequently at loggerheads with the Air Ministry because of his no-nonsense way of dealing with problems.

ABOVE Inside the English Electric shadow factory at Preston, Lancashire, where Handley Page Halifax fuselage sections wait to join the final assembly line.

ABOVE RIGHT The contribution made by Sir Wilfred Freeman to Britain's wartime aircraft production was immeasurable. *(Getty Images)*

year. The production of complete bombers and spare parts in 1944 was also particularly strong: as a proportion of all heavy bombers built, Lancaster output reached 60% in December, while for the full year the repair organisation fixed and returned 3,285 heavy bombers to RAF squadrons – largely thanks to Freeman's emphasis on the importance of spares production (in 1942 this figure had been only 711).

Repair options

Civilian firms that were mostly already engaged in building, maintaining and repairing military aircraft in Britain were issued with individual contracts from the CRO. They were supported by other companies from the engineering and cabinet making industries, the latter being especially important where repairs to the wooden de Havilland Mosquito were concerned.

The Air Ministry and MAP devised a three-tiered repair system: the first level (simple repairs and minor damage) was done by squadron ground staff; a second, where the aircraft had crashed, was undertaken by civilian work gangs who dealt with it on the spot; and the third when the repair needs were extensive or complex and the aircraft had to be returned to a CRO depot or the manufacturer's works for rectification.

Another option for an aircraft in need of minor repairs that could be completed quickly was for it to be flown in to a CRO contractor based at an airfield, where it was repaired and usually flown out the following day by the same pilot. This sort of quick 'while-you-wait' repair was known as a 'fly-in'.

For an aircraft that had crashed and was therefore immobile, the second and third of the options were applicable. If it was repairable on site then this was done; but if it was assessed as requiring more extensive repairs then its damaged airframe and wings were dismantled into their main constituent sections and transported on a 'Queen Mary' low-loader to

LEFT The most vulnerable part of most bombers was found to be the bomb doors, and so more of these were built than any other section. Being fitted underneath the fuselage they were regularly damaged in belly landings and constantly peppered with shrapnel in action. This is 196 Squadron's Wellington Mk X, HE165, which was damaged by flak in a minelaying operation on 14/15 March 1943. Her pilot made a successful belly landing at its base, Leconfield, in Yorkshire. Note the rubber air bags for lifting.

the aircraft repair depot. (The trailers were so named because their great length resembled that of the passenger liner the *Queen Mary.*)

Those aircraft that were not damaged but simply in need of a major overhaul were usually flown in to the repair depot from their units. First, guns and ammunition were removed and returned to the home airfields, then the airframes were disassembled and the sections farmed out to small workshops and garages in surrounding towns (and even villages) to be worked on. Here they were examined by a manufacturer's inspector (*eg*, from Avro or Handley Page) who assessed the amount of work needed to

bring the section up to the required standard for return to use. In turn, an inspector from the MAP's Aeronautical Inspection Directorate (AID) checked the assessment and, if satisfied, authorised work to proceed. Double-checking continued all the way through the repair process until the constituent parts of the aircraft were finally brought together again at the main repair depot and reassembled.

Following a final inspection by an AID inspector a 'Certificate of Safety for Flight' was granted, without which no aircraft was permitted to fly. Several test flights were then made before all aspects of an aircraft were deemed to be

ABOVE LEFT There was no hope of returning this 1668 CU Lancaster to service again after it caught fire following a rough landing at RAF Fiskerton on 3 March 1945.

ABOVE In a stately procession led by two motorcycle outriders, a convoy of Queen Mary trailers transports sections of 1660 HCU's Lancaster B Mk I, YW-T/R5845, to RAF Langar for repair. *(Leonard McCombe/Picture Post/ Getty Images)*

BELOW The damage suffered by 550 Squadron's Lancaster B Mk I BQ-O/DV305 in a savage mauling from a night-fighter over Berlin on 30/31 January 1944 that left both gunners dead, meant she was beyond economical repair and was 'reduced to produce'. She is pictured at Woodbridge Emergency Landing Ground in Suffolk.

Type of Aircraft		Mark	R.A.F. Number
LANCASTER		I	D.V.305
Contractor		Contract No.	Engine installed :—
Mel: Vickers.		69275/40	Merlin 22.
			Maker's airframe No. :—
Unit or Cat'y/Cause	Station or Contractor	Date	Authority	41 or 43 Gp. Allot.
23.9.43	A.V. Roe	28/9	25/9	419/46734
	100 Sqdn	2.10.43	193 6/10	
	550 Sqdn	25.11.43	151 20/11	
Cat E1		31.1.44	F8/T.d	
S.O.C		21.2.44	Romfull	

A.M. Form 78

LEFT The Air Ministry Aircraft Movement Card for DV305 records she was struck off charge on 21 February 1944, three weeks after her devastating combat experience. *(RAF AHB)*

acceptable, whereupon it was flown out by an Air Transport Auxiliary (ATA) pilot to an RAF MU for storage, where it remained until reissued to a front-line squadron or a training unit.

Shortages of essential parts

If an aircraft was grounded awaiting receipt of spares that were not available locally, an urgent signal was sent to the manufacturer starting with the letters 'AOG', which stood for 'Aircraft on the Ground'. Immediate dispatch of the appropriate part would be expected.

During 1943 and 1944 when the level of heavy bomber operations had increased to fever pitch, Bomber Command was faced with two serious shortages of equipment – radio valves in 1943, and main-wheel tyres in 1944. With the latter, all unserviceable aircraft at HCUs were jacked up and their tyres removed to keep serviceable aircraft in the air. At one point, squadrons were collecting tyres from the factory and taking them straight to the airfields to be fitted direct to aircraft. Ground staff worked hard to prolong the life of tyres and avoid blow-outs by carrying out regular 'fod-plods' of runways to remove loose stones and debris.

However, Bomber Command considered that the problem of short tyre life – and that of tyre bursts in particular – could have been avoided completely using treaded tyres instead of slicks. The former began to be introduced towards the end of the war.

Manufacturers' repair organisations

A.V. Roe

Damaged Lancasters and any that had miraculously survived for 500 flying hours were taken for repair or major overhaul to the London Midland and Scottish Railway (LMS) locomotive works, and the LMS carriage and wagon workshops in Derby, or to one of Avro's own repair works on the airfields at RAF Langar or Bracebridge Heath in Lincolnshire.

Avro opened a large hangar and workshop complex on the west side of Langar airfield in September 1942 where they carried out modification and repairs on 5 Group's Lancasters for the duration of the war. It was also used for the reassembly of fuselage, wings and tailplanes.

At Bracebridge Heath some of the former airfield buildings were taken over by Avro in 1942, mainly to repair Lancasters (but they also included Whitleys and Hampdens), which were worked on inside the airfield's Belfast Truss hangars. Much of the work was delegated and undertaken at many dispersed sites in the East Midlands including Loughborough, Northampton and Derby. Airframe sections and parts were brought back together again at Langar for reassembly, with completed aircraft towed 1 mile down the road to RAF Waddington for test-flying.

Handley Page

Handley Page's York Aircraft Repair Depot (known locally as 'The Yard') was based at RAF Clifton near York, where Halifaxes were taken to be repaired, overhauled or modified. Situated plumb in the centre of Halifax country – home to the squadrons of 4 and 6 (RCAF) Groups – Clifton and its adjoining site at Rawcliffe employed close to 3,000 skilled tradesmen and women, where some 2,000 Halifaxes were repaired or overhauled during the war years. As with the Avro Lancaster, the LMS railway workshops at Derby

RIGHT After being raked by cannon and machine-gun fire from a Focke Wulf Fw 190 fighter over Essen on 13/14 January 1943, 106 Squadron's Lancaster B Mk I, ZN-G/R5700, made it home to a crash-landing on the USAAF base at Hardwick, Norfolk. Although outwardly she appears to be more badly damaged than DV305, R5700 was deemed repairable and was later reissued to 9 Squadron. She finally went down in a raid on Hannover on 22/23 September the same year.

were also involved in repairing Hampdens in the early years of the war.

Mosquito Repair Organisation (MRO)

In October 1941, de Havilland's factory at Hatfield was destroyed by the Luftwaffe but it was subsequently rebuilt as the Mosquito Repair Organisation (MRO), where parts were salvaged from written-off Mosquitoes before the remaining wooden shell was scrapped. The MRO also carried out work at RAF airfields around the country, with its craftsmen travelling by road or air to front-line airfields to repair damaged aircraft on site. More severely damaged aircraft were brought by road to Hatfield for repair. In all, 1,505 damaged aircraft were repaired by the Hatfield-based MRO (the majority were Mosquitoes, but this total included 150 Hawker Hurricanes).

Ken Collison was a civilian technician working at RAF Marham for de Havilland. Two Mosquito squadrons, 105 and 139, were stationed there between 1942 and 1944. He recalled:

At the time I was working for the Mosquito Repair Organisation (MRO), one of the sections of the de Havilland Aircraft Co that could repair aircraft on site. These units varied greatly in size, some having only two or three people, but Marham grew to at least 25 strong. . . . At Marham airfield we had the use of one hangar. Contact with the RAF was kept to a minimum, restricted only to visits from pilots and their navigators, checking on repair progress of their particular aircraft and looking for shrapnel etc removed from the wooden parts of the aircraft. We knew little about the targets as security was very strict; our only information came from the newspapers.

Short Brothers Repair Organisation (SEBRO)

Known by its acronym SEBRO, the Short Brothers Repair Organisation was located in Cambridgeshire, close to the airfields of 3 Group's Stirling units. With offices located initially at King's College in Cambridge and hangars at RAF Wyton, the rapid increase in repair work necessitated a move in 1941 to

purpose-built accommodation at Madingley Road on the outskirts of the city, with additional repair and flight-testing facilities at RAF Bourn.

At its peak SEBRO employed some 4,500 people in seven purpose-built hangars repairing accident- and battle-damaged Stirlings for return to service, or salvaging and recycling parts from airframes that were considered beyond repair.

Work continued to grow so Hangars 6 and 7 were extended soon after completion to triple-length capacity. This allowed them to house 18 Stirling fuselages side by side down the full length of Hangar 6, with mainplanes lined up along both sides of Hangar 7. With these two facilities acting as main production areas,

ABOVE After being hit by flak over Essen, Mosquito B XVI, HS-D/ML957, was written off in a crash-landing at RAF Bradwell Bay in the early hours of 9 April 1944. The pilot, Flg Off R.H. Pattison DFC, RCAF, and his navigator Sqn Ldr J.V. Watts, RCAF, were uninjured. ML957 was subsequently 'reduced to produce'.

BELOW Next stop the SEBRO works at Madingley Road, Cambridge – 1660 CU's Mk III, EF146/TV-B, suffered an undercarriage collapse when landing on 8 March 1944. Here the fuselage, shorn of its mainplanes, tail unit and fin, is hoisted from the grass by two heavy cranes in preparation for lowering on to a trailer. The guns have been removed from the turrets, as have the rear undercarriage doors. Note also the damage to the fuselage bomb bay doors. EF146 was repaired and joined 1332 CU on 28 August. *(Dave Welch)*

the other hangars were repurposed as factory support with No 1 becoming the main supplies store, Nos 2 and 3 for paint spraying and finishing and Nos 4 and 5 for breaking up and parts salvage of Category E scrap aircraft.

The initial grading of battle- and accident-damaged Stirlings was done at the parent airfield or wherever the aircraft had crashed in Britain. In the case of minor damage (Category A) the RAF dealt with any repairs, but aircraft requiring major rectification work were stripped of radios, loose instruments and any secret equipment (eg H2S and Gee sets) before the wings were detached and the airframe dismantled for transportation by road to SEBRO.

Damaged but airworthy Stirlings were flown in to Bourn for damage assessment. Those classified as Category Ac (damage repairable beyond unit capacity) were repaired at Bourn; Category B (damage beyond repair on site, but repairable at an RAF MU or at a contractor's works), together with Category C and D aircraft, were dismantled either at their home base or at Bourn (with the Hercules engines going to a Bristol Aeroplane Company engine repair depot) and transported to the Madingley Road site on Queen Mary trailers for attention.

On arrival at SEBRO the damaged but repairable Stirlings were taken to the Category B hangar, while those considered beyond repair were moved to the Category E hangars (Nos 4 and 5) where they were stripped of instruments and working parts, much of which was returned to the Stirling factory production lines for reuse.

Repairable fuselages were carefully examined and received an assessment of the time considered necessary to complete the repairs and then a target date was set for delivery back to the RAF. Once the work had been done, the aircraft were reassembled at Bourn airfield and flight-tested before delivery either to an RAF MU or direct to a squadron.

Emily Hayward was one of many women who had been drafted by the Ministry of Labour to take on men's jobs in the factories, thus freeing the men to join the forces. She worked at SEBRO in one of the inspection departments. Emily recalled:

As soon as a crashed fuselage came in I had to go and list all missing and damaged items and then order replacements. The RAF usually cleaned the worst of the mess from the fuselages before they came to us, but as bombing missions increased so too did the crash-landings on return. The undercarriages were almost always damaged and there were many belly landings. Often we had to deal with the fuselage in the same state as it had come home, with the smell of blood and urine – and on one occasion a severed finger on the navigator's table. The pilot's seat had armour plating to protect the back and sometimes the seat had been shot through from below. The horror of war was brought home to us every day.

During the repair process particular attention was given to the Stirling's electrical installation, since the aircraft's primary systems were all electrically operated (compared to the Lancaster and Halifax where it was mainly hydraulic), which called for considerable technical know-how and practical effort. The vast network of wiring and multi-cable conduit runs to interconnecting junction boxes, instrument panels and wing root connectors posed a formidable practical challenge. When a repaired aircraft left the factory for reassembly at Bourn it was essential to ensure that the electrical systems in the wings and fuselage were in full working order and the circuit wiring had been thoroughly checked.

Engine repair

Rolls-Royce and Bristol Aeroplane Company aero engine divisions set up dispersed systems for repairing their engines, centred on the parent factories but overseen by the Air Ministry's Air Member for Development and Production.

Damaged engines arrived at the repair works where inspectors categorised them under three headings:

- Category B – repairable engines.
- Category E – engines damaged beyond repair and likely to be reduced to produce spares.
- Investigation engines – engines on which special investigation of some failure had been requested by the Air Ministry or the manufacturer's technical department.

Those engines graded as Category E (beyond repair) were often at first sight a hopeless mass of tangled and burned metal, usually covered with mud and turf, but when cleaned and stripped down they yielded a varied selection of reusable components. These were subjected to rigorous inspection and testing before being passed to the stores for reissue.

Category B repairable engines were subdivided into the following classes:

- Engines which had completed their full life hours and were due for a complete overhaul.
- Engines damaged or 'shock-loaded' due to aircraft crash or forced landings.
- Engine failures owing to external factors such as oil supply failure, debris entering the supercharger, etc.
- Incorporation of essential modifications.
- Enemy action.

The degree of stripping down depended on the amount of repair required and the previous history of the engine as recorded in its logbook. While most engines were completely dismantled, a few were stripped to the various sub-assemblies to rectify minor damage. For example, the amount of overhaul needed for a carburettor depended on its previous history. This might have included splitting the body for examination of the internal components; a partial overhaul to the extent of removing various units for examination; or a complete strip-down.

Rolls-Royce

Rolls-Royce established a Repair Engineering division located in workshops in and around Nottingham, as well as at their Hillington shadow factory in Glasgow. At both locations the repair and overhaul of engines was undertaken that had either reached their life limit, or had been damaged by accident or in combat. The Hillington factory was geared up to deal with Packard-built Merlins, which had been manufactured under licence in the USA to boost the supply of engines to British aircraft builders.

Merlin overhaul and repair facilities were also set up in the car factories of Sunbeam-Talbot in London and Alvis in Stafford. On Barlby Road at Ladbroke Green in the London suburb of

North Kensington, Sunbeam-Talbot's production of civilian cars was suspended after 1940 and the facility turned over to Rolls-Royce for overhaul and repair (although parent company Rootes continued to build the Hillman Minx and Humber Super Snipe for military use).

The Alvis factories were also kept busy at Stafford in the north Midlands. On the Freemand Street site Merlins were overhauled and repaired, while the Blackheath Covert factory was responsible for testing, rectification and dispatch. At the peak of production Alvis was turning out 50 refurbished Merlin engines every day.

In 1944 the de Havilland Engine Company also set up a Merlin engine overhaul facility on Stag Lane airfield at Edgware in north London. By the end of the war Merlin overhaul facilities in Britain had repaired and returned to service some 50,000 engines.

Bristol

Bristol Aeroplane Company's engine repair facilities in the West Country were transferred from the main factory at Patchway in north Bristol almost as soon as the war started. They were moved to the harbour waterfront in Bristol city centre and relocated in the bonded tobacco warehouses at Canon's Marsh (11 Bond) and along the Cumberland Basin. An engine test area was also built in a stone quarry near the new repair facilities.

There was another repair depot for Bristol aero engines in the north of England at Guiseley near Leeds, which may have been housed in the Crompton Parkinson factory. It is understood to have been managed from Bristol No 3 Shadow Factory at Clayton-le-Moors near Accrington.

ABOVE Rolls-Royce Merlin engines under repair at one of several Repair Engineering workshops that were located around Nottingham. *(Rolls-Royce Heritage Trust)*

'An Operational Research
Section is indispensable to every
Command in modern war. . . .
The large research section at my
Command saved thousands of
lives and hundreds of aircraft.'

**(Air Chief Marshal Sir Arthur Harris,
AOC-in-C Bomber Command 1942–45)**

Chapter Thirteen

Operational research

‘Bomber’ Harris could not have directed Bomber Command’s operations single-handedly – not without the crucial support of his backroom ‘boffins’ and analysts in the Command’s Operational Research Section. They were needed to collect, organise, analyse and act on the profusion of data and circumstances that were vital to their commander-in-chief’s daily and long-term decision making.

OPPOSITE With the Battle of Berlin at its height in February 1944, Bomber Harris confers with his senior staff officers over bomb damage plots. Left to right: AVM Sir Hugh Walmsley, AVM R. Oxland, Sir Arthur Harris and Senior Air Staff Officer AVM Sir Robert Saundby. *(Popperfoto/Getty Images)*

Operational Research

In the 21st century the saying goes that 'data is king'. Its mining, processing and uses loom large in almost every area of our lives. The importance of data has been likened to other big 'boom' commodities of the 19th and early 20th centuries like gold or oil, where the technology and methods for refining were as important as the ore or crude itself, and the same goes for data.

Data is surprisingly similar to gold and oil: in its raw unrefined state it has far less utility or value. Algorithms have been developed to comb data for trends, patterns and hidden nuances, which add value and make it useful. Processed data is converted into actions that affect everything from consumer behaviour to supply chain efficiency, scientific research to healthcare.

In the opening months of the Second World War the Air Ministry recognised the need for applying scientific know-how to problem solving as well as gathering and analysing data to improve the operational efficiency of its front-line commands. Civilian scientists and engineers (known as 'Operational Researchers') were brought in to Fighter and Coastal Commands to pit their intellects and skills against complex problems of immediate operational importance. Their vital contribution was first appreciated in the development of Britain's air defence network and the Chain Home radar system in 1939–40, particularly in the way it informed their use; and later, these researchers were key to the introduction of Air to Surface Vessel (ASV) radar, followed by their conclusion that Coastal Command's flawed tactics and weapons were the reasons behind its low rate of U-boat sinkings.

By mid-1941 the Air Ministry decided that the many benefits of this collaboration with scientists and engineers should be extended to its other commands. Henceforward, the scientific and empirical analysis of operational problems was increasingly broadened to include matters which, until then, had often been left to chance, conjecture or to ad hoc investigations like the infamous Butt Report in 1941.

Up until then most operational researchers had been members of the Telecommunications Research Establishment (TRE) at Malvern, from whom they were 'borrowed' by the Command in which they served, but under the new proposal for Operational Research (OR) the job was brought 'in-house' under Air Ministry control. OR personnel were officially transferred to the staff of the MAP and then seconded to the Air Ministry for attachment to the various RAF Commands. These groups of scientists became collectively known as 'Operational Research Sections' and reported direct to the commander-in-chief of the Command concerned.

Bomber Command's Operational Research Section is formed

On 1 September 1941 an Operational Research Section (ORS) was formed within Bomber Command at the request of the (then) Commander-in-Chief, Air Marshal Sir Richard Peirse. Dr B.G. (Basil) Dickins, a highly experienced statistician, was made officer in charge of the Section. On its formation the relatively small team comprised 10 scientific officers and 11 administrative staff, but with the rapid growth of the bomber offensive this grew to a maximum of 55 scientific officers by August 1943.

The ORS always worked as an integral part of the Command and in close collaboration with other sections in Bomber Command HQ at High

RIGHT An eccentric English gentleman and a consummate fly fisherman, Senior Air Staff Officer (1940) and Deputy C-in-C (1943) Robert Saundby became Bomber Harris's right-hand man after his appointment as C-in-C Bomber Command in 1942. Together with his boss, Saundby gave the fullest encouragement to ORS and did much to facilitate their research.

DR B.G. (BASIL GORDON) DICKINS (1908–96)

The son of a south London car dealer, Dickins excelled in his studies at King Alfred School in Streatham before being accepted to study physics at the Royal College of Science in London. He continued with postgraduate study before joining the Royal Aircraft Establishment in 1932. Dickins was working for the MAP in 1941 when he was appointed to lead the ORS at Bomber Command HQ.

Dickins was criticised by the mathematician Freeman Dyson, a member of the ORS from July 1943 to September 1945, whose main duty was theoretical investigations concerning bomber losses, who labelled him 'a career civil servant' who was in thrall to Bomber Harris and only told the C-in-C what he wanted to hear. (After the war Dyson was elected a Fellow of the Royal Society and became Professor of Mathematics at Princeton University in the USA.) Churchill's scientific adviser on bombing strategy, Solly Zuckerman, also questioned Dickins's impartiality, but it is beyond doubt that under his leadership the Command's ORS contributed significantly to the operational efficiency of Bomber Command, particularly in the last two years of the war.

After the war Dickins continued to work at the highest levels of the Civil Service as Director General of Atomic Weapons at the Ministry of Supply in 1959, and Director General of Guided

ABOVE LEFT Dr B.G. Dickins was the head of Operational Research at Bomber Command.

ABOVE RIGHT Solly Zuckerman, who was scientific adviser to the Allies on bombing strategy in the Second World War, was also a pioneer of operational research. His influence as a scientist on British and American governments during peace and war was unique in the 20th century.

Weapons at the Air Ministry (1962). His final appointment was Deputy Controller of Guided Weapons at the Ministry of Technology from 1966 to 1968.

Basil Gordon Dickins CBE, OBE, BSc, ARCS, DIC, PhD, died in Jersey in 1996.

Wycombe. Most ORS staff were based at HQ but many were also detached to the six front-line bomber groups in Britain. Bomber Harris was effusive in his praise for the ORS, which he described in his memoir *Bomber Offensive* as: '… a body of brilliant young civilian scientists and technicians at Bomber Command headquarters who did work of inestimable value in subjecting all aspects of our operations to an impartial scrutiny.'

The objective of the Bomber Command ORS was to improve the operational efficiency of the Command's squadrons, determine how this could be increased in terms of bombs on targets per aircraft lost and provide the AOC and his senior commanders with analyses on which future action could be based, including the selection of targets. In short – getting 'more bang for your buck'.

Its initial duties were to study bomber losses, the success or otherwise of bombing operations, the vulnerability of bombers and the problems associated with the use of radio and radar. In due course a fifth section for the study of daylight operations was formed. The subjects for research within these areas usually originated within the Section itself, but from time to time urgent assignments could be received from the Command's senior staff.

In time it became increasingly clear that the investigation of radar problems was too closely related to both the study of bomber operations and that of bomber losses for it to be undertaken in a separate section. As a result, the branch was reorganised in early 1942 into three sections under the control of the Head of Branch, Dr B.G. Dickins: ORS 1 pursued research into the success of night operations (Officer in Charge, Mr G.A. Roberts); ORS 2 investigated losses on night operations (Officer in Charge, Dr R.J. Smeed); and ORS 3 carried out research into day operations (Officer in Charge, Mr H.L. Beards). The latter was disbanded in early 1943 when the Command ended daylight operations; when they were resumed in mid-1944 the task was taken over by ORS 1.

In mid-1942 a miscellaneous section (ORS 4) was created to deal with research that did not fit easily with the tasks of the rest of the organisation, including airfield control, air photography in the Command and training. In early 1943, ORS 3 was re-established as the statistical section, recording a massive amount of crucial data on Hollerith punch cards relating to each night sortie flown by Bomber Command from March 1944, of which more on page 176.

External contacts

The work of the Bomber Command ORS was closely related to other government research organisations, with whom research was shared and who were all carrying out their own investigations into certain aspects of Allied bombing operations. This exchange of information and data was essential to the work of ORS.

Among the most notable were the Air Warfare Analysis Section (AWAS) of the Air Ministry, responsible for preparing charts associated with ground-based navigational and bombing aids and the calculation of target coordinates; the RE8 (Research and Experiments) Division of the Ministry of Home Security, who were concerned with the economic effects of Allied bombing (the ORS provided RE8 with operational information, who in return supplied the ORS with bomb plots for analysis purposes); and 'N' Section of the Central (later Allied Central) Interpretation Unit, from whom bomb plots were also obtained. 'N' Section specialised in the interpretation of night photographs taken at bomb release (the 'aiming-point photograph' as bomber crews called them), as well as developing methods of analysing the activities of bombers in the target area together with the distribution of bombs and markers which, together, were essential to the proper analysis of raids.

In the latter stages of the war ORS maintained close links with RE8, and all the other bodies that were studying bomb performance, to keep the Air Staff up to date and to advise them (in conjunction with the Armaments Branch) on the types of bombs that were most effective against the various kinds of target attacked.

RIGHT Basil Megaw edited the *Bomber Command Quarterly Review* produced by ORS. He was typical of the many academics who served in back-room roles with the British military during the Second World War, putting their specialist skills and knowledge at the service of their country.

BOMBER COMMAND QUARTERLY REVIEW

Not to be outdone by the *Coastal Command Review* produced by Coastal Command's ORS, in early 1942 Bomber Command's AOC Sir Richard Peirse commissioned his ORS to produce a similar publication. The first issue of the *Bomber Command Quarterly Review* covering April–June 1942 was produced by an unlikely editor in the form of B.R.S. (Basil) Megaw (1913–2002), an archaeologist and anthropologist with experience of journals publishing. Megaw had been assistant director of the Manx Museum before the war and after his war service as a scientific officer with Bomber Command's ORS he became the first director of the School of Scottish Studies at Edinburgh University.

The Daily Express front page, No. 13,107, Monday, June 1, 1942, One Penny, headlined:

ONE BOMBER EVERY 6 SECONDS, 3,000 TONS IN 90 MINUTES

THE VENGEANCE BEGINS! The ruins of Cologne are hidden under a pall of smoke rising 15,000 feet after the first thousand-bomber raid in history

Investigating the bomber offensive

In basic terms there were two kinds of analyses that the ORS was called upon to perform – qualitative and quantitative. The former allowed quick estimation of the success or failure of a raid, with the results published as soon as possible in ORS reports for distribution within Bomber Command HQ and to the Groups involved. With the latter, quantitative analysis, data was used to compare different operational techniques and the accuracy of an attack under varying conditions, as well as enabling estimates of the weight of attack needed in future operations.

ORS made vital contributions to the development of bomber tactics (concentration over targets, wave plans, evasive manoeuvres, tracer ammunition, etc), escape hatches in the Lancaster and Halifax, fuel and engine fires, the introduction and application of Gee, G-H, Oboe and H2S, the creation of the Pathfinder Force (the formation of 'specialist squadrons to initiate raids' was recommended by the ORS as early as December 1941) and the subsequent detailed analysis of the first 21 attacks led by the PFF; problems affecting navigation, target identification and loss reduction; and the use of 'Window'.

An early success of ORS was in drawing up detailed plans for testing the effectiveness of TR1335 – otherwise known as the radio-navigation aid Gee (see page 105 for a description). Two simulated experimental attacks were made on 13 February 1942 by 3 Group against Selby railway station on the Isle of Man (where the Gee lattice lines were similar to those over the Ruhr) and again on the 19th using Brynkir railway station in North Wales, to

ABOVE ORS data analysis led to the choice of Cologne as the target for the RAF's first 1,000-bomber raid on 30/31 May 1942, which was within range of Gee for accurate navigation and where the bomber stream tactic could be used to overwhelm the enemy defences.

confirm the soundness of the 'Shaker' attack protocol. With 'Shaker', selected crews using Gee dropped flares blindly over the centre of the target at the beginning of the attack as markers for the main force – foreshadowing the techniques of the Pathfinders later in the war. The first use of Gee operationally was on 8/9 March against Essen when the leading aircraft were fitted with the aid.

ORS also established early on through data analysis that the concentration of bombers in time and space over a target resulted in lower losses in the attacking force. Days after Harris took over at Bomber Command, the concentration theory was tested and proved on what was a hugely successful attack on the lightly defended Renault factory at Billancourt on the outskirts of Paris on 3/4 March. Some 235 bombers were dispatched in three waves, with an average of 121 aircraft per hour

concentrated over the target, which exceeded Bomber Command's hitherto best rate of 80 per hour. Only one Wellington was lost.

The two key elements of Gee and bomber-stream concentration were soon incorporated into the first 1,000-bomber raid on Cologne on 30/31 May – Gee to get the bombers to the target, and concentration to swamp enemy defences.

In April 1943 ORS stated that the introduction of the newly developed countermeasure codenamed 'Window' (metal foil strips cut to a certain length and dropped over Germany to 'fog' enemy radar screens) might save one in three of the bomber aircraft then being lost to enemy action. It took until the Hamburg fire raids of late July for it to be used operationally for the first time (for fear of alerting the Germans to its existence and for them to develop their own version to use against Britain), where it proved devastating for the German defences.

Data capture and analysis

The Hollerith system

With the growing volume of information coming out of night sorties from aircrew debriefing reports, post-raid and special equipment analysis, the need was never greater for an effective means of capturing and processing this data to inform decision making at Bomber Command. At the heart of Operational Research from March 1944 was a punch card data processing system that used a device called a Hollerith machine and tabulator. Until the first commercial electronic computers arrived in the 1950s the Hollerith system was the pre-eminent form of data processing.

Hollerith was a system for coding data into punched cards, which was read by electromechanical counters (called tabulators) that captured and processed the data. Invented by Herman Hollerith, the machine had been developed originally to help process data for the 1890 US Census.

Tabulating data
Each horizontal row on a Hollerith punch card was assigned a different value, and

BELOW The use of punched cards to analyse data was devised by the German inventor Dr Herman Hollerith (1860–1929) in response to a contest to process data for the 1890 US census. The later machine shown here is a printer and listing tabulator that combined several functions in one. After the punched cards were sorted they were passed through the tabulator and the information they contained was transmitted to the adding and printing mechanisms. The tabulator calculated quantities and printed out the data. The Hollerith Company later evolved into International Business Machines, known today as IBM. *(SSPL/Getty Images)*

letters, numbers or special characters were encoded as combinations of these values in a vertical column.

To begin tabulating the data, information contained in the Raid Reports (for example) received from each bomber group were transferred to paper punch cards using gang punches and pantographs. Using this equipment, data coding clerks known as 'Initial Coders' 'punched' each card to represent specific data on the raid report schedule. The completed card was then checked several times by a Secondary Coder and any discrepancies noted on a proforma before the correct coding was passed over to a Specialised Coder for final coding. The ultimate version of the card was then passed to the Punch Operator for punching, after which the data was signed off as 'verified' before statistics could be produced for the final cards.

To operate the mechanism the operator manually positioned the punching stylus over the appropriate hole in a punch card template. Each hole in the template corresponded to a specific category, eg squadron, letter, aircraft type and mark. Pressing the stylus into the template created a punched hole in the paper card that was in turn read by the Hollerith tabulator's card reader.

Reading the punched holes

Each Hollerith tabulator was equipped with a card reading station. The card reader consisted of two hinged plates operated by a lever (similar to a toasted sandwich maker). Data clerks opened the reader and positioned a punched card between the plates. When the plates were closed, spring-loaded metal pins in the upper plate passed through the punched data holes in the cards and through the bottom plate to make an electrical circuit, which activated the magnetic dials on the Hollerith tabulator and operated the counting hands. With completion of the electrical circuit (signalled by the ringing of a bell), the clerk transcribed the data indicated by the dial hands before opening the card reader, removing the punch cards, and resetting the dials and positioning a new card in the reader to repeat the process. An experienced tabulator clerk could process 80 punch cards per minute.

Other users of the Hollerith machine system

With an inventory of more than 750,000 stock items in RAF Maintenance Command, the Air Ministry recognised the great benefits to be had from the use of automated data processing. In 1943 it rushed in Hollerith punched-card and electromechanical reading machines for stock control at the first of its seven principal equipment depots. The benefits were great in terms of standardisation of stores accounting across 40 Group (Maintenance) and more efficient distribution, not to mention the time savings and increased accuracy in record keeping.

At the government's top secret code-breaking centre at Bletchley Park, the essential task of cracking German military and naval codes generated vast amounts of data. Some 2 million punched Hollerith cards were used each week for storing decrypted German signals.

Forward planning

Getting the most from resources

Before 1944, detailed operational data was scarce on which to base any estimates for the size of a bomber force needed to destroy any particular target. However, with the Transportation Plan that focused on northern France and Belgium in the three months leading up to D-Day in June 1944, ORS used the Hollerith system to help develop methods of

ABOVE An operator enters data into punch cards for processing by the Hollerith machine. A typical office suite would consist of a punch, a sorter, a collator and a tabulator. *(Underwood Archives/Getty Images)*

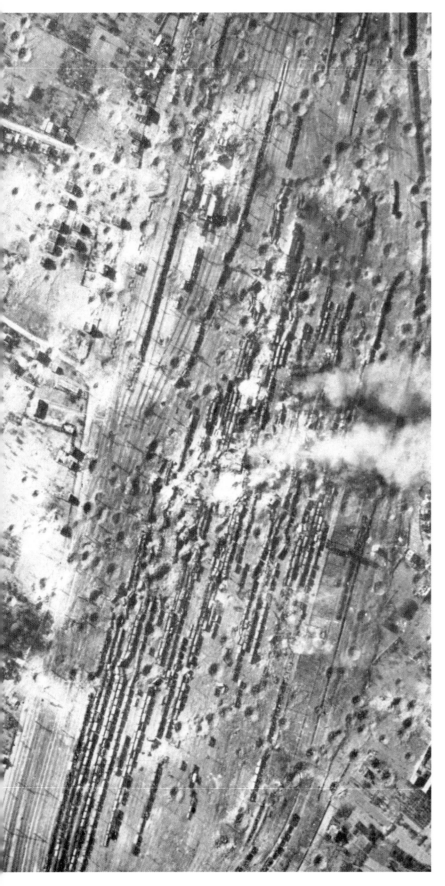

forward planning that enabled it to calculate the effort needed to achieve the level of damage to the enemy's transport infrastructure required by Overlord's planners.

These methods were first applied with considerable success in raids against French railway marshalling yards and were later used in planning attacks on gun batteries, followed later by marshalling yards, synthetic oil plants and U-boat assembly facilities in Germany itself. Towards the end of 1944 forward planning was further developed to allow ORS to give estimates for attacks on large targets such as towns and cities. As Bomber Command became increasingly heavily tasked throughout the summer of 1944 in support of the advancing Allied armies on the ground, forward planning became critical in making sure that its resources were utilised in the most economical way possible.

Raid Reports

Raid Report cards were usually produced two to three days after receipt of Raid Reports from the Groups, or six to eight days after an operation. They judged the success of bombing by measuring and comparing the following variables:

■ Standard deviation – a measure of the concentration of bombing by calculating the scatter of bombs about their Mean Point of Impact (MPI).
■ Systematic error – the distance of the MPI of the distribution from the detailed aiming point, which gave a measure of the accuracy with which an attack was centred.
■ Ineffectiveness – bombs that did not contribute to the normal bomb-fall distribution owing to abortive sorties, gross errors or other causes.

LEFT The Hollerith system was crucial in the selection of targets in Bomber Command's raids on the transportation infrastructure in northern France and Belgium in the lead-up to D-Day. This is the railway marshalling yard at Orléans after a particularly accurate raid by 118 Lancasters and 4 Mosquitoes on 19/20 May 1944.

CODING SHEET No. 3
Special Equipment & Damage Card – Card No. 3

	Card No.	Coders No.	Aircraft		Date and Target	Special Equip.				Controls			Miscellaneous						Engines												Fires General
			Sqdn.	Letter		Monica & Fishpond	MLF & Boozer	H2S, H2X OBOE	Carpet Type 2	All.	Elev.	Rud.	Fuel	Hydr.	Bombs	Oil	Inst.	Air Fr.	P.O.			P.I.			S.I.			S.O.			
																			Dam. Fail	Fires	Gen.	Dam. Fail	Fires	Gen.	Dam. Fail	Fires	Gen.	Dam. Fail	Fires	Gen.	
Col. No.	44	45	46-48	49-50	51-54	55	56	57	58	59	60	61	62	63	64	65	66	67	68	69	70	71	72	73	74	75	76	77	78	79	80
1	3																														
2	3																														
3	3																														
4	3																														
5	3																														
6	3																														
7	3																														
8	3																														
9	3																														
		A	A	A	A	A/P	A/P	A/P	P	A/P	A/P	A/P	A	A	A	A	A	A	P	P	P	P	P	P	P	P	P	P	P	P	P

Timing and height distribution

The analysis of different bombing techniques was made possible by compiling a list of aircraft by their time over the target, giving the method of bombing used, in conjunction with information showing the plotted position of aiming-point photographs provided by the Central Interpretation Unit at Medmenham.

Concentration in time of the bomber stream was considered important in reducing fighter losses and information was required that showed the number of aircraft bombing in each minute of an attack. Consequently Hollerith enabled a tabulation to be extracted from the raw data giving the number of aircraft attacking the target in each minute of a raid. From the figures obtained it was possible to see if the raid had been carried out as planned.

Aircraft losses

Investigations into the cause of aircraft losses over the target focused on the number of each aircraft type attacking at each height band (eg, Lancasters 18,000ft, Halifaxes 15,000ft, Stirlings 10,000ft). From this information it was not only possible to see if the planned height distribution had been maintained but also, when combined with data of timing distribution, the incidence of collisions and the concentration of 'Window' could be estimated.

Special equipment analysis

Punched card systems were used to record and analyse data concerning the use and serviceability of special equipment on board aircraft (IFF, H2S, Gee, Oboe, Monica, Fishpond etc). From this it was possible to make the calculations necessary to estimate the effectiveness of each piece of special equipment.

Returned aircrew data

From May 1943 ORS became responsible for interrogating evaders and escapers, with their accounts written up in narrative form and published internally with a limited circulation. These were known as Bomber Command ORS 'K' Reports, of which some 282 were released. Evaders were also interrogated by MI9.

From autumn 1944 the number of escaped and returned aircrew had increased so much that a new method of recording the data was needed. The Hollerith punch card system was used with a bespoke coding method to capture data.

After the end of the war in Europe the rapid return of repatriated POWs took the authorities by surprise. They realised that returnees had to be interrogated otherwise valuable information might be lost – for example, concerning fires in aircraft and aircrew safety, much of which could be helpful in the future designs of aircraft. Some

ABOVE One of many different data coding sheets. This particular one is for recording the performance of special equipment (H2S, Oboe, etc) and any damage to the aircraft's controls, systems and engines.

ABOVE The rapid influx of some 10,000 RAF prisoners of war returning to England between April and June 1945 put the ORS under considerable pressure to record data from intelligence reports as quickly as possible before the men were demobbed. Here, Australian, British and New Zealand former POWs wait eagerly to board 463 (Australian) Squadron's Lancaster RA573 at Juvincourt near Rheims, for the return flight to England on 6 May 1945.

10,000 Bomber Command aircrew ex-POWs were interviewed between 11 April and 22 June 1945 and the information they gave in the questionnaires was prepared for analysis using the punch card system. A master number code system was devised covering all the particular points of information likely to be obtained. Each POW account was then read and coded using the appropriate number codes.

Investigating the effectiveness of bombing

From September 1944 a ground survey unit known as the Bombing Analysis Unit (BAU) was formed in France to investigate the effectiveness of Allied bombing. Its brief was to undertake investigations of areas that had been subjected to RAF attacks in support of the Army. This included tactical targets like bridges and railways as well as close-support operations and V-weapons sites. Three members of ORS were permanently attached to BAU, while the officer in charge of ORS, Dr B.G. Dickins, also spent occasional periods with the unit. The BAU worked closely with the United States Air Evaluation Board (USAEB) and by January 1945 all the studies it had been given were complete and the reports ready for editing and publication.

Bomber Harris decided that the time had

now come for his ORS staff to focus their attention on the effects of strategic bombing. However, such targets were outside the remit of BAU and so ORS staff were withdrawn from the unit and duly attached to the British Bombing Research Mission (BBRM). This Mission had the gargantuan task of surveying targets in Germany as they became available for inspection. The United States Strategic Bombing Survey (USSBS) was also working on similar investigations and both teams maintained close contact, benefitting from each other's experiences as well as their own.

Initial bomb damage surveys were attempted at Aachen and Krefeld during March and April, but the chaotic conditions on the ground were not conducive to good scientific and quantitative assessments being made. It was not until the end of April that the Ruhr pocket was secured and with it the important industrial cities of the region. In May the BBRM was merged with the BAU to form the British Bombing Survey Unit (BBSU).

ORS staff within the BBSU were now able to survey four major towns in the Ruhr – Essen, Bochum, Dortmund and Düsseldorf, as well as several sites of synthetic oil production. Using a combination of written questionnaires and formal interviews with selected executives and municipal officers, the ORS were able to establish the level of damage sustained by industry and its effect on production, as well as assessing the effects of bombing on civic life. The data was collected, analysed and presented as a written report.

While investigating the Krupp industrial behemoth in Essen it was discovered that a large number of pistols from unexploded bombs had been retained and these were made available to the bomb disposal teams. German ARP personnel from surrounding districts were also questioned about unexploded bombs to discover the reason for their failure, which was found to be high.

The BBSU continued its studies of German towns with Hamburg, Bremen and Kiel (which included U-boat production) in July, then Hannover and Kassel. By this time the war in the Far East had come to an end and the BBSU had revised its approach to the study of

bombing by using instead the data collected by the USSBS.

Activities of the Bomber Command ORS were wound down in September 1945 when it called a halt to its data-gathering programme once Kassel was completed. Before leaving Germany and returning to the UK, Dr Basil Dickins, the Officer-in-Charge of ORS, and one research officer visited Berlin where they interviewed the executives of several important companies, although no attempt was made at a formal survey.

BELOW One year on from the devastating firestorm of 13/14 February 1945 that burned the heart out of the baroque city of Dresden, the streets are virtually empty of people and the gutted buildings stand forlorn. For observers from the British Bombing Research Mission investigating the effectiveness of strategic bombing, the results were only too plain to see. *(BA Bild 212-103)*

Appendix

Orders of battle, 1939, 1943 and 1945

27 September 1939

No 1 Group. *HQ: Forming at Benson, Oxon.*

No 2 Group. *HQ: Wyton, Cambs.*

21 Sqn ⎤
82 Sqn ⎦ 79 Wing Watton Blenheim I, IV

114 Sqn ⎤
139 Sqn ⎦ 82 Wing Wyton Blenheim I, IV

107 Sqn ⎤
110 Sqn ⎦ 83 Wing Wattisham Blenheim I, IV

101 Sqn West Raynham Blenheim IV

No 3 Group. *HQ: Mildenhall, Suffolk.*
9 Sqn Honington Wellington I
37 Sqn Feltwell Wellington I
38 Sqn Marham Wellington I
99 Sqn Mildenhall Wellington I
115 Sqn Marham Wellington I
149 Sqn Mildenhall Wellington I
214 Sqn Feltwell Wellington I
215 Sqn Bassingbourn Wellington I, Harrow

No 4 Group. *HQ: Linton-on-Ouse, Yorks.*
10 Sqn Dishforth Whitley IV
51 Sqn Linton-on-Ouse Whitley II, III
58 Sqn Linton-on-Ouse Whitley III
77 Sqn Driffield Whitley III, V
78 Sqn Dishforth Whitley I, IVa, V
102 Sqn Driffield Whitley III

No 5 Group. *HQ: St Vincent's, Grantham, Lincs.*
44 Sqn Waddington Hampden
49 Sqn Scampton Hampden
50 Sqn Waddington Hampden
61 Sqn Hemswell Hampden
83 Sqn Scampton Hampden
106 Sqn Cottesmore Hampden
144 Sqn Hemswell Hampden
185 Sqn Cottesmore Hampden

February 1943

No 1 Group. *HQ: Bawtry Hall, Yorks.*
12 Sqn Wickenby Lancaster I, III
101 Sqn Holme Lancaster I, III
103 Sqn Elsham Wolds Lancaster I, III
166 Sqn Kirmington Wellington III, X
199 Sqn Ingham Wellington III
300 Sqn Hemswell Wellington III
301 Sqn Hemswell Wellington IV
305 Sqn Hemswell Wellington IV
460 Sqn Breighton Lancaster I, III

No 2 Group. *HQ: Castlewood House, Hunts.*
21 Sqn Methwold Ventura I, II
88 Sqn Oulton Boston III
98 Sqn Foulsham Mitchell II
105 Sqn Marham Mosquito IV
107 Sqn Great Massingham Boston III, IIIa
139 Sqn Marham Mosquito IV
180 Sqn Foulsham Mitchell II
226 Sqn Swanton Morley Boston III, IIIa
464 Sqn Feltwell Ventura I, II
487 Sqn Feltwell Ventura II

No 3 Group. *HQ: Exning, Suffolk.*
15 Sqn Bourn Stirling I, III
75 Sqn Newmarket Stirling I
90 Sqn Ridgewell Stirling I
115 Sqn East Wretham Wellington III
138 Sqn Tempsford Halifax II, V
149 Sqn Lakenheath Stirling I, III
161 Sqn Tempsford Lysander, Halifax, Hudson, Havoc, Albemarle
192 Sqn Gransden Lodge Wellington I, III, X, Mosquito IV
214 Sqn Chedburgh Stirling I, III
218 Sqn Downham Market Stirling I, III

No 4 Group. *HQ: Heslington Hall, Yorks.*
10 Sqn Melbourne Halifax II

51 Sqn Snaith Halifax II
76 Sqn Linton-on-Ouse Halifax II/V
77 Sqn Elvington Halifax II
78 Sqn Linton-on-Ouse Halifax II
102 Sqn Pocklington Halifax II
158 Sqn Rufforth Halifax II
196 Sqn Leconfield Wellington X
429 Sqn East Moor Wellington III, X
466 Sqn Leconfield Wellington X

No 5 Group. *HQ: St Vincent's, Grantham, Lincs.*
9 Sqn Waddington Lancaster I, III
44 Sqn Waddington Lancaster I, III
49 Sqn Fiskerton Lancaster I, III
50 Sqn Skellingthorpe Lancaster I, III
57 Sqn Scampton Lancaster I, III
61 Sqn Syerston Lancaster I, III
97 Sqn Woodhall Spa Lancaster I, III
106 Sqn Syerston Lancaster I, III
207 Sqn Langar Lancaster I, III
467 Sqn Bottesford Lancaster I, III

No 6 (RCAF) Group. *HQ: Allerton Park, Yorks.*
405 Sqn det Beaulieu, Hants Halifax II
408 Sqn Leeming Halifax II
419 Sqn Middleton St George Halifax II
420 Sqn Middleton St George Wellington III, X
424 Sqn Topcliffe Wellington III, X
425 Sqn Dishforth Wellington III
426 Sqn Dishforth Wellington III
427 Sqn Croft Wellington III, X
428 Sqn Dalton Wellington III

No 8 (PFF) Group. *HQ: Wyton, Hunts.*
7 Sqn Oakington Stirling I, III
35 Sqn Graveley Halifax II
83 Sqn Wyton Lancaster I, III
109 Sqn Wyton Mosquito IV
156 Sqn Warboys Wellington III, Lancaster I, III

22 March 1945

No 1 Group. *HQ: Bawtry Hall, Yorks.*
12 Sqn Wickenby Lancaster I, III
100 Sqn Grimsby Lancaster I, III
101 Sqn Ludford Magna Lancaster I, III
103 Sqn Elsham Wolds Lancaster I, III
150 Sqn Hemswell Lancaster I, III
153 Sqn Scampton Lancaster I, III
166 Sqn Kirmington Lancaster I, III
170 Sqn Hemswell Lancaster I, III
300 Sqn Faldingworth Lancaster I, III
460 Sqn Binbrook Lancaster I, III
550 Sqn North Killingholme Lancaster I, III
576 Sqn Fiskerton Lancaster I, III
625 Sqn Kelstern Lancaster I, III
626 Sqn Wickenby Lancaster I, III

No 3 Group. *HQ: Exning, Suffolk.*
15 Sqn Mildenhall Lancaster I, III
75 Sqn Mepal Lancaster I, III
90 Sqn Tuddenham Lancaster I, III
115 Sqn Witchford Lancaster I, III
149 Sqn Methwold Lancaster I, III
186 Sqn Stradishall Lancaster I, III
195 Sqn Wratting Common Lancaster I, III
218 Sqn Chedburgh Lancaster I, III
514 Sqn Waterbeach Lancaster I, III
622 Sqn Mildenhall Lancaster I, III

No 4 Group. *HQ: Heslington Hall, Yorks.*
10 Sqn Melbourne Halifax III
51 Sqn Snaith Halifax III
76 Sqn Holme Halifax III, VI
77 Sqn Full Sutton Halifax III, VI
78 Sqn Breighton Halifax III
102 Sqn Pocklington Halifax III, VI
158 Sqn Lissett Halifax III
346 Sqn Elvington Halifax III, VI
347 Sqn Elvington Halifax III, VI
466 Sqn Driffield Halifax III
578 Sqn Burn Halifax III
640 Sqn Leconfield Halifax III, VI

No 5 Group. *HQ: Moreton Hall, Swinderby, Lincs.*
9 Sqn Bardney Lancaster I, III
44 Sqn Spilsby Lancaster I, III
49 Sqn Fulbeck Lancaster I, III
50 Sqn Skellingthorpe Lancaster I, III
57 Sqn East Kirkby Lancaster I, III
61 Sqn Skellingthorpe Lancaster I, III

ABOVE No 467 (Australian) Squadron's veteran Lancaster, R5868, S for Sugar, with her representative air and groundcrews on a goodwill tour of USAAF bases in East Anglia during February and March 1945. *(US National Archives)*

106 Sqn Metheringham Lancaster I, III
189 Sqn Fulbeck Lancaster I, III
207 Sqn Spilsby Lancaster I, III
227 Sqn Balderton Lancaster I, III
463 Sqn Waddington Lancaster I, III
467 Sqn Waddington Lancaster I, III
617 Sqn Woodhall Spa Lancaster I, III, Mosquito VI
619 Sqn Strubby Lancaster I, III
630 Sqn East Kirkby Lancaster I, III

On loan from No 8 (PFF) Group
83 Sqn (PFF) Coningsby Lancaster I, III
97 Sqn (PFF) Coningsby Lancaster I, III
627 Sqn (PFF) Woodhall Spa Mosquito IV, IX, XVI, XX, XXV

No 6 (RCAF) Group. *HQ: Allerton Park, Yorks.*
408 Sqn Linton-on-Ouse Halifax VII
415 Sqn East Moor Halifax III, VII
419 Sqn Middleton St George Lancaster X
420 Sqn Tholthorpe Halifax III
424 Sqn Skipton-on-Swale Lancaster I, III
425 Sqn Tholthorpe Halifax III
426 Sqn Linton-on-Ouse Halifax VII
427 Sqn Leeming Lancaster I, III, Halifax III
428 Sqn Middleton St George Lancaster X
429 Sqn Leeming Lancaster X, Halifax III
431 Sqn Croft Lancaster X
432 Sqn East Moor Halifax VII
433 Sqn Skipton-on-Swale Lancaster I, III, Halifax III
434 Sqn Croft Lancaster I, III, X

No 8 (PFF) Group. *HQ: Castle Hill House, Hunts.*
7 Sqn Oakington Lancaster I, III
35 Sqn Graveley Lancaster I, III
105 Sqn Bourn Mosquito IX, XVI
109 Sqn Little Staughton Mosquito IX, XVI
128 Sqn Wyton Mosquito XVI
139 Sqn Upwood Mosquito IX, XVI, XX, XXV
142 Sqn Gransden Lodge Mosquito XXV
156 Sqn Upwood Lancaster I, III
162 Sqn Bourn Mosquito XX, XXV
163 Sqn Wyton Mosquito XXV
405 Sqn Gransden Lodge Lancaster I, III
571 Sqn Oakington Mosquito XVI
582 Sqn Little Staughton Lancaster I, III
608 Sqn Downham Market Mosquito XX, XXV
635 Sqn Downham Market Lancaster I, III
692 Sqn Graveley Mosquito XVI

No 100 (SD) Group. *HQ: Bylaugh Hall, East Dereham, Norfolk.*
23 Sqn Little Snoring Mosquito VI
85 Sqn Swannington Mosquito XXX
141 Sqn West Raynham Mosquito VI, XXX
157 Sqn Swannington Mosquito XIX, XXX
169 Sqn Great Massingham Mosquito VI, XIX
171 Sqn North Creake Halifax III
192 Sqn Foulsham Halifax III, Mosquito IV, XVI
199 Sqn North Creake Halifax III, Stirling III
214 Sqn Oulton Fortress III
223 Sqn Oulton Liberator IV
239 Sqn West Raynham Mosquito XXX
462 Sqn Foulsham Halifax III
515 Sqn Little Snoring Mosquito VI

Bibliography and sources

Primary sources

Air Historical Branch (RAF), London
RAF squadron histories
Operational Research in Bomber Command (draft MS)

The National Archives, Kew
AIR 27 Class – RAF Squadron Operations Record Books – various piece numbers
AIR 40/3023 – British Air Scientific Intelligence Report No. 23

National Archives of Australia
A705, 163/24/255, Casualty, repatriation file: Bourke, Thomas Harrington, Flight Lieutenant, Service Number 407192

Letters, diaries and interviews
Leslie Fry, flight engineer, 429 Squadron RCAF, unpublished diary, 92pp, March–October 1944
Ken Kemp, air gunner, 578 Squadron 1944–45, interview with the author, 7 September 1988
Air Marshal Sir John Whitley, AOC 4 Group 1945, unpublished memoirs (not dated)

Other sources
The Air Force List (various)

Secondary sources

Books

Aders, G., *History of the German Night Fighter Force 1917–1945* (London, Jane's, 1979)
Ashworth, C., *RAF Bomber Command 1936–1968* (Sparkford, PSL, 1995)
Bennett, D.C.T., *Pathfinder* (London, Frederick Muller, 1958)
Blanchett, C., *From Hull, Hell and Halifax: An Illustrated History of 4 Group 1937–1948* (Leicester, Midland Counties Publications, 1992)
Bowyer, C., *Path Finders at War* (Shepperton, Ian Allan, 1977)
Bowyer, C., *Bomber Barons* (London, William Kimber, 1983)
Bowyer, M.J.F., *2 Group RAF: A Complete History 1936–1945* (London, Faber & Faber, 1974)
Bowyer, M.J.F. and Rawlings, J.D.R., *Squadron Codes 1937–56* (Cambridge, PSL, 1979)
Bramson, A., *Master Airman: A Biography of Air Vice-Marshal Donald Bennett* (Shrewsbury, Airlife Publishing, 1985)
Brickhill, P., *Escape or Die* (London, Pan, 1952)
Brookes, A., *Bomber Squadron at War* (Shepperton, Ian Allan, 1983)
Chorley, W.R., *To See the Dawn Breaking: 76 Squadron Operations* (privately published, W.R. Chorley, 1981)
Chorley, W.R., *Bomber Command Losses*, various volumes (Leicester, Midland Publishing)
Cormack, A. and Volstad, R., *Men at Arms 225: The Royal Air Force 1939–45* (London, Osprey, 1996)
Cosgrove, E., *Canada's Fighting Pilots* (Toronto, Clark, Irwin & Co., 1965)
Delve, K., *The Source Book of the RAF* (Shrewsbury, Airlife Publishing, 1994)
Eyton-Jones, A.P., *Day Bomber* (Stroud, Sutton Publishing, 1998)
Falconer, J., *RAF Bomber Airfields of World War 2* (Shepperton, Ian Allan, 1992)
Falconer, J. and Rivas, B., *de Havilland Mosquito Manual* (Sparkford, Haynes, 2013)
Falconer, J., *Handley Page Halifax Manual* (Sparkford, Haynes, 2016)
Franks, Norman, *Ton-up Lancs* (London, Grub Street, 2015)
Green, W. and Swanborough, G., *RAF Bombers Parts 1 and 2* (London, Macdonald and Jane's, 1979, 1981)
Greenhous, B. et al., *The Official History of the RCAF, vol. III: The Crucible of War 1939–1945* (University of Toronto Press, 1994)

Greer, L. and Harold, A., *Flying Clothing: The Story of its Development* (Shrewsbury, Airlife Publishing, 1979)

Hadaway, S., *Missing Believed Killed: Casualty Policy and the Missing Research and Enquiry Service* (Barnsley, Pen & Sword, 2012)

Harris, Sir A., *Bomber Offensive* (London, Collins, 1947)

Harris, Sir A., *Despatch on War Operations, 23 February 1942 to 8 May 1945* (London, Frank Cass, 1995)

Hastings, M., *Bomber Command* (London, Michael Joseph, 1979)

Held, W. and Nauroth, H., *The Defence of the Reich: Hitler's Nightfighter Planes and Pilots* (London, Arms & Armour Press, 1982)

James, J., *The Paladins: The Story of the RAF up to the Outbreak of World War II* (London, Macdonald, 1990)

Jefford, Wg Cdr C.G., *RAF Squadrons* (Shrewsbury, Airlife Publishing, 1988)

Mason, F.K., *The British Bomber since 1914* (London, Putnam, 1994)

Merrick, K.A., *Halifax: An Illustrated History of a Classic World War II Bomber* (Shepperton, Ian Allan, 1980)

Middlebrook, M. (ed.), *The Everlasting Arms: The War Memoirs of Air Commodore John Searby* (London, William Kimber, 1988)

Middlebrook, M. and Everitt, C., *The Bomber Command War Diaries* (London, Viking, 1985)

Muirhead, C., *The Diary of a Bomb Aimer* (Spellmount, 1987)

Munson, K., *Aircraft of World War II* (Shepperton, Ian Allan, 1972)

Musgrove, G., *Operation Gomorrah: The Hamburg Firestorm Raids* (London, Jane's, 1981)

Price, A., *Bomber Aircraft* (London, Arms & Armour Press, 1989)

Prodger, M.J., *Luftwaffe vs. RAF: Flying Clothing of the Air War 1939–45* (Atglen, PA, Schiffer Publishing, 1997)

Richards, D., *The Hardest Victory: RAF Bomber Command in the Second World War* (London, Hodder & Stoughton, 1994)

Saward, D., *'Bomber' Harris* (London, Cassell, 1984)

Streetly, M., *Confound and Destroy: 100 Group and the Bomber Support Campaign* (London, Jane's, 1978)

Thorne, A., *Lancaster at War 4: Pathfinder Squadron* (Shepperton, Ian Allan, 1990)

Townsend Bickers, R., *Home Run* (London, Leo Cooper, 1992)

Wallace-Clarke, R., *British Aircraft Armament vol. 1: RAF Gun Turrets from 1914 to the Present Day* (Sparkford, PSL, 1993)

Wallace-Clarke, R., *British Aircraft Armament vol. 2: RAF Guns and Gunsights from 1914 to the Present Day* (Sparkford, PSL, 1994)

Webster, C. and Frankland, N., *The Strategic Air Offensive against Germany, 1939–1945*, 4 volumes (London, HMSO, 1961)

Wells, M.K., *Courage and Air Warfare: The Allied Aircrew Experience in the Second World War* (London, Frank Cass, 1995)

Who Was Who, various volumes (London, A & C Black)

Who's Who, 1995 (London, A & C Black, 1995)

Journals, magazines and newspapers

Jones, Edgar, '"LMF": The use of psychiatric stigma in the Royal Air Force during the Second World War', *The Journal of Military History* (70), April 2006, pp. 439–58

FlyPast Magazine (various issues)

The Times and the *Daily Telegraph* (various issues)

Internet

www.bbc.co.uk/history/ww2peopleswar/ stories – BBC WW2 People's War, article ID: A4023316; contributed on 7 May 2005, Lily Newick.

www.dorsten-unterm-hakenkreuz.de – *Dorsten unterm Hakenkreuz*.

ww2talk.com – thread: the killing and ill-treatment of Allied airmen in the former Gau Baden.

www.raf.mod.uk/rafmarham

www.cdvandt.org – Aspects of the Giant *Würzburg/Würzburg-Riese* FuMG 65.

www.gyges.dk – Luftwaffe night-fighter control methods.

www.cdvandt.org/seeburg-tisch.htm – *Seeburg Tisch*: a survey.

Index